Anthropology and Tribal Development

About the Editors

Subir Biswas is the Professor & Head, Department of Anthropology, West Bengal State University, Barasat, Kolkata, West Bangal. Earlier, he was an Assistant Professor, Department of Anthropology of North Bengal University (since 2001). His areas of interests are Anthropological Demography, Health and Bioethics. He has to his credit several research projects of UGC, ICSSR, CWS (NBU), UGC-IUC associateship at IIAS, Shimla; and successfully guided five doctorate scholars. He has published four edited books as well as several research articles of anthropological interests published in national and international journals.

Abhijit Das is a student of Anthropology, obtained his M.Sc. and Ph.D. Degree from the University of Calcutta. Dr. Das is an Assistant Professor in the Department of Anthropology, West Bengal State University, West Bengal. He has successfully guided one Ph.D. scholars, and has over 14 years of teaching experience in Anthropology. His areas of teaching and research interests include tribal culture, rural society and culture along with different fields of Modern Socio-Cultural Anthropology. He has published a number of research papers and articles (both in English and Bengali) in the reputed local, national, and international journals and books.

ANTHROPOLOGY AND TRIBAL DEVELOPMENT

Edited by
Subir Biswas
Abhijit Das

CONCEPT PUBLISHING COMPANY PVT. LTD.
NEW DELHI-110059

ISBN-13: 978-93-86682-40-6

First Published in 2018

Published and Printed by

Concept
Since 1974

Concept Publishing Company Pvt. Ltd.
A/15-16, Commercial Block, Mohan Garden,
New Delhi-110059 (INDIA)
T : 91 11 25351460, 91 11 25351794
E : publishing@conceptpub.com; *W* : www.conceptpub.com

Cataloging in Publication Data--Courtesy: D.K. Agencies (P) Ltd. <docinfo@dkagencies.com>

National Seminar on "Anthropology, Tribal Policies and Tribal Development in India" (2016 : Bārāsata, India)
Anthropology and tribal development / edited by Subir Biswas, Abhijit Das.
pages cm
"A National Seminar on "Anthropology, Tribal Policies and Tribal Development in India" as organized by the Department of Anthropology, West Bengal State University, was held at Proggalaoy (Barasat, North 24 Parganas) from 21 to 22 march, 2016"—Preface and acknowledgement.
Includes bibliographical references and index.
ISBN 9789386682406

1. Tribes—India—West Bengal—Social conditions—Congresses. 2. Tribes—India—West Bengal—Economic conditions—Congresses. 3. Tribes—Government policy—India—West Bengal—Congresses. I. Biswas, Subir, 1974- editor. II. Das, Abhijit (Assistant professor of anthropology), editor. III. West Bengal State University. Department of Anthropology, organizer. IV. Title.

LCC GN635.I4N38 2016 DDC 307.772095414 23

Preface and Acknowledgements

Anthropology is constantly struggling to evolve as a sophisticated theoretical and methodological apparatus; conducting intensive fieldworks, and unswervingly subscribing to the premises of human rights, democratization, welfare and the development of people of all shades and spheres of life. It is this new millennium anthropology which is still responding to the call of tribal development and policy formations.

The tribal situation in India presents a varied and complex picture and poses peculiar problems of economic development. Demographically speaking, there are some 250 Scheduled Tribes with several sub-groups speaking some 100 languages/dialects. Most of these tribes constitute separate socio-cultural groups having distinct customs, traditions, marriage, kinship and property inheritance systems and living largely in agricultural and pre-agricultural level of technology. There are food gatherers, hunters, forest-land cultivators, shifting cultivators and minor forest produce collectors among these tribes. Their geographical isolation and impoverished economy have made them object of exploitative economic and trade practices of the non-tribals living in or entering the tribal areas.

Tribal people, the *Adivasis*, literally autochthones, i.e. "original people of the forest", comprise a substantial indigenous minority of the population in India. Tribal peoples are particularly numerous in the Indian states of Odisha, Madhya Pradesh, Chhattisgarh, Rajasthan, Gujarat, Maharashtra, Andhra Pradesh, Bihar, Jharkhand, and West Bengal and in extreme north-eastern states such as Mizoram. Officially, they are recognized by the Indian

Government as "Scheduled Tribes" in the Fifth Schedule to the Constitution of India.

The key issues which perturb the tribal people are atrocities, land alienation, bondage, displacement, money lending, forest destruction, education, health and nutrition, drinking water supply etc.

It is observed that, next to Africa, India has the largest concentration of tribal population in the world. Tribals in India, traditionally known as "*Adivasis*", constitute 8.08 per cent of the total population of the country according to the Census 2011. The major identified tribal groups in the country amount 250. They are scattered along the length and beneath of India from Himalayas to the Indian Ocean and from the Arabian Sea to the eastern frontiers. There are over 134 tribal communities as the *Adivasis,* the original inhabitants; *Vanyajatis,* the caste or ethnic groups of forests; *Paharis,* the hill dwellers and so on. These tribal communities are concentrated in the three major zones of the country, like (i) North and North-Eastern Zone, (ii) Central or Middle Zone, and (iii) Southern Zone (Pawde, Bhise and Takla, 2008).

Although Scheduled Tribes are over 8 per cent of Indian population, they occupy 20 per cent of the country's geographical area which contains as much as 70 per cent of the total natural resources like forests, minerals, and ores (Singh, 2002).

Tribal population and development are inter-dependent. In fact we cannot conceive of development in a vacuum. Development is a very broad term which encompasses various changes that are taking place due to human intervention.

The paradox is that while enclaves within the large tribal areas have burst into unprecedented economic activity, the tribal communities living in and around them have been depressing into a morass of poverty and misery. They have been facing eviction from their ancestral lands on account of the national mainstream's exploitation of the natural resource reserves.

A National Seminar on "**Anthropology, Tribal Policies and Tribal Development in India**" as organized by the Department of Anthropology, West Bengal State University, was held at *Proggalaoy* (Barasat, North 24 Parganas) from 21 to 22 March, 2016. The seminar was sponsored by West Bengal State University, West Bengal.

The seminar was attended by senior professors, teachers, and scholars from universities, colleges and organizations of the country. The seminar, which brought together experts in the field of Anthropology, Sociology, and Tribal Studies largely, achieved its aims and objectives of acquainting themselves with each other's works and ideas, thoughts and engendering mutual respect which was a prerequisite for the joint efforts.

It has already been mentioned that Indian Subcontinent has the largest concentration of tribal population in the world and constitute 8.08 per cent of the country's total population. After independence various measures have been devised and implemented for the upliftment of the tribals, but tribal welfare and development have remained very slow and steady. These measures have not disseminated significant benefits, at least for some tribal communities, who remain practically untouched as well as far from the mainstream Indian society and culture. The objective of the seminar was to give a momentum to slow and steady growth of tribal policies and development along with the status and role of Anthropology in these issues. More than thirty papers were presented during the Seminar besides few lectures by the invited Speakers as resource persons from the leading universities in India.

At the end of the Seminar, the following recommendations as well as concluding remarks were drawn up after due discussion for two days.

1. Anthropology with its distinctiveness as well as uniqueness in studying human being has been an added advantage for dealing and approaching tribal issues.
2. There is a greater realization among scholars, planners and programme implementers about anthropological approach and methodologies in varieties of policies and development programmes with special emphasis on the tribal issues in India.
3. The tribal communities have been conscious about their cultures and rights should be protected and better socio-economic safeguards should be provided.
4. Some new researches should be carried out and concentrated on multiple and ethno-medicinal/

epidemiological determinants *vis-à-vis* socio-cultural determinants of health to examine the failure of certain health related welfare programmes.

5. At the grassroots level, the institutions for tribal communities and other development agencies should be made more transparent and women's participations at the decision-making level should be included.
6. The universities and other academic organizations should modify their syllabi and include applied perspectives more rather than only theoretical/general tribal issues as well as ethnography of tribes.
7. A well-planned national policy for tribal development and policies should be introduced by the Government of India with the help of anthropologists, sociologists, social workers etc.
8. The inter-disciplinary collaborations should be encouraged mainly in the spheres of health, education and economy.
9. All developmental plans, programmes and policies should be culture-specific and should be implemented after proper evaluation of the situations. All these can be better fulfilled by the anthropologists because of their unique orientations in fieldwork, relativism and holism.
10. In a nut-shell, anthropology of the present century studies socio-cultural process within communities of all types. It helps in need-based planning implementation, monitoring and evaluation of the developmental programmes.

Last of all, we on behalf of the organizing committee must convey our heartiest thanks to Prof. Basab Chaudhuri, the Hon'ble Vice Chancellor, all the research scholars and students of the department of Anthropology, West Bengal State University as well as to all the delegates from various parts of India, for their co-operation and active participation in all stages of the seminar to make it successful.

We are thankful to Shri Ashok Kumar Mittal, Managing Director, Concept Publishing Co. (P) Ltd., New Delhi to publish this volume within short time.

Subir Biswas
Abhijit Das

Contents

Preface and Acknowledgements v

List of Contributors xi

1. Barriers and Opportunities in Tribal Development: A Case Study among the Rava Tribe Living in Fringe Forest Areas of North Bengal, India 1
   Suman Chakrabarty
2. Education and Development among the Tangkhul Nagas Tribe of Manipur 15
   Rangya Gachui
3. Development and Dichotomous Challenges in Patalkot and Amarkantak: Rethinking the Ethnographic Ways of Knowing the Tribal Social Landscape 25
   Amlan Kanti Ray and *Binod Kumar Singh*
4. Socio-Economic Growth Through Women Education: A Case Study on the Santal at Ballipara of Birbhum, West Bengal 63
   Sampa Das
5. Occupational Change and Its Influence on the Cultural Tradition of the Lohras in West Bengal 78
   Suman Das and *Suchismita Sen Chowdhury*
6. Development of Thrifting Habit Among the Tribes of West Bengal: A Study on the Tribal SHGs under LAMPS 99
   Ananya Chanda and *Sanjay Basu*
7. Indigenous Communities, Livelihoods and Displacement: A Socio-Ecological Approach 131
   Biswajit Parida

8. Life Style of the Dukpas: A Little Known Ethnic Group of West Bengal 145
Soumyajit Das and *Suchismita Sen Chowdhury*

9. Media and Nation Building: An Empirical Study with Special Reference to Tribals Living in Birbhum District, West Bengal 167
Debasis Mondal

10. Social Media and Tribal Development: A Case Study of Bolpur, Birbhum District, West Bengal 179
Munshi Ismotara

Index 189

List of Contributors

Basu, Sanjay, Deputy Director, Cultural Research Institute, Government of West Bengal.
email: *cridir100@gmail.com*

Chakrabarty, Suman, Assistant Professor, Department of Anthropology, Mrinalini Dutta Mahavidyapith, Vidyapith Road, Birati, Kolkata-700051.
email: *sumanshabr@gmail.com*

Chanda, Ananya, Research Assistant, Cultural Research Institute, Government of West Bengal.
email: *ananyachanda15@gmail.com*

Das, Sampa, Research Scholar, Department of Anthropology, Visva Bharati, Santiniketan, West Bengal-731235.
email: *sampadas09111990@gmail.com*

Das, Soumyajit, Junior Research Fellow, Department of Anthropology, University of Calcutta, West Bengal.
email: *withluvbittuegmail.com*

Das, Suman, Research Assistant, Cultural Research Institute, Government of West Bengal & Research Scholar, Department of Anthropology, West Bangal State University, West Bengal.
email: *anth.sumangmail.com*

Gachui, Rangya, Assistant Professor, Department of Anthropology, Visva Bharati, Santiniketan, West Bengal-731235.
email: *rangyagachui@yahoo.co.in*

Ismotara, Munshi, Research Scholar, Department of Anthropology, Visva Bharati, Santiniketan-731235, West Bengal.
email: *munshi.ismotara@gmail.com*

Mondal, Debasis, Research Scholar, Centre for Journalism and Mass Communication, Visva Bharati, Santiniketan-731235, West Bengal.
email: *d.mondal82@gmail.com*

Parida, Biswajit, Research Scholar, Department of Anthropology, Sambalpur University, Jyoti Vihar, Burla-768019, Odisha. email: *parida.biswa85@gmail.com*

Ray, Amlan Kanti, Research Coordinator, Spectrum Clinic and ERI, Kolkata, West Bengal. email: *humanedestiny@gmail.com*

Sen Chowdhury, Suchismita, Assistant Professor, Department of Anthropology, Mrinalini Dutta Mahavidyapith, Vidyapith Road, Birati, Kolkata-700051. email: *chowdhury.suchi@gmail.com*

Singh, Binod Kumar, Senior Geographer, Directorate of Census Operations, Uttar Pradesh. email: *bkscensus2011egmail.com*

1

Barriers and Opportunities in Tribal Development

A Case Study among the Rava Tribe Living in Fringe Forest Areas of North Bengal, India

Suman Chakrabarty

Introduction

It is an established fact that the tribal development policy is one of the key issues in national development policy even after 70 years of independence in India (Rao and Ramu, 2014). Currently, tribes constitute 104.3 million people which account around 8.60 per cent of India's population (Census of India, 2011). Majorities of these people live in and around the forest areas and collect forest resources on a regular basis for their livelihood (Ghosal, 2011). But, presently free and abundant forest resources are no longer available (MSSRF and WFP, 2001). On the other hand, constant economic, political and intellectual marginalization acts upon them (Hebbar, 2014).

The marginalization towards tribal people was begun by the British Government through the implementation of Scheduled Districts Act in 1874. After independence, the founders of Indian Constitution, policy-makers and social scientists were genuinely focused their attention towards the condition of the Indian tribes and tried to frame various policies for mainstreaming the population. Policy-makers were exponentially formulated the various development policy and plans for tribes through first (1951-1956) to twelve (2012-2017) five year plans along with specific proposal by the different committees related to tribal development like Renuka Roy Committee, Elwin Committee, Dhebar Committee etc. However, the implementation of those plans may remain debatable.

Indeed, the major barriers of the implementation of those tribal development policies started right after the creation and implementation of the *Wildlife Protection Act, 1972* in order to conserve biodiversity in Indian forest. As a result there have been situations where needs were curtailed among local communities' or specifically Indian tribal communities' and also their economic sources were constricted from the forest (Hegde and Enters, 2000). Although in 1988, *National Forest Policy* made a significant shift in forest policy by stating the need to consider local community interests for utilization of forest resources and for involvement of local communities in protection and regeneration of forests (National Forest Policy, 1988). However, the deforestation and violation of local community interests continued to be endangered due to dual interests as conserving endangered natural resources and promoting economic development in forest community, which often result in conflicting policies that fail to protect forests (FAO, 2003). In view of the above difficulties, *Recognition of Forest Rights Rules, 2007* for the Scheduled Tribes and other traditional forest dwellers regarding conservation of their forest rights and also documenting biodiversity and wildlife and delineation of areas significant from the perspective of biodiversity such as heritage sites, ecologically sensitive areas, sanctuaries and national parks (Ministry of Environment and Forest, 2007). Throughout the above process, government is trying to rehabilitate the tribal people from conserve to outside conserve areas by respective forest departments, which is also a major problem in all over India (Nayak *et al.*, 1996). There is growing evidence that without reducing people's dependence on the forests, it is likely that protected areas or natural forests are difficult to conserve (Gunatilake, 1998; Hedge and Enters, 2000) because of higher dependency of population on natural resources for their agriculture, energy, nutrition, medicinal, and other needs (Putz, 1988). Furthermore, in countries like India where remote populations endure social and economic inequities, protected areas have further narrowed down their livelihood options (Salafsky and Wollenberg, 2000). Studies show that subsistence activities and sustenance have become the major problems of the Kadars, when their traditional habitat became a Wildlife Sanctuary (Mahendrakumar, 2005). The restrictive biodiversity conservation strategies also affect livelihoods of indigenous communities in Mudumalai Wildlife Sanctuary, Southern India (Hedge and Enters, 2000). Living Condition is further complicated among those tribal groups who live in fringe forest areas due to regular harassment from the forest authorities, economic, political and intellectual marginalization, crop damage by wildlife animals and also rights of habitation (Rashed, 2003; Hebbar, 2014; Ramkumar *et al.*, 2014). Therefore, the present study aims to understand the living condition, barriers of implantation of development projects and future opportunities of the tribal group living in the forest fringe areas of India.

Materials and Methods

Population and the Study Area

For the present study, the Rava tribe was selected who are perhaps the most backward and autochthonous tribal group in North Bengal. They belong to the Indo-Mongoloid group of people and mainly inhabit the States of Assam, Meghalaya, and West Bengal of India and a few areas of Bangladesh. In North Bengal, the Ravas occupy the Dooars region (in and around forest areas) between the Rivers Teesta and Sarnakosh (Sankosh), specifically in the Jalpaiguri and Cooch Behar districts of West Bengal. About 70 per cent concentration of the Rava villages can be found in newly formed Alipurduar district and specifically in Kalchini block of Alipurduar Sub-division (Sarkar, 2011). They have their own dialect and matriarchal society, but now-a-days, their culture have been influenced by Christianity to a great extent (Mandal and Ray, 2013). The total Rava population is around 15,000 (Census of India, 2001). The present study was conducted in Kalchini block of Alipurduar district of West Bengal.

Sample Size and Sampling

At the first stage, a sample size was calculated to estimate a hypothesized prevalence of 50 per cent with a margin of error of

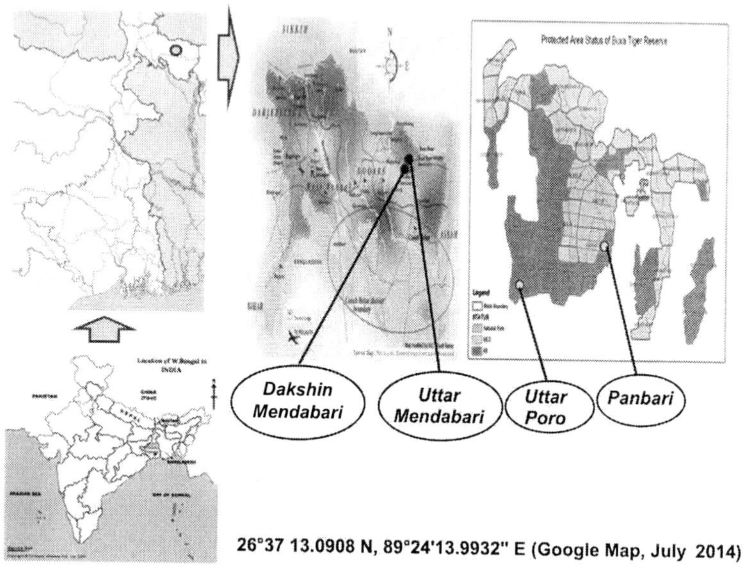

Fig. 1.1: Maps showing Study Areas and Villages under Study (four marked areas)

10 percentage points and 95 per cent confidence, assuming a design effect of one. Approximately 5 per cent non-response rate was considered. Overall, 207 households (HH) were selected by using cluster sampling from 4 villages (as four clusters) out of 11 forest villages in the Kalchini block. The households within a village were selected by using random sampling. Consent from was used to get the consent of the participants in this study. This study was approved by both the ethical committee of Mrinalini Datta Mahavidyapith, Birati, Kolkata and University Grants Commission, New Delhi, India. Data was collected from September 2015 to February 2016.

Data Collection

The primary data were collected from forest villages and secondary data were collected from Forest Department, Block Office, District Agricultural Office and other secondary sources. The cross-sectional data of household socio-demographic and socio-economic characteristics like age, sex, marital status, education, occupation, income, expenditure, food expenditure, house type, household size,

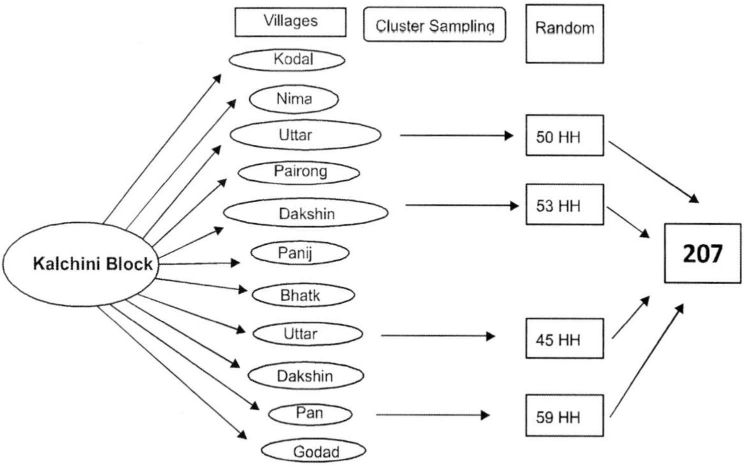

Fig. 1.2: Diagram showing Different Stages of Sample Size and Sampling

household assets (like Pressure-cooker, Bicycle, Radio, Mobile, T.V. with cable, Car, Tractor, Motor cycle, Fan, Sewing machine, Refrigerator, Fishing net, Plough, and Axe), item-wise household food production, and live stock possession data was collected by using semi-structured questionnaires. Besides four Focused Group Discussion (FGD) and eight Key informant's interview were performed during field survey from four selected villages.

Analytical Procedure

The Measure of Uncertainty in Paddy Production

The uncertainly in paddy production was done by considering following formula as Uncertain paddy production = (Annual paddy production of a household – Household annual consumption of paddy).

Standard of Living Index (SLI)

Standard of Living Index (SLI) was estimated by using score of household assets as suggested by NFHS-III, 2005-06. The score was categorized by using 50th (median) percentile values in order to understand the inequalities within the group (Chakrabarty and Bharati, 2012).

Results and Discussion

Living Condition

Table 1.1 demonstrates the individual level variables of the study population from four selected villages of the Rava tribe. Out of total 971 total sample populations, the males (53.35%) were outnumbered than females (46.65%) with low sex-ratio (874.51 females per 1000 males). The dependency ratio was 50.3 per 100 working age group. The percentage of illiteracy was 45.93 per cent and higher among females compared to males counterparts, though the percentage of literate individuals was higher in the recent generation their parental generation. However, majorities of the individuals were studied up to secondary level and there after the percentage was suddenly dropped (table not shown). The Rava group mainly engaged in four primary occupation, where highest percentage of individuals engaged in agricultural activity (21.21%) followed by daily-wage, migratory labour and very few depended on wood cutting exclusively throughout the year.

Table 1.1: Individual Level Variables of the Study Population (n = 971)

Variable	*No.*	*Per cent*
Sex		
Male	518	53.35
Female	453	46.65
Literacy status		
Illiterate	446	45.93
Literate	525	54.07
Occupation (Primary)		
Agriculture	206	21.21
Daily wage	72	7.41
Migratory labour	53	5.45
Only wood cutting	30	3.08

Source: Present Fieldwork.

Table 1.2 shows the household level socio-economic variables of the population under study and it was found that 85 per cent of the household was transformed into Christianity compared to only 15.0 per cent population retained their traditional mode of religious beliefs. They majorly used tube-well for sources of their drinking

Table 1.2: Household Level Summery Variables of the Rava Community ($n = 207$)

Variables	*No*	*Per cent*
Religion		
Christian	176	85.0
Traditional	31	15.0
Drinking water sources		
Well	6	2.9
Tube-well	136	65.7
Pond	1	0.5
Other (borrowed from others tube-well)	64	30.9
Toilet facility at home		
Present	60	29.0
Absent	147	71.0
Electric facility at home		
Present	185	89.4
Absent	22	10.6
Fuel Sources		
Wood	207	100.0
Other	00	0.0
Family involved wood cutting and selling (if required)		
Yes	121	58.45
No	86	51.55
Cultivable land		
Present	160	77.3
Absent	47	22.7
Irrigation facility at the cultivable land (n = 160)		
Present	14	8.8
Absent	146	91.2
Amount of paddy production (annual) (n = 160)#		
No cultivation	16	10.0
Up to 500 kg	105	65.63
Above 500 kg	39	24.37
Crop damaged by wild life (n = 144) #		
Yes	108	75.0
No	36	25.0
Homestead Land		
Present	137	66.2
Absent	70	38.8
Livestock		
Present	190	91.8
Absent	17	8.2
Standard of living index		
Low (score up to 4)	104	50.2
High (score 5 and above)	103	49.8

considered only the last year

Source: Present Fieldwork.

water (65.7%), which was located in their own courtyard. However, 71 per cent of the household was not possessed any toilet in their own house but, they had electric facility (89.4%). About 100 per cent of the households used wood as their fuel resources for cooking purpose. They had collected it from their nearby forest everyday. Besides 58.45 per cent household occasionally engaged wood cutting and selling it in the nearby market mainly during the post-harvest seasons. 77.3 per cent household possessed own agricultural land, but only 8.8 per cent of them were received irrigation facilities. It was interesting to observe that out of 77.3 per cent cultivable land holder, 90 per cent were performed cultivation in the last rainy season. On the basis of the last year paddy production, about 65 per cent household produced up to 500 kg. paddy annually. In addition to that 75 per cent of the households reported about damaged crop by wild life attack specifically by Elephants and Bison in the last agricultural season. As a result it was created a huge uncertainly in their staple consumption during the post harvest seasons (Figure 1.3). However, besides cultivation, they also grew some vegetable in their homestead land (66.2%) and engaged in animal husbandry (91.8% of the HH). The overall standard of living index (SLI) based on the basis of household durable assets showed equally percentages of low and high SLI of the population. It designates a socio-economic inequality persisted among the study group. Irrespective of socio-economic group within population, they have collected various non-timber forest products (NTFPs) in a restricted way (Figure 1.4). They mainly used those NTFPs for their own livelihood purpose, which contained different kinds of roots (*Dioscorea* sp.) locally known as *Han*, different kinds of leaves, fruits etc. However, currently the abundance of the NTFPs was very limited in and around the periphery of the forest. Therefore, they have to cross long distance (about 4-5 km) for the collection of forest products.

Barriers of Implantation of Development Projects

On the basis of focus group discussions and key informant interviews in the studied populations, the various pros and cons regarding the implementation of various development plans in the studied villages were documented. As the studied people mainly depended on agricultural activities for their staple food, they need various agricultural development inputs for getting the

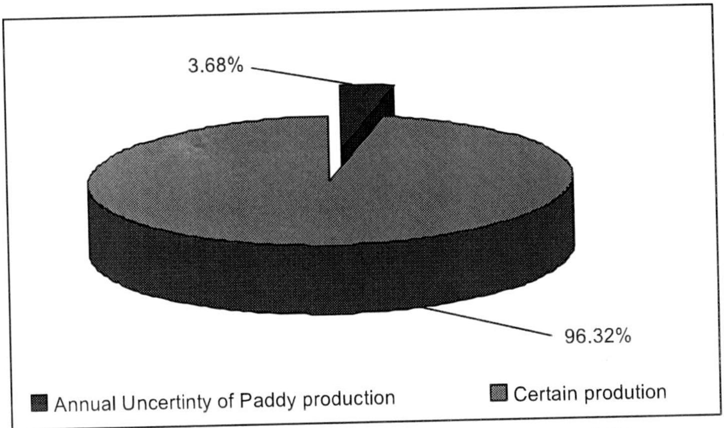

Fig. 1.3: Uncertain Production to Meet Consumption (n = 160)

Fig. 1.4: Types of Non-Timber Forest Products (NTFPs) Collected by the Studied Group

Source: Present Fieldwork.

desire amount of paddy for their consumption throughout the year. But, they were deprived of various agricultural development programmes like irrigation facilities, bank credits, agricultural facilities from District Agricultural Department, crop insurance etc. The major barrier behind this problem was non-availability of legal rights over their agricultural land and habitation. It was suppressing to observe the requirement of "No Objection Certificate" (NOC) at every occasion of developmental activities from forest department in these fringe forest areas as these areas located under the jurisdiction of Jaldapara and Buxa reserve forests. However, as per Recognition of Forest Rights Act, 2006 and its amendments, the Governments should take initiative to convert the forest village into revenue village and subsequently their cultivable land will also be converted and villagers may get legal rights over their agricultural land and all sorts of development activities may be implemented in that area. Therefore, presently their livelihood options have narrowed down as shown in other tribes in India (Salafsky and Wollenberg, 2000). As a result, they have to depend on other unstable means of subsistence. The Rava people engaged heavily in daily wage labour, wood cutting and most importantly involved as migratory labour. The youth mainly interested to go outside the state and engaged in various unskilled and temporary jobs in hotels and industry in Sikkim, Kerala, Gujarat states in India. These occupations were also insufficient in meeting their overall earning. Similar situation has been found among the Shabar tribes of Odisha living in the edge of Chandaka-Domapara Elephant Sanctuary (Chakrabarty and Bharati, 2012). Besides man-animal conflict, there was another important problem in the studied areas. Majority of the studied people said that the elephant attack had increased over the last 10 years and it is mainly due to cumulative effects of human induced de-vegetation, climate change and other related factors. These associated factors have lead to decline of forest resources for elephant feeding and forced them to come in the food resources in the studied villages. On the basis of focus group discussion, it was documented that the households are gradually becoming unwilling to cultivate paddy and/or other crops like jute, maize, wheat, muster etc. due to repeated crop failure owing to wild animal attacks, lack of irrigation facilities, lack of bank loan and other governmental facilities in agricultural activities (due to forest village), improper knowledge of cultivation (as they traditionally are a hunting-gathering group). It was evident from field observation that majority of the land has either been converted to plantations like coconut, teak, and betel nut or left unused. Similar conditions were reported from Kerala where there was a decrease in paddy production over the years and a gradual shift to rubber cultivation on agricultural land (Karunakaran, 2013). Moreover, Xaxa (2014) argued that for obtaining food security, possessing agricultural land was indispensable for Indian tribes because they are mainly marginal farmers.

Future Opportunities

Similarly, on the basis of focus group discussions and key informant interviews along with secondary data and personal observation, there are several opportunities noted in the studied areas and population as:

(i) *Irrigation from nearby rivers / use river's bed for cultivation*—Irrigation from nearby river trough canal may be the best option for desire irrigation facilities in the studied areas. While the use of river bank (River Torsha and other) for seasonal cultivation is another way to meet the production of the community mainly during the dry season.

(ii) *Motivation regarding multiple cropping*—The majorities of households possessed cultivable land and they cultivate only during rainy seasons. The production of paddy is not sufficient to meet their annual consumption. Therefore, awareness regarding multiple cropping should be generated in the studied villages. For that community cultivation may be the best option to get the optimum benefits of production. Modern technology should be incorporated for enhancing the production.

(iii) *Awareness generation of biodiversity loss*—Some awareness camps should be generated related to biodiversity loss of the studied areas and its adjacent forest. Some alternation programme should be launched by involving local villager and using their indigenous knowledge of protecting the forest.

(iv) *Use of traditional knowledge in cultivation*—Presently, the Rava people mainly produced paddy by the abundant use of modern hybrid seeds. However, they had less technologically equipped along with absent of proper irrigation facilities and finally, unwillingness of the use of chemical fertilizer (as they believed that the modern chemical fertilizer may decrease the soil fertility). These factors have resulted to low production even in rainfed agriculture. Therefore, the use of traditional knowledge may help them more familiarity in cultivation by the use of the wild varieties of paddy. But, the studied people argued that the quantity of paddy production from wild varieties was questionable as per their annual requirement.

(v) *Consistent involvement in forest protection*—There should a provision in the government and forest department to recruit the local villagers specifically the Rava youth in the protection of the forest as they may be the best reader of their immediate environment and able to meet the necessary protection of the forest.

(vi) *Forest livelihood intervention*—The present Rava people collected various non-timber forest products (NTFPs) from their nearby forests and used it for their own livelihood purpose. However, the roots and tubers as well as other products have well effective for food and medicinal uses. A project may be launched to enhance the revenue from NTFPs by adding some values and also negotiation should be made by them in the market for the commercialization of the valued forest product.

(vii) *Teak/Rubber plantation*—There is ample opportunities for teak or rubber plantation in the home garden or unused agricultural land among the Rava group in these areas. At the edge of their cultivable land or at some portion of the land, they may plant the teak or rubber trees, which may be beneficial to biodiversity conservation and also they can use it commercially.

(viii) *Forming small industry (Areca nut)*—As the area is best suited for cultivating areca nut or betel nut and majorities of the households have possessed betel nut trees. They were given lease those trees for 2-3 years to the businessman from outside the community. Therefore, small industry related to various products of betel nuts should be implemented by involving the community as a whole and to build a network chain from cultivation, production and selling to the markets. It helps them to generate secondary means of earring.

Conclusion

The Rava tribes living in forest fringe areas of Kalchini block need immediate intervention in their livelihood promotion and other tribal development strategies but the foremost step for getting these opportunities is to convert these forest villages into the revenue villages, which is one of the major directions as per Recognition of Forest Rights Act, 2006.

Acknowledgements: My special thanks to the study participants and to UGC for its grant under UGC-Minor Research Project (PHW-266/13-14 dated 18th March, 2014). I would like to extend sincere thanks to the BDO (Shri Chandra Sen Khati), PDO (Mr. Saurav Mandal) of Kalchini block and forest authorities of Jaldapara and Buxa Forest Division for their constant support during my venture.

References

Census of India. 2001. *Census of India.* Registrar General of India, Government of India, New Delhi.

Census of India. 2011. *Census of India 2011.* Registrar General and Census Commissioner of India, Government of India, New Delhi.

Chakrabarty, S., Bharati, P., 2012. Household economy and nutritional status among the Shabar tribe living in a protected forest area of Odisha, India. *Human Biology Review,* 1: 16-33.

Food and Agriculture Organization (FAO). 2003. *Proceedings of workshop on tropical secondary forest management in Africa: Reality and perspectives,* held at Nairobi, Kenya, 9-13 December, 2002.

Ghosal, S., 2011. Importance of non-timber forest products in native household economy. *Journal of Geography and Regional Planning,* 4: 159-168.

Gunatilake, H.M., 1998. The role of rural development in protecting tropical rainforests: Evidence from Sri Lanka. *Journal of Environmental Management,* 53: 273–292.

Hebbar, R., 2014. Reflections and marginalization of tribes in South India. *Yojana,* 58 (January): 49-51.

Hegde, R., Enters, T., 2000. Forest products and household economy: a case study from Mudumalai Wildlife Sanctuary, Southern India. *Environmental Conservation,* 27: 250-259.

Karunakaran, N., 2013. Shift to rubber cultivation and consequences on environment and food security in Kerala. *Journal of Rural Development,* 32: 395-408.

Mahendrakumar, M.S., 2005. Ecocultural Adaptation of the Kadars of Kerala. *Studies in Tribes and Tribals,* 3: 99-104.

Mandal, B., Roy, M., 2013. The Rabha and Their Social Movement (1925-1950): A Case Study of North Bengal. *IOSR Journal of Humanities and Social Science* (IOSR-JHSS), 10: 5-8.

Ministry of Tribal Affairs. 2007. *Recognition of Forests Rights*. Government of India, New Delhi.

M.S. Swaminathan Research Foundation (MSSRF), World Food Programme (WFP). 2001. *Food Insecurity Atlas of Rural India*. M.S. Swaminathan Research Foundation, Chennai.

National Family Health Survey (NFHS-III). 2005-06. International Institute of Population Sciences, Mumbai, India.

National Forest Policy. 1988. Government of India, Ministry of Environment and Forest.

Nayak, A.K., Panigrahi, R., Mishra, M.R., 1996. *Site report for the relocated village of Chandaka—Dompara Wildlife Sanctuary. Documenting peoples' knowledge and priorities for biodiversity conservation*. Bhubaneswar: Vasundhara.

Putz, F., 1988. Blueprint for saving the tropical forest. *Garden*, 12: 5.

Rao, M.S., Ramu, P., 2014. An Overview of the tribal development policy of India. *International Journal of Academic Research*, 1: 1-24.

Rashed, K.B.S., 2003. *Vulnerability of the forest-fringe population in a degraded forest area of central Bangladesh*. XII World Forestry Congress, Canada. Retrieved from http://www.fao.org/docrep/ARTICLE/WFC/XII/0839-A1.html

Salafsky, N., Wollenberg, E., 2000. Linking livelihoods and conservation: a conceptual framework and scale for assessing the integration of human needs and biodiversity. *World Development*, 28: 1421-1438.

Sarkar, B.C., 2011. Geography of Tribal People in Jalpaiguri District of West Bengal. *International Referred Research Journal*, 2(21).

Ramkumar, K., Ramakrishnan, B., Saravanamuthu, R., 2014. Crop Damage by Asian Elephants *Elephas maximus* and Effectiveness of Mitigating Measures in Coimbatore Forest Division, South India. *International Research Journal of Biological Sciences*, 3: 1-11.

Xaxa, J., 2014. Problem of Food Security: A brief Analysis of Tribal Area in India. *International Journal of Scientific and Research Publication*, 4: 1-4.

2

Education and Development among the Tangkhul Nagas Tribe of Manipur

Rangya Gachui

Introduction

Education in all respects is an essential entity for the development of human qualities and personalities. In true sense, it is the backbone of a development of society which makes good and responsible citizen. It is an activity, or a series of activities, or a process which may either improve the immediate living conditions or increase the potential for future living. Education is an input of only for economic development but also for inner strength of the tribal communities so that they can meet the new challenge on some degree of equality (Narayan, 1997). It is the single most important means by which individuals and society can improve personal endowment build capacity levels, overcome barriers, and expand opportunities for a sustained improvement in their well-being. Education is crucial to development as it provide the individual with adequate skill for participating in various economic activities. It enables human beings to understand the interrelationship among the tangible phenomena surrounding them and give skill to translate the knowledge into action. Acquisition of education helps workers to take advantage of technical changes which increases their productivity and earnings (Basu, 2002). Education may, however, influence social and economic change directly as a consequence of its role in the discovery and dissemination of new knowledge (Shah, 2005).

Realising the importance of education, the Government of

India formulated various measures to promote education. Article 45 of the Directive principle of state policy emphasised the role of state to provide free and compulsory education to all children up to the age of 14 years. The National Policy on Education in 1968 and 1986 also gave a stimulus for the expansion of education. These promotional measures helped to improve literacy rate. Though, we were able to achieve an increase in general literacy rate, educational status of the disadvantaged groups, in particular, of the Scheduled Tribes is in pathetic condition both in respect of coverage and achievement even after seventy years of independence. Being illiterate, the tribal people cannot become acquainted with the development in science and technology. Due to illiteracy, people of these communities are totally ignorant of basic principles of health which makes them an easy prey to disease. For a tribal family to send a boy or a girl is essentially a matter of economics and entails dislocation in the traditional pattern of their labour force. Many tribals refrain from sending children to school due to loss of good characteristic of the labour force and the fear of expenditure on education (Venkataramana, 2001). Sujatha (2002) revealed that though education was not a critical demand among Scheduled Tribes, Government policy focused on education as the main avenues by which to integrate them into mainstream society.

Shah (2005) mentioned the modern forces have been actively moulding the life of the tribals and changing them. The forces affecting them are several. They include (a) Christianity; (b) the development of communication within the tribal areas and between tribal and non-tribal areas; (c) the opening up and extension of modern economic and political processes of tribal people; (d) the welfare and development work by the voluntary as well as Governmental agencies; (e) the introduction of advanced technology to exploit the mineral, forest, power and other industrial resources; and (f) the spread of literacy and formal modern education. All these go together towards affecting social change. The present topic makes an attempt to analyse the education and development among the Tangkhul Nagas of Manipur.

Methodology

Both primary and secondary sources are used for this study. Primary sources are interview and observation technique. The primary sources are supplemented with the secondary sources like literature of the earlier researchers.

The Tangkhul Nagas

Tangkhul Naga lives in the present North-eastern part of India and north-western part of Burma (Myanmar). Tangkhul inhabited mainly the Ukhrul district in Manipur covering an area of 4544 sq. kms. with the population of 1,83,998 (2011 census). Some Tangkhul villages are found in the adjoining Senapati, Thoubal and Chandel districts in Manipur and sizeable numbers of Tangkhuls are found in the Somrah tract of Sagaing division in Burma. As to their origin, the Tangkhuls believe that they have originated out of stone in a cave in the Samshok village in Burma and later on, their ancestors migrated to the North-Eastern part of India. The Tangkhuls live in villages and firmly uphold the doctrine that one never abandons ones village home and clan. The villages are generally thickly populated and are situated on the top of the hills. The village has been the highest political, social, economic and religious unit and the main source of spiritual, social and cultural bonding among the people. The hereditary chief (*Awunga*) and his clan-based village council (*Hanga*) is the highest decision-making body in the village hierarchy who take the responsibility of looking after the welfare of the villagers. All village festivals, social and religious functions begins with rites and sacrifices by the *awunga*.

Christianity and Education

The Tangkhul Naga did not evince significant social change till the commencement of British rule in India because due to the inaccessibility and remoteness of the areas generally inhabited by the Tangkhul, it was not possible for them on the part of others to establish contacts. Due to lack of contact and interaction, Tangkhul Naga remained within bounce of their social contours and cultural boundaries of long ago. In socio-cultural change, contact with reference groups is a major factor, in other words tribal communities did not have contact with significant others whom they could have accepted as reference groups in situations of cultural contact. Due to this and other inherent limitations it is not easy to study the progress of education among them, prior to independence. There is no doubt that a few anthropologist, welfare workers, missionaries and government officers posted in these areas, who established contacts with the Tangkhul, have left valuable information about the conditions in which the Tangkhuls were living, but the information is rather scanty and does not give complete account of the deplorable conditions prevailing at that time. It appears that the colonial government in India also never thought seriously of taking any constructive steps for the educational and for that matter even social and economic development of the Tangkhul people. For this reason, the Tangkhul remains educationally extremely backward. Educational backwardness accounted for their socio-economic backwardness. Lack of education is a retarding factor. Credit must be given to the Christian missionaries for their efforts in spreading education among the tribals people in certain selected pockets. Their work in this respect carried out in North-eastern India is particularly commendable of course, they succeeded in converting significant proportion of tribal in this area to Christianity.

The British paved the way for entry of education into tribal societies through Christian missionaries. They spread Christianity in concurrence with the introduction of education from the late nineteenth century. They brought education and introduced the Roman script, and made communication easier between the Nagas as well as with the outside world (Chasie, 2005). Unlike military expeditions which burnt villages and instilled terror of the colonial authority among the people, missionary expeditions presented themselves as carriers of 'peace and love' that has come to soften their 'hard hearts'. One way in which the missionaries did this was to package this message in an attractive and appealing manner. For instance, on reaching a village, the touring party would set up a camp and then the evangelists would send out in pairs to different parts of the village. They would then hang up the Bible pictures rolls and preach for an hour or so. The pictures rolls created quite an excitement among the villagers and the missionary saw that as an effective way of catching the attention of the people. Most missionaries also preached the gospel with the help of equipment, like the gramophones and the magic lantern, which created much excitement among the villagers. Providing modern medical services was an integral part of the evangelizing activities of the missionary. During their preaching tours, it was common for the sick to be gathered together and brought to the tent of the missionary for medical treatment. During one of the tours in 1907, missionary among the Tangkhul Nagas, William Pettigrew claims to have treated over two hundred patients. While not on tours, the missionaries established and ran dispensaries in the places where they were stationed. Some of the trained medical missionaries toured around nearby villages to vaccinate a considerable section of the villagers against malaria and small pox, especially during the times of epidemic. For the missionaries, providing of medical services was quite generally and wisely accepted as one of the most effective means of gaining the attention, sympathy, and goodwill of the people.

The evangelical practice also socialized and disciplined the Nagas into civilized American notions of time, hygiene and clothing. From the moment missionaries first attempted to work among the Naga, they felt the need to instill certain time discipline. The missionary also made consistent effort towards instilling principles of cleanliness and hygiene among the Nagas. For the missionaries, maintenance of a clean body and surroundings was one of the characteristics of becoming Christian. Missionaries even included hygiene as part of the school curriculum (Serto, 2000, as cited in Thiyam, 2007) asserted that tribal people in the hills generally lack education, training, communication facilities etc. among the Nagas of Manipur, the Tangkhuls were the first to receive Christianity; therefore, they were more educated and better adapted to the modern and Western cultures than other tribes (Pukharambam, 2012). It appears that Christianity has played a major role for the tribals in Manipur. As a result large tribal population is not only literate but also educated.

Until the coming of education, the Tangkhul Nagas economic, social, cultural and religious activities revolved around nature and were closely intertwined with their livelihood and culture. Tangkhul Nagas lived by adapting to changes in their immediate environment. Horam (1977) talks of how "the early tribal life centred round the soil, the ancestral fields, sowing and harvesting. Village feast were dictated by the agricultural calendar and the seasons. Most religious ceremonies and festivals are directly connected with the fields. Gods and spirits are placated so as not to bring blight and frost and to bless the village with good harvest." Nature in this context has provided the Tangkhuls with a solid foundation for the formation of distinct ethno-cultural trait. Everything in nature has direct impact on them and plays pivotal role in contributing to their material, social and spiritual well-being and thus shapes their cultural community life. Therefore, nature is considered in Tangkhul as fundamental elements of their life wor ld.

The traditional centre of education among the Tangkhul was the youth dormitory *Longshim*. There are two *Mayarlong* and *Ngalalong*. *Mayarlong* means boys dormitory and *Ngalalong* meaning girls dormitory. Boys dormitory or bachelor's dormitory was strictly forbidden for womenfolk, for it was their belief that if they wanted to perform any manly activities as considered by them, such as hunting, fishing, trapping, preparation of waging war etc., and if womenfolk entered in their dormitories freely, ill luck might befall them. In this way menfolk never enter the girls dormitory if they would perform something which they felt to be serious and even a married person did not sleep with his wife at home, but spent the night either in the boy's dormitory or in the village camp outside the village gate. In the *Longshim* they were given instruction in matters necessary for their practical life. From the technical know-how in constructing their houses, various arts and crafts to the learning of their folklore, dance, music and discipline were all imparted to them there. However, with the introduction of the British rule and Christianity and Western education youth dormitory lost its importance and is gradually disappearing.

The new religion proved beneficial in countless ways such as removal of superstitions, introduction of schools and hospitals, cleanliness, and a turning away from head-hunting and such other practices (Horam, 1977). Christianity reigned through the spread of rudimentary education among the Tangkhul tribes who could render the least any resistance movement to the Christian missionaries. At the beginning of the Nineteenth century the Christian missionaries started to establish educational institution and Churches which held out certain pledges for modernisation and reformation in the style of social life. The Tangkhul embraced Christianity at the beginning of Nineteenth century. In 1896, when a lower primary school was established at Ukhrul, not a single boy came to take education in the school. With the help of the then political Agent, Mr. A.E. Wood, 20 boys from Ukhrul came to get admission in the school. One Manipuri teacher, Mangolchao Singh, by name came to assist the missionary teacher, Pettigrew who was the teacher of that school. As month and years passed, the Tangkhuls began to learn modern education and modern life. They started cutting their hair in the Western style and they learnt the use of pants and shirts. Gradually, they embraced Christianity. Today with more than 90 per cent literate population, Ukhrul is considered as the most educated town of the State next to the capital city Imphal. Some of the well-known schools of the town are: Sacred Heart Higher Secondary School, Alice Christian Higher Secondary School, Little Angels School, Savio School, Blesso Montessori School, Holy Spirit School, Patkai Academy, Juniors Academy, Sentinel College, Saint John School and Pettigrew College, Kendriya Vidyalaya and Jawahar Lal Navodaya Vidyalaya. Almost all parents are eager to give their children education and with this rapid increase in literacy and higher education many people have gone away from the land and are seeking white-collar jobs.

In the past, inter-tribal marriage was not common but today such marriages are not rare among them after the establishment of lower primary school at Ukhrul in 1896 and subsequent advancement of education among the Tangkhuls, now, it may be found that the first matriculate and graduate among the Naga tribe belong to Tangkhul community. Not only that today we find many of them are qualified as doctors, engineers, theologists etc. some of them are I.A.S. Officers, and many are scattered in different fields. In the political field also many of them are found in the Manipur Assembly and Council of Ministers. Almost in every Tangkhul village, we may find a school at present. Though the Tangkhul are now modernised, still the process of modernisation has not suddenly cropped up. For their advancement, many of them had to dedicate for the community. Now, they have changed from primitive to the modern life. Their beliefs in wild spirits and deities have been discarded as the things of the past. Most of their expensive social ceremonies have been left out and discarded as those ceremonies caused heavy expenses. Christianity and modern education have changed their life style. They have brought a variety of change in their society is not free from undesirable elements generated by modern times. It is all to the credit of Christian missionaries who have brought, the Tangkhul on the way to progress as citizen of Indian Union. They have not only broken the political isolation of the Tangkhuls but have brought in radical socio-economic and political transformation (Singh, 1987).

At a closer look, Tangkhul society actually experienced crises on several fronts. Horam (1977) remarks that "the present century has witnessed sudden and drastic changes, and these are more gradual changes that are occurring daily, have caused the present age to be labelled an age of transition. There is no aspect of these people's life which has not been touched by change. Whether look at the Tangkhul Naga economically, politically, socially or in religious field, many transformations have taken place." This transition from traditional to the modern way of life not was a simple one. While the people frequently give up their antecedent religious belief in favour of Christianity, their relations to custom and cultural practices and their outlooks on the nature's providence have also undergone changes.

Conclusion

Culture and social change was brought by Christian education in the Tangkhul Naga. With Christian education the message of love and forgiveness were installed upon the minds of the people. With the introduction of Christian education the message a feeling of love and peace was aroused in the area where this was lacking. Secondly, a common language and written literature were given to the people by the Christian missionaries which brought about a sense of togetherness and common understanding through the medium of language and literature. Language is always a cementing factor that brings people of the same tongue together. With the introduction of modern education Tangkhul came into contact with civilized world and they came under the influence of other people. So, changes took place in their social, cultural, ideological, religious and many other aspects of life. Their attitude towards life, morality and day-to-day living are affected. Their material culture, habits, dress and customs, profession and all style of life are greatly affected. Their old village cultural ways of life were disintegrated, defused and displaced by new ideas and practices. They have been transformed from universal illiteracy to literacy. Political consciousness is another remarkable contribution of education to the Tangkhul people. The rapid and radical changes in their social life from a primitive and unsophiscated life to a high standard modern life style are all the impact of education. Education also brought the tribal skill necessary to function effectively within the new society that modernization was bringing.

"Once upon a time Nagas were known as head-hunters before Christianity came to our land. It was also true that Nagas were savages, wild, illiterate, half-clad, poor, sickly, and all that; and there were constant tribal feuds among them. Our ancestors were left to the mercy of nature. The Nagas also worshipped unknown gods and many spirits; they were narrow minded and superstitious. They were isolated from the rest of the world; others did not know them. This land was an unknown land, Terra incognita. It was proverbial among the Assamese kids that the whole of Naga hills disappeared in the cloud where the people lived like monkeys in the branches and whoever penetrated close into their hills would lose their heads. This was our past. Now, we are grateful to American missionaries that they brought to us the Good News of God which opened our eyes and liberated us from the bondage of darkness. Now, our land is in progress with growing education; we breathe the air of civilization as good as with the rest of the world" (Nuh, 1986).

References

Basu, Ashok, 2002. Primary Education, human development and India's disadvantaged groups, In: Ruddar Datt (ed.) *Human Development and Economic Development*, Deep and Deep Publication, New Delhi.

Chasie, Charles, 2005. Nagaland in transition, *India International Centre Quarterly*, 32(2/3), pp. 253-264.

Horam, M., 1977. *Social and Cultural Life of Nagas (The Tangkhul Nagas)*, B.R. Publishing Corporation, Delhi.

John Thomas, Missionaries, colonialism and the writing of history among the Nagas, http://www.biblicalstudies.org.uk/pdf/jcta/07-05_thomas.pdf, as viewed on 12th August, 2015.

Marchang, Reimeingam, 2013. Educational development among the Scheduled Tribes of Manipur, *Journal of North East India Studies*, 3(1): pp. 1-17.

Narayan, Sachindra, 1997. *Perspective on Tribal Development (Gandhian Approach to Plan Development)*, Commonwealth Publishers, New Delhi.

Nuh, V.H., 1986. *Nagaland Church and Politics*, Kohima, pp. 207-208.

Ruivah, Khashim, 1984. Long Shim (Dormitory) of the Tangkhuls, In: Sebastian Karotemprel (ed.), *The Tribes of Northeast India*, Firma KLM Private Limited, Calcutta.

Shah, B.V., 2002. Eduction and social Change among Tribals in India. In: Pariyaram M. Chacko (ed.), *Tribal Communities and Social Change*, Sage Publications, New Delhi.

Singh, Ramgopal, 1987. The Tangkhuls of Manipur, In: Sudhanshu Bikash Saha (ed.), *Tribes of North East India*, Rupali Publishing, Agartala.

Sujatha, K., 2002. Education among Scheduled Tribe; In: R. Govinda (ed.), *India Education Report: A Profile of Basic Education*, Oxford University Press, New Delhi.

Thiyam, Bharat Singh, 2007. Poverty in Manipur, *Economic and Political Weekly*, 42(3), pp. 251-254.

Venkataramana, M., 2001. Tribal literacy and the total literacy campaign, *Social Change*, 48(8), p. 25.

3

Development and Dichotomous Challenges in Patalkot and Amarkantak

Rethinking the Ethnographic Ways of Knowing the Tribal Social Landscape

Amlan Kanti Ray and *Binod Kumar Singh*

Introduction

From colonial to post-independent period, perception of tribes in India has undergone a paradigm shift from 'protective' to 'scheduled' form, as an administrative category, pertaining to economic and political context. British government in colonial period, envisaged initiating development programmes for taking these forest dwellers into confidence along with debating the plight of tribal for being the dichotomous status—'assimilated' or 'preserved' (Eriksen, 2010), who got divided the two distinct groups—nationalists *versus* colonialists. This debate still continues. In an investigation of the tribal—national conflict, the rationale of 'the cultural stuff' (Jenkins, 2008) has got a point in giving required value to the community, and being a tribal with a notion being Bharias, Baigas, Kols, Gonds and so on referring to certain individual or people at large is extremely important issue. In the name of protecting tribal during colonial India in order to gain control over forest based populations and their resources through census surveying and mapping of regions (Upadhya, 2011) and uplifting tribal under Scheduled category, Government of India (GOI) visualizes an aura of opportunity for all 705 tribes (Census of India, 2011) to get them access towards reasonable upward mobility, availing material benefits as a kind of "the economic logic..." (Firth, 1939) such as access to free education, government's job against minimal competition, health service etc., appears to be a slow process towards proposed modernity. However, vision of modernity always unfolds within a specific cultural and civilizational context, and different starting points for the transition to modernity lead to different outcomes (Gaonkar, 1999) are exemplified in two different premises such as rural Patalkot Valley (PKV) and urban Amarkantak Nagar Panchayet Town (AKNPT). Modernization is a phenomenon, overcoming traditional societies and cultures "in the European-Western sense" (Taylor, 1999). The "socio-cultural formations" (Demmer, 2008) of tribes in this subcontinent do not simply disappear by a "tide of modernization". Argumentarily, it could be said that "Modernities are not artifacts of a pre-determined time and place, rather is a product of processes which define the modern period: the expansion of capitalism" (Giddens, 1991 Rabinow 2008), heavy industries, built-in projects in areas, where tribes live there for more than centuries (Merrifield *et al.*, 2013).

The notion of development and modernity appears to be as a quasi-symmetric alliance. Modernity is being injected into the tribal belief as a kind of vehicle moving them towards modern version of self-sufficiency to seek an alternative way of living. After having consistent investigation of the treasure of tribal intergenerational repository like better physical and mental status, endogamous practice in nested rhythm of age old social structure, and "traditional ecological knowledge and wisdom" (Turner *et al.*, 2000) intertwined with complex social landscape has been reflected in the present study of pluralistic independence among tribes within respective "cultural and political-economic contexts" (Merrifield *et al.*, 2013).

Given the developmental context, Government infrastructural projects related to the construction of the motorway, connecting Jabalpur, Dindori, Pendra Road and Bilaspur with AKNPT, along with upcoming market place, technical institute, university and many *ashramas*, which virtually carry a strong symbolic meaning of modernity. Unlike AKNPT, small but fruitful initiative has been found in PKV settlement having a motorway up to Ghatlinga village from Tamia tahsil of Chhindwara district for the purpose of providing government's amenities to Bharias. Interestingly, both show the official discourse of government's honesty, attempting to match the requirements in two different settlements.

The argument might rely on one probable hypothesis—that the trend of tribal life be it in archaic context (Patalkot is a case) or in urban milieu (Amarkantak is a case) deeply involves the passage of time. The former adjusts with the geological driven settlement pattern in different crater rims mingling with the upland forest compared to the lower level of Dudhi river basin and the latter engages them in urban economy with readiness to the acquisition of professional knowledge, facilitates sustainability in growing market place. Using ethnographic details from fieldwork, conducted in Patalkot and Amarkantak, the present scenario of tribes are elucidated and argumentarily explained. The present chapter considers four key components such as Boundary, Demography, Livelihood and Ecological Wisdom to underpin the debate about the intractable realities of highly mandated tribal development for assertive transformation from traditional identity to urbanity.

Materials and Methods

Study Subjects

We do not make many claims on the ethnographic fieldwork among Bharias in Patalkot Valley (October 2014) and Kols, Baigas and Gonds in Amarkantak NP (October 2014 and February 2016) in Madhya Pradesh. We have meticulously drawn an outline of their emic social response against the etic political governance along with their uncanny knowledge on forest environments. But we contemplate and we have designed this research paper as a contribution to the ethnography in both the places covering those aspects, which appear on the surface of tribal life in 'everyday reality', rest we have used secondary information in other aspects of different tribes, which are retrieved from the archival materials and other sources of secondary data.

Reflection from Study Areas

During our my stays in Amarkantak, a multi-ethnic, Bundeli-Hindi speaking town on the border of Madhya Pradesh and Chhattisgarh, we have often found ourselves somewhat embarrassed as various town people have seen us as a possible resource in implausible schemes for going local sight-seeing or boarding train from Pendra Road or long tour, or even as pilgrims only. Similar situation we were to face in Chhindwara—our base camp for Patalkot Valley. To begin with, we only saw these occurrences as a distraction from our purpose of finding out how tribes react and interact in their new found land of economy and subsistence in support of their livelihood in case of Amarkantak and forest land in case of Patalkot Valley (PKV) to response government's support.

Study Area

The blend of savanna and deciduous forest of Patalkot Valley (PKV) (Figs. 3.1 and 3.2) and emerging urban Amarkantak Nagar Panchayat Town (AKNPT) (Fig. 3.3) offer the view of sub-humid region 35°-2° C of vast undulating plain, interspersed by Vindhya-Satpura range mixed with Panchmarhi Biospere Reserve (PBR) and mighty Mekkal mountain (AKNP) between which lie rugged mountain ranges from crater rim to undulating plain, enriched by Dudhi river basin in PKV and Narmada rift valley in AKNPT. PKV brings about pristine, archaic settlement of Bharias and Gonds (few in number) embedded in different crater rims processed through orogenic phases from PBR construct, comprises Dewana, Sonbhadra, Bainganga, Tawa, Nagduari and Dudhi drainage system. AKNPT on the other hand, is a place metamorphosed into urban complex, where we cover Kols, Baigas and Gonds. PKV, with a total land area of 79 km^2 includes 2785.9 hectares of land with forest coverage of 27.5 per cent, Pastures of 19.31 per cent and Net Area Sown of 19.63 per cent (Census of India, 2011) (Figs. 3.1-3.4 and 3.6) and AKNPT with a land area of 46.57 km^2 (Census of India, 2011) under NP is surrounded by Mekkal mountain range.

(a) Patalkot Valley (PKV)

(a.1.) *Geomorphic Formation*

Tectonic geomorphology in association with processes of rivers, debris flow and hill slope likely to lie in a state of natural law plays an important role in hypotheses linking climate to tectonics from discrete events like earthquakes, landslides and storms, to the evolution of orogens over millions of years. Pachmarhi plateau

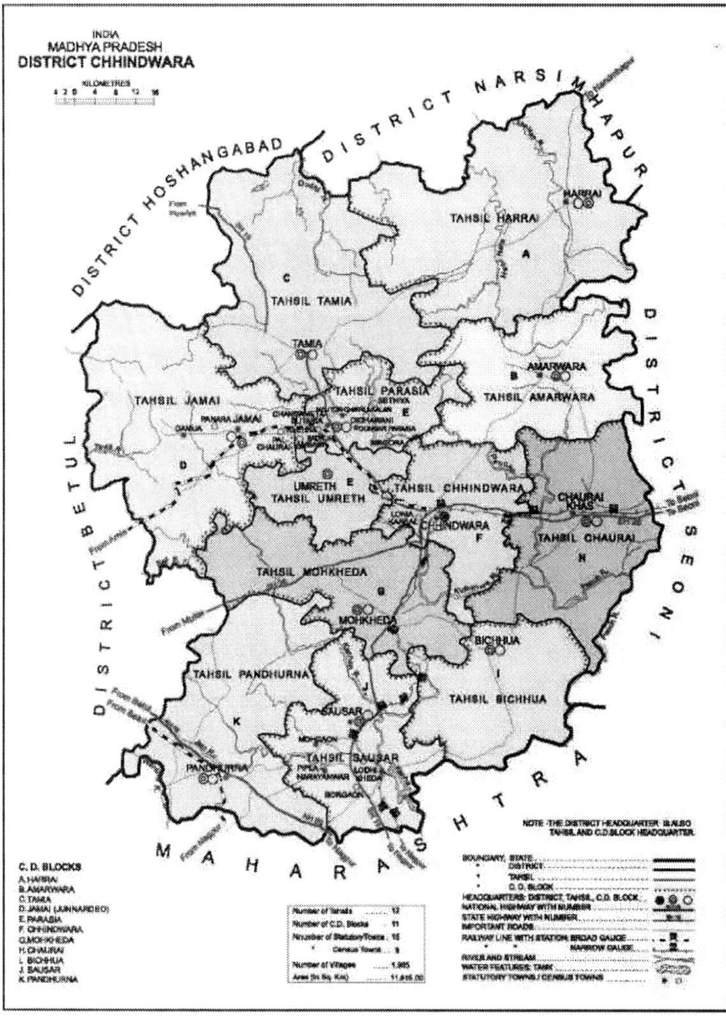

Fig. 3.1: Location of Patalkot valley of Tahsil Tamia in Chhindwara District of Madhya Pradesh

Source: Dr. Binod Kumar Singh, *Senior Geographer*. Ministry of Home Affairs, Government of India. Directorate of Census Operations, Uttar Pradesh, Lucknow, Janaganana Bhawan, Plot No. CC-1, Sector-G, Aliganj, Lucknow-226024, UP, India.

Fig. 3.2: Location of Patalkot Valley exhibiting all code number of 12 and other villages of Tahsil Tamia in Chhindwara district of Madhya Pradesh

Source: Dr. Binod Kumar Singh, *Senior Geographer*. Ministry of Home Affairs, Government of India. Directorate of Census Operations, Uttar Pradesh, Lucknow, Janaganana Bhawan, Plot No. CC-1, Sector-G, Aliganj, Lucknow-226024, UP, India.

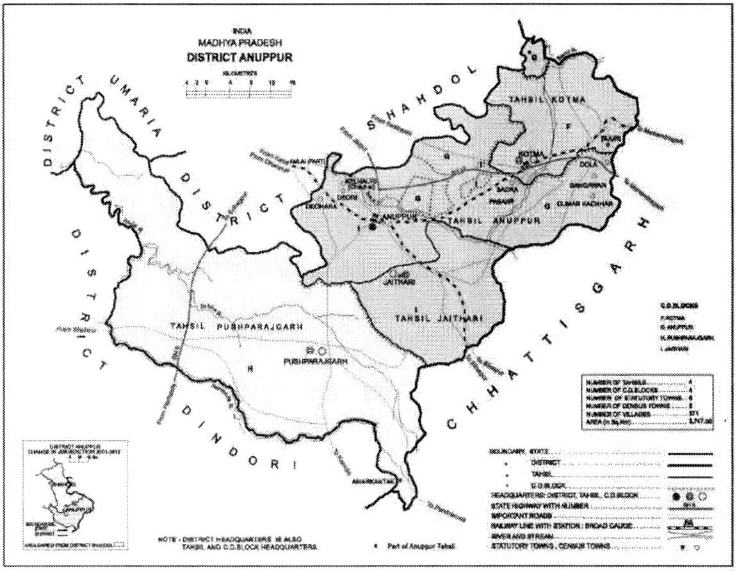

Fig. 3.3: Location of Amarkantak of Tahsil Pushparajgarh in Annupur district of Madhya Pradesh

Source: Dr. Binod Kumar Singh, *Senior Geographer*. Ministry of Home Affairs, Government of India. Directorate of Census Operations, Uttar Pradesh, Lucknow, Janaganana Bhawan, Plot No. CC-1, Sector-G, Aliganj, Lucknow-226024, UP, India.

comprises basalt and sandstone rocks and its drainage system in the form of Tawa, Dewana, Sonbhadra, Dudhi, Bain Ganga and Nagduari basins have been documented demonstrating such tectonic geomorphic details (Dongre, 2015, 2012). These rivers are flowing down through geological fault angles cutting gorges across mountain blocks of Pachmarhi across Satpura Dome and flow emerge north to debouch into the Narmada rift valley. These streams have laterally planated and vertically eroded the valley (Verma, 1972).

(a,2.) Patalkot Valley Formation

This triad of Vindhya-Satpura hills and contours is the governing chord of the symphony of the PKV landscape. Dudhi basin is floored by the sandstone and Deccan trap rocks, has produced a wide valley bottom. All four springs viz., two in the southern zone

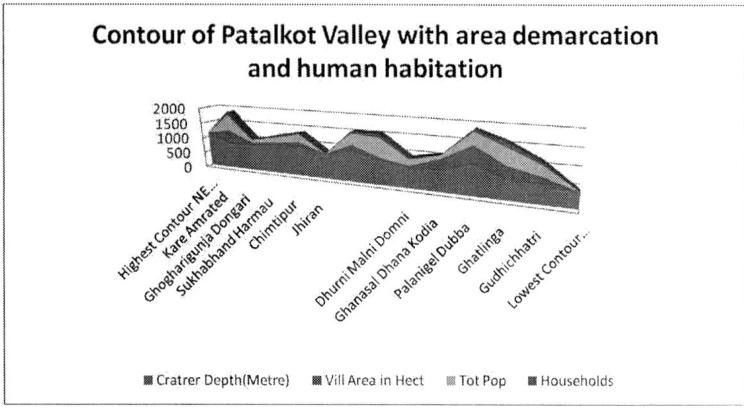

Fig. 3.4: Contour of Patalkot Valley showing 12 villages, viz. *Chimtipur, Kare Amrated, Sukhabhand Harmau, Dhurni Malni Domni, Ghatlinga, Ghanasal Dhana Kodia, Ghogharigunja Dongari, Palanigel Dubba, Jhiran, Jadmadal Harra Kachhar, Sehrapachgol Khamarpur, Gudhichhatri* in different Crater Depth (Metre), Area in Hectare, Population and Household size ranges from North-West Ridge (457 m) to North-East Ridge (1143 m) with location of 12 villages with serial number of each village in Patalkot Valley in different crater depth.

Source: Bhattacharya and Bhattacharya, 2002, Census of India, 2011.

near Chimtipur and Palanigel Dubba and other two in the north-eastern zone near Sehtapachgol Khamarpur and Dhurni Malni Domni, plummet in a single respective vertical drop in the Dudhi river basin in the bottom of the valley (Census of India, 2011; Dongre, 2015). Three physical markers, namely alluviation, Dudhi basin and the stepped land-forms (Venkatakrishnan, 1975) are supposed to be the strongest contenders for Patalkot Valley formation are exemplified by the presence of all 12 villages in different contours of the valley (Fig. 3.4). The Dudhi flows over a level sheet of basalt, in a PKV, bounded by low and distant sandstone rocks. The river's course is dotted with numerous trees, shrubs and herbs, which decrease in number as the river approaches down in the basin area.

(a.3.) Human Habitation

Human habitation and its approachability to the upland areas mingled with shades of greeneries—the 'residence' of Bharias and Gonds. Presence of stepped land-forms enriched with alluvial soil in the higher crater depth and Dudhi flows down the level of lower crater depth along with spring channels suggest that tectonic factors along with the drainage river architectures played a major role for this grandeur. Patalkot, as a region to be placed approximately in the middle of south of Madhya Pradesh is based on the basis of physical criteria with its distinct cultural properties of Bharias with small number of Gonds and characterized by a cultural landscape of tribe known as PVTG (Particularly Vulnerable Tribal Group) according to the Census of India, 2011.

(a.4.) Geographical Location

PKV, situated between the steep hilly ridges and valleys covered with good growth of *Sal, Teak* and other deciduous trees of PBR known as Pench forest, is geomorphically confined in bowl shaped area in the Satpura Plateau. Though not reaching the upland area of Tamia, it has access to Dudhi river catchment area of PBR drainage system in geological sense from south to north-west course of Dudhi. PKV's potential strength lies in its nodality having contour specific settlement, but has a great deal of communication among themselves with an advantage of natural fortification of three sides of hilly ridges and one side open only in north-west side towards Dudhi River (Fig. 3.5). The fertile soils and undulating cultivable and grass lands are an important prerequisite to its economic livelihood. PKV is differently endowed with natural wealth—vegetation in the form of medicinal plants, NTFP (Non-Timber Forest Products) and fertile soils are more closely linked

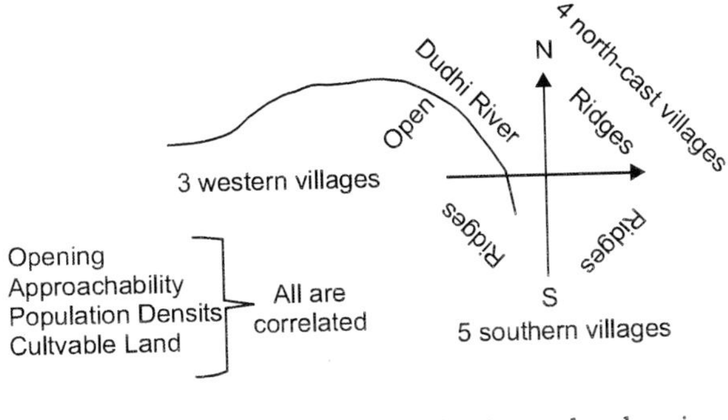

Fig. 3.5: Diagram showing the Patalkot Physiography showing the Path of Dudhi River

Source: Census of India, 2011.

with Bharias. Since, the river drains to the north-west originating apparently from south near Karaem-rated village (Fig. 3.6), a first glance at the drainage pattern might lead to the erroneous conclusion that it feeds the entire community from agriculture to daily use but actually it is not the case.

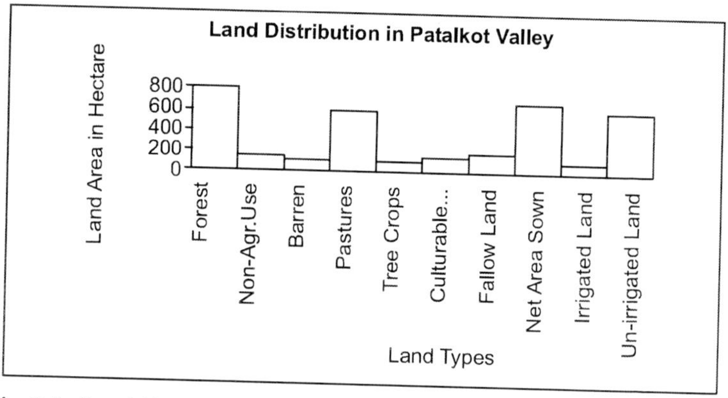

Fig. 3.6: Land Distribution showing the Highly Dependence Pastures, Net Area Sown and Un-irrigated land by Bharias within the forest coverage.

Source: Census of India, 2011.

(b) Amarkantak Nagar Panchayat Town (AKNPT)

An enormous fleet of inter town taxicabs from Tata-Mahindra-Toyota-Maruti-Suzuki-Force automobiles between Pendra Road Station and Amarkantak which ply on undulating hilly tract of Maikal (Mekkal Parbat) hills under Vindhya-Satpura ranges with an average speed, used to ferry the pilgrims to the destination safely, could be at some risk during night. Amarkantak has an etymological meaning of Amar is *immortal* and Kantak is obstruction (Bhattacharya, 1977)—a pilgrimage for Goddess Narmada in Annupur district under Nagar Panchayat of Annupur, Madhya Pradesh at 22.67°N 81.75°E at an altitude of 1048 metre. The distance from Pendra Road is about 43 km via Keonchi. The region is the meeting point of Vindhya and Satpura ranges with Maikal hills as the fulcrum. Three rivers, *viz.*, Narmada, Son and Johila originate from this region is enriched with Achanakmar Wildlife Sanctuary at a distance of about 40 km from AKNPT, which falls on the corridor of Kanha-Achanakmar dense forests with medicinal properties (Kapale and Kumar, 2011) (Fig. 3.1).

The hallmark of Amarkantak landscape is gradualistically transforming from pilgrimage to tourist centre. This brings about great changes in town and adjacent villages throwing the traditional tribal way of life into the oblivion under the influence of urban expansion of AKNPT (Fig. 3.2). The only presence of their existence is in terms of documented identity for enumeration.

(c) Ethnographic Sketch

Tribal knowledge is likely to be applied in the material culture of daily schedule which further maintains its tempo in contemporary situation, thereby comprehending a reflexive self-awareness or identified with a sort of wisdom is still valid in the present, is the focus of our research. For the purpose of elucidating this argument, this chapter explains the temporality of development encountering the timeless wisdom. Dealing with Bharias, Kols, Baigas and Gonds in PKV and AKNPT, we critically step in trying to explore their state of affairs in the contemporary situation against the pre-conceived notion against their political relevance *vis-à-vis* the development projects executed by GOI. Here timeless wisdom *per se* is immanent in the passage of time. It is nested inside the long history of tribal custom in such simple human society, seems not plausible to be superseded by development programmes as a tool for systematic transformation in totality.

(c.1) Tribes in PKV

(c.1.1) Bharia

Bharias (Fig. 3.7) are settlers of more than centuries are distributed in 12 villages of PKV. They are Chimtipur, Kare Amrated, Sukhabhand Harmau, Dhurni Malni Domni, Ghatlinga, Ghanasal Dhana Kodia, Ghogharigunja Dongari, Palanigel Dubba, Jhiran, Jadmadal Harra Kachhar, Sehrapachgol Khamarpur, Gudhichhatri, in different crater rim (Fig. 3.1) comprises 3419 population in PKV compared to 1.93 lakh in Madhya Pradesh (Census of India, 2011). Although they belong to Dravidian group, they predominantly communicate in Bundeli-Hindi language. They engage themselves in hunting and fishing, collecting NTFP, cultivating, involve in other

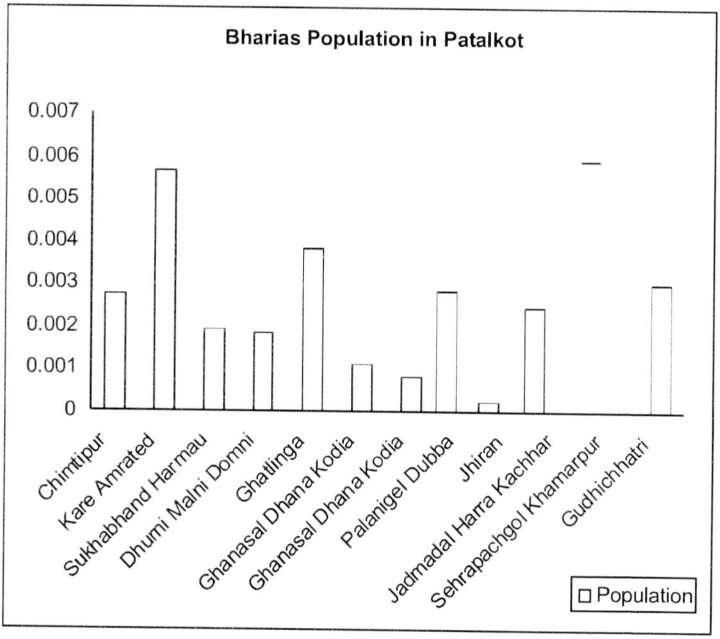

Fig. 3.7: Village wise Bharias Population in Patalkot Valley
Source: Census of India, 2011.

agricultural fields, threshing floor as agricultural labour.

(c.2) Tribes in AKNPT

The area of AKNPT is inhabited by population which is predominantly tribal, where Kol, Baiga and Gond are focused under study.

(c.2.1) *Gond*: Gonds have their largest concentrations in Madhya Pradesh and Chhattisgarh. They are believed to be originated from Amarkantak, belong to Dravidian language group has Gondi dialect. According to the Census of India, 2011, Gond population was 50.93 lakh in Madhya Pradesh.

(c.2.2) *Baigas*: The Baigas have been placed under primitive tribe category. The changes that have come about in their lifestyle and beliefs are comparatively negligible. As per the Census of India, 2011, their population was merely 4.15 lakh. The Baigas mainly live in dense forest and hilly regions of Mandla, Dindori, Shahadol, Umaria, Balaghat and Amarkantak in Madhya Pradesh. They are considered as an offshoot of the Bhumias of Chhota Nagpur.

(c.2.3) *Kols*: Kol is the second largest tribe of Madhya Pradesh. They also reside in Uttar Pradesh, Bihar, Odisha and Maharashtra. In Madhya Pradesh, the people of this tribe live in Rewa, Sidhi, Satna, Shahadol, Jabalpur and Mandla area. The Kols consider themselves as native of Farenda and Kurali villages in Rewa district. Their most dense population is in Rewa, Sidhi and Satna in Madhya Pradesh. On the basis of the Census of India, 2011 the total population is 11.68 lakh in Madhya Pradesh belongs to Mundari language group.

By and large, Gonds, Kols and Baigas and non-tribals live in AKNPT used to modify their economic livelihood linked to pilgrim based economy to associate with the expanding AKNPT market with the systematic consumption of the natural resources which is predominantly Forest produce and Medicine (Census of India, 2011) and enjoying civic amenities.

(d) Key Components

(d.1.) Boundary

The term 'Scheduled Tribes' (henceforth interchangeably used with the term tribal) is a vague and ambiguous denomination to identify India's 8.6 per cent (Census of India, 2011) of ethnic minorities under so called tribal boundary. On the contrary, it is the demarcated area in which tribal social and cultural mobility is ensured in the form of boundary. Notion of such boundary lies in a particular language; social elements and certain beliefs. In other words, tribes are "discrete groups of people" (Barth, 1969) or clusters called 'ethnic units', who correspond to respective culture. Indian sub- continent is the witness of the huge diversity of much local and segmented population in various geographical regions, nevertheless, their life style has been almost synonymous with ecological wisdom is a signature of their entity.

(d.2.) Demography

There is almost coincident features, took place from the second half of the twentieth century onwards between the resurgence of ethnic question in the world and the emergence of tribal question in India. Unlike conflicts (the Balkans and Central Africa), "nationalist struggles" (the Basque country, Quebec and Belgium)

(Simon *et al.*, eds., 2015), tribes of India do not undergo of any such struggle. Further, the term "ethnic renewal" is used in US in the 1960s has been attributed to the kind of ethnic diversity to the people of US, who come from all the way from the other continents (Simon, *et al.*, 2015) is not the case of tribal people in India. Here is a different legacies from the huge diversity of many local and segmented population in various geographical regions, who have undergone a series of political and cultural metamorphosis to witness a long historiography of more than thousand years or so, from the history of several kingdoms to the colonial era followed by post-Independent India. At the turn of century, Census of India, NASSO (National Sample Survey Office) and the Ministry of Tribal Affairs have been processing data on respective tribes in India which include the assessment of the impact of development projects, demography profile and interpretative details of social and demographic dynamics through different lenses. These data help in policy-making by the Planning Commission and make a contribution for establishing the national identity [Alonso and Starr (ed.) 1987, Anderson, 1991].

(d.3.) Livelihood

Livelihood can be emically viewed as "a point of entry" (King, 2011) in order to integrate rural region with "external markets and network" is likely to be the driver of social change. Tribal system of livelihood was stigmatized with marginalization, so that modernity blends with alternative way of livelihood appears to be a better option comparing marginality. Linking migration as a compulsory event to supplement and maintain the sustainable living condition could be revealed as integral to the production and maintenance of livelihoods systems across space which could be "temporally and spatially fixed"(McSweeney, 2004). Spatialising livelihood, demonstrates that tribal communities need to be rigorously evaluated in order to appreciate the socio-spatial livelihood variations that exist within specific places has been implicated in collecting forest produce, cultivation and earning money superseded by the development interventions of GOI mission. Tribal livelihood strategies are supposed to be adherent to traditional practices which had an advantage over proper utilization of ingenuity that seems to have greater sway with the reasonable authority.

(d.4.) Ecological Wisdom

More than 1000 years old population living in isolation intertwined with the rhythm of nature such as forest, season, water bodies like, lake, river, rivulets—these tribal people must have their own "corporations, personhood and ritual" (Schnepel, 1990) in building their respective society in different point of time. Tribal's reciprocity with forest eco-system, particularly in PKV and AKNPT, lay in the field of time tested belief pertaining to wisdom—stemming from inter-generational knowledge that might provide useful advice to forest management, plantation and thereby strengthens a strong forest based eco-system. It contrasts the trend of predictable progression from traditional practice to urban reality. On the contrary, they perceive time in every bit of daily life is spontaneous with in-built philosophy of being protected in forest habitat (Geertz, 1973). The selecting skill of medicinal herbal parts sourcing from intergenerational wisdom from the gorgeous greenery and the tool of wisdom are very much structured, time specific, having clarity and consistency. It is through this understanding, that they make sense of self-improvization against physical danger is the only capital for existence. Such cultural practice by Bharias and Gonds in PKV and Kol, Baigas and Gonds in AKNPT employ to orient themselves in their own community as healer and in larger community as cash driven 'herbalists' (Geertz, 1973). Herbal medicine is defined by the World Health Organization (WHO) as "herbs, herbal materials, herbal preparations and finished herbal products, that contain as active ingredient parts of plants, or plant materials, or combinations thereof" —is used to treat a multitude of ailments throughout the world (World Health Organization, 2002). This forest (Census of India, 2011) and herbal medicine (World Health Organization, 2002) has created a huge knowledge repository practiced by healers of Central Indian tribes who compound their own remedies and further, it does provide a stimulus to advance the anthropological research of tribal folk medicine.

Results

Boundary

PKV

Tribals are always in continuous contact with one another to justify the compact unit. Bharias and Gonds for example, used to come to Tamia for trading and other purposes. The mechanisms of boundary transcendence have been reflected in Patalkot, in Tamia tahsil, district Chhindwara, Madhya Pradesh. The relationship between Gond and Bharia, both of them are sedentary cultivators and healer by virtue of their traditional knowledge about medicinal plants. The two tribes do not differ in life style, subsistence pattern, and overt cultural features like language, house types, and place of rituals with permeable ethnic boundary. The relationship between Gond and Bharia can be described in the form of economic complimentarity. Despite the respective identity practiced by individuals, they live in 12 villages of Patalkot valley apparently having no boundary among them.

AKNPT

Tribes in Amarkantak are under no circumstances organized socially along each tribal line such as Baiga, Kol, Bhil, Gond, Agaria, Panika etc. (Ahirwar and Sandhya, 2013) and like but they develop self-consciousness of their respective identity keeping in extensive interaction with other town people. They practice a sort of town style decorum to be acceptable from different corners. As a matter of fact, they gradually mingle with the general customs to avoid conflict and competition. Apparently, there are hardly any cultural differences in business or religious situations and all of them communicate in Hindi language. Although, the members might have particular notions about the virtues and vices of other people, have no impact at all in various religious events in the temple of Goddess Narmada. When such events become a regular exercise, would by all means develop togetherness among them.

Case Study

(a) A Kol person for example behaves as a 'tribal' in family, but as a 'town-dweller' in AKNPT premise. Ethnicity of tribal identity hardly matters; rather there remains a cultural pervasiveness in such poly-ethnic situations (Mitchell, 1966). "This holds well not only in intra-ethnic relationships, but also in inter-ethnic ones". A Kol family involves in daily economic performance as road side tea and snax and herbal parts trader having medicinal value which might hide their identity because it does not matter to customers, but they cannot represent the town dwellers either. "Life, it would seem, is a market, or a cafeteria" (Worsley, 1984: 246).

(b) Baiga fuel wood supplier is another example used to deliver to all designated stalls against money, because the situation here is meant by their respective statuses, i.e., buyer-seller relationship. In several instances, self identity is not accountable. It only becomes possible, if someone asks like we did, during our fieldwork. Such fluidity among AKNPT dwellers including Kol, or Baiga or Gond are ubiquitously present particularly epitomized in Narmada festivals. There is apparently no distinct variation in their life style – be in dress and language spoken, unless if they are not asked. Allegiance to town-dwellership does not lose their membership. Firstly, in assuming particular identity, whether it is Kol, or Baiga or Gond, they are acknowledged as *adivasis*, what they do not deny and does not have no impact in their livelihood pattern. Secondly, living with the modern times is "socially effective" focus in inter-ethnic relations. Though the identity of these tribes are "categorical ascriptions" (Barth, 1969a:11) to characterize individuals, whose membership must be acknowledged by the respective members.

Demography

In Table 3.1, Total Scheduled Tribe (ST) population was shown along with rural and urban distribution. Male percentage in rural and urban sector was hovering around 50 per cent against the 70.89 per cent female in rural *vis-ā-vis* 5.08 per cent suggest that to and fro movement of male folk between rural and urban is quite likely may be due to job, business and education.

Table 3.2 demonstrates the almost balanced male-female sex-ratio among Baigas (49.88% and 49.64%), Bharias (50.26% and 49.74%), Gonds (50.07% and 49.93%), Kols (50.94% and 48.97%) and Amarkantak (NP) (53.71% and 46.43%). Barring Kols, where the density of female population in urban sector is significantly higher (48.89%) compared to male counterpart, support the argument of female empowerment in earning livelihood. However, we have not validated it.

Table 3.1: Number and Percentage of Total Scheduled Tribe Population by Sex in Rural and Urban Categories in Madhya Pradesh, 2011

In Rs. Lakh

Madhya Pradesh			*Total*	*M*	*%*	*F*	*%*
State Code-23	MP ST	Total Pop	153.17	77.19	50.39	75.97	49.59
		Rural	142.77	71.88	50.35	70.89	49.65
		Urban	10.4	5.32	50.96	5.08	49.04

Source: Census of India, 2011.

Table 3.2: Number and Percentage of Baigas, Bharias, Gonds and Kols Population by Sex in Rural and Urban Categories including Amarkantak (NP) in Madhya Pradesh, 2011.

In Rs. Lakh

	Tribes		*Total*	*M*	*%*	*F*	*%*
ST Code-503	Baiga	Total Pop	4.15	2.07	49.88	2.06	49.64
		Rural	3.94	1.97	50	1.96	49.75
		Urban	0.2	0.1	50	0.1	50
505	Bharia	Total Pop	1.93	0.97	50.26	0.96	49.74
		Rural	1.83	0.92	50.27	0.91	49.73
		Urban	0.1	0.053	50	0.051	50
516	Gond	Total Pop	50.93	25.5	50.07	25.43	49.93
		Rural	47.72	23.87	50.02	23.85	49.98
		Urban	3.21	1.63	50.78	1.58	49.22
524	Kol	Total Pop	11.68	5.95	50.94	5.72	48.97
		Rural	10.33	5.27	51.02	5.06	48.98
		Urban	1.35	0.68	5.04	0.66	48.89
802421	Amarkantak (NP)	Total Pop	0.84	0.45	53.71	0.39	46.43

Source: Census of India, 2011.

Table 3.3 depicted the percentage of both main and marginal workers are uniform. Both Gonds (58.4%) and Kols (54.33%) are having higher presence in main worker category compared to Baiga (48.83%) and Bharias (47.37%). On the contrary, both Baigas (51.17%) and Bharias (52.63%) are having higher presence in marginal worker category. Interestingly, Gonds show substantial

Table 3.3: Distribution of Workers by Sex among Baigas, Bharias, Gond and Kols Population of Economic Activity in Towns, 2011

ST Code	*Tribe*	*Total Workers (lakh)*	*Main Workers*	*%*	*Marginal (lakh)*	*%*	*3:6 M*	*0:3 M*
503	Baiga	2.13	1.04	48.83	1.09	51.17	0.88	0.21
505	Bharia	0.95	0.45	47.37	0.5	52.63	0.39	0.11
516	Gond	26.25	15.33	58.4	10.92	41.6	8.81	2.11
524	Kol	5.54	3.01	54.33	2.53	45.67	2	0.53

Source: Census of India, 2011.

quantity of < 3 month (8.81 lakh) and < 6 months (2.11 lakh) marginals workers in Madhya Pradesh according to Census of India, 2011 compared to Baigas, Bharias and Kols.

Table 3.4 shows the village-wise distribution of population in PKV. Percentage of population explains the different size and shape of 12 crater rims in different elevation echoes a strong geomorphologic link of the settlement (Fig. 3.5).

Table 3.4: Village-wise Bharias Population in PKV, 2011

(Population in Lakh)

Patalkot CD	*Villages*	*Population*	*%*
493819	Chimtipur	0.0025	0.73
493822	Kare Amrated	0.00539	15.76
493820	Sukhabhand Harmau	0.00171	5
493807	Dhurni Malni Domni	0.0018	0.53
493796	Ghatlinga	0.00486	14.21
493806	Ghanasal Dhana Kodia	0.00107	3.13
493821	Ghogharigunja Dongari	0.0008	23
493805	Palanigel Dubba	0.00361	10.56
493813	Jhiran	0.00006	0.17
493809	Jadmadal Harra Kachhar	0.00342	10
493808	Sehrapachgol Khamarpur	0.00597	17.46
493795	Gudhichhatri	0.003	0.09
	Total Population	**0.03419**	

Source: Census of India, 2011.

Table 3.5 shows that there is a trend of highest concentration of other category of workers (male: 85.78% and female: 78.91%) compared to the rest of three categories of workers *viz.*, cultivators (male: 2.91% and female: 0.55%), agricultural labourers (male:

6.74% and female: 15.30%) and household industry workers (male: 4.57% amd female: 5.25%). This trend reciprocates the slow transformation of built-in urban AKNPT which holds sway the tribal population in unison.

Table 3.5: Amarkantak: Distribution of Workers by Sex in Four Categories of Economic Activity in Towns, 2011

Person	*Total population*	*Total workers (main + marginal workers)*	*Category of workers*							
			Cultivators		*Agricultural labourers*		*Household industry workers*		*Other workers*	
			Number	*%*	*Number*	*%*	*Number*	*%*	*Number*	*%*
Persons	8416	3081	68	2.21	286	9.28	147	4.77	2580	83.74
Males	4514	2166	63	2.91	146	6.74	99	4.57	1858	85.78
Females	3902	915	5	0.55	140	15.30	48	5.25	722	78.91

Source: Census of India, 2011.

Livelihood

Kols, Baigas and Gonds involve in the trend of struggling "with the rules of the market economy" for maintaining the livelihood and the constant pressure of the market economy encroaching in the bastion of traditions of moral economy as in case of PKV tribes.

PKV

Bharias and Gonds engage in cultivating seasonal crops, vegetables, animal rearing and collecting NTFP (Non-Timber Forest Products). They weave bamboo and *chhind* (date-palm) baskets with different kinds of grass (Pachauri, 2014). The administration has time and again also promoted several trekking camps so as to promote tourism in the region. For instance, the Satpura Adventure Tourism Festival was organized in 2012. Such initiatives contribute to rural livelihoods by creating opportunities for local youth, for instance, as tourist and trekking guides. Similarly, realising the developmental concerns of the area, Patalkot Development Agency, a dedicated wing of the district administration, is working towards tribal welfare and subsequently, increasing outreach of Government Schemes in this difficult topography.

Case Study

(a) There is a universal trend in agriculture based economy, that young people are reluctant to take over small scale production from their parents—is often sustained by the elderly. Young people are virtually lured to metropolitan wealth and consumption to adopt "migratory lives" rather staying local and digging soil. For them, the village remains a form of belonging to come once or twice a year or it could be considered "a memory or a family link" (Kalb, 2007).

(b) Sushil Dhurbe (Name changed): We are Gonds by birth and permanent settlers in Chhindwara town for three generations. My Father is in Madhya Pradesh Police Force. I am a graduate, sitting in competitive examinations and trying to get a government job. I engage myself in driving tourist car to earn my livelihood. While weaving our way up through vast and zigzag undulating plain with ups and down shades of greenaries—simply amazing, patch of forest, reaching a gravelly strade patalkot, flanked by upheaval land on both the side of the road, standing to attention as though guarding one of Chhindwara's most valuable treasures—Patalkot. "I had been there in my student days up to Chimtipur took whole day to go and come back" said Sushil. "Once get opportunity, will not hesitate but to visit once again".

(c) Baigas involvement in selling dry woods collected from Amarkantak forests (Fig. 3.13) to street hawkers is the daily phenomenon. They used to collect wood almost every day and covered quite a vast forest area by foot. They deliver to the traders near Goddess Narmada temple stalls same day in the afternoon is the end of the day's work. They also earn their livelihood by collecting NTFPs (Fig. 3.15), herbal parts of medicinal plants and sell it to the local market.

(d) Bharias used to grow Maize, Jowar, Millets, vegetables etc. They collect and process herbal pars and NTFP and sell it to Tamia market etc. But crossing the boundary in metaphorical term is aptly relevant in the context of tribal migration in terms of "*chaitu* (onset of summer), *palayan*"(migration) (Acharya, 2016), seasonal movement from Gaildubba, Kareyam-Rated, Chimtipur to brick klin, and to town market as quasi-permanent trader could expand their activities as agricultural labourers, cultivators, hawkers, street sellers to adjacent towns like Bhopal, Hoshangabad, Pipariya, Jabalpur, Betul, Chhindwara, Tamia, Parasia, in Madhya Pradesh state while maintaining their original base in Patalkot valley.

AKNPT

The trend of Amarkantak transformation into NP (Nagar Panchayat) town status followed by commissioning master plan of inroad of built-in urban projects stimulate "the entrepreneurial propensity" of Amarkantak dwellers preferably tribes who have reasonably adapted to the market economy, primarily based on pilgrimage customers. While remaining in new configuration of livelihood economy blending with tribal wisdoms in Amarkantak as a case, demands sheer challenges against predictabilities in growing urban market and negotiating political crevices such as police raid, Panchayat's dictum, administrative vigilance etc. in order to lead an unencumbered life of Kols, Baigas, Gonds and others of said status.

Case Study

Incident happened in 2014 during our fieldwork in Amarkantak. There was massive theft took place inside the temple of Goddess Narmada. Thieves took all money leaving *Dan Box* (devotees pour money and coins in the box) empty. The matter has reached to Annupur DM, who has immediately come to give a political pressure to SP Amarkantak to solve the matter and arrest the criminals. Incident happened in front of us. Since almost stalls were present behind the boundary wall of the temple started demolishing by the Panchayat officials in presence of MP Police. We watched that a police constable murmured a Kol elderly, Dadaji (name changed) Dadaji replied in smiling face. After having enquired, he explained that Panchayat was not in mood to keep all stalls intact because criminals are still abscond. Asked whether he would be in position to make stall—the only source of livelihood in future, "*Koi chinta nahi, baad me sab thik ho jayega*" (There was no question of hesitation, it will be sorted out shortly) replied Dadaji.

Ecological Wisdom

Table 3.6 shows that usage of aP-aerial parts (leaves, fruits, seeds, flowers, roots, bark, milky latex, and oil seeds) is much higher than uP-underground parts (roots, rhizome, bulb) counterpart in

Table 3.6: Tribe's Use of Herbal Parts on Respective Group of Diseases

Disease	*Herbal Parts*	*%*	*Herbal Parts*	*%*	*Value*		
Groups	*aP*		*uP*		*Odds Ratio*	*CI*	*P-Value*
Fever	23	19	4	3	1	1	1
Resp Dis	70	57	25	20	1.156	0.948-1.409	0.3
Gut Dis	76	62	20	16	1.076	0.891-1.298	0.59
Repro Dis	74	56	31	23	1.209	0.989-1.477	0.14
Hepatitis	25	40	10	16	1.193	0.0.917-1.55	0.23
Inflammatory	74	61	21	17	1.094	0.904-1.303	0.58
ENT & Dental	31	50	4	6	0.961	0.789-1.172	0.71
Neuro	10	25	3	8	1.107	0.790-1.551	0.66
Won & Wor	44	54	11	13	1.065	0.867-1.308	0.76
Systemic Dis	47	55	11	13	1.051	0.860-1.785	0.76
Misc Cellaneous	22	39	7	13	1.123	0.866-1.454	0.5

Notes: aP=Aerial Part, uP=Underground Part, CI= Confidence Interval
Source: Pandey, A.K. and Shukla, P.K. 2008. Role of Medicinal Plants in Health Care and Rural Economy in the Tribals of Satpura Plateau Region of Central India. *Indian Forester*. 2008. November, pp. 1438-1446.

treating various ailments under eleven disease groups (Table 3.6). Our data are not statistically significant to identify the prognostic factors of herbal parts of aP over uP. But both OR and (95% CI) against the fever as control, reveals the higher level of potency in association with the time of harvesting both aP and uP for better prognosis (Figs. 3.8-3.9). This has been validated by the laboratory experiments of the said plant parts (Pandey and Shukla, 2008) containing "optimum ingredients". Highest prevalence of gut and inflammatory diseases are cured from the usage of 62 per cent and 61 per cent aP of plant sources. Tribes are extremely concerned of all eleven group of diseases. The range of treatment varies from fresh to processed plant parts. The widely use of aPs compared to uPs tells that they ingenuously utilize the medicinal plants in curing various illness which they collect from the forest.

Table 3.7 shows the empirical usage of parts of pteridophytes in different reproductive diseases irrespective of statistical insignificance (Fig. 3.10). These findings reveal that 23 species of pteridophytes belonging to 15 families and 18 genera are traditionally used by tribal women of *Korku, Gond, Bharia, Bhil,*

Table 3.7: ***Herbal parts used in diseases***

Diseases	Herbal Parts	%	Herbs	%	Value		
					Odds Ratio	CI	P-Valu
Infection					1	1	
Ven. Dis.	4	44	3	33	0.87	0.189-4.031	1
Mens Dis	7	58	3	25	0.71	0.168-3.028	1
Leucorrhoea	4	57	1	14	0.62	0.146-2.625	1
Increase Fertility	5	71	0	0	0.5	0.125-2.00	0.28
Aphrodisiac	2	50	0	0	0.5	0.125-2.00	1
Family Planning	10	77	1	8	0.55	0.135-2.228	0.29

Source: Singh and Singh, *IJPSR*, 2012; Vol. 3(12): 4780-4790.

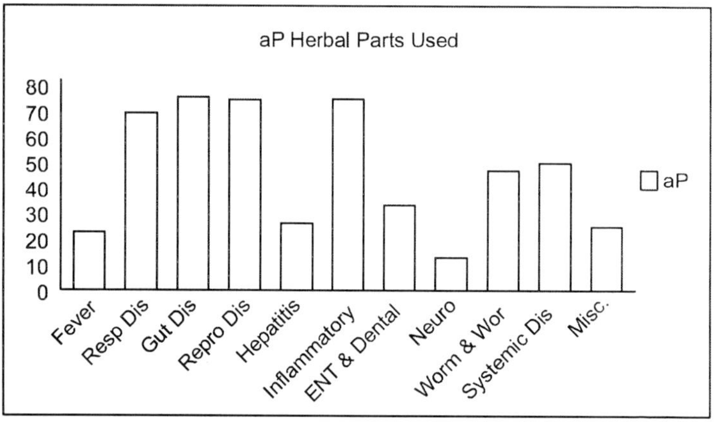

Fig. 3.8: Number of Aerial Parts used per Disease Group
Source: Adopted from: Pandey and Shukla, 1997.

Mauria, Maria, Paria, Bhatara and *Baigas* communities in reproductive health problems which contribute about 18.66 per cent of total pteridophytic diversity (134 species) of the area (Singh, S. and Singh, R., 2012).

Discussion

The chapter has assessed and analysed the development and dichotomous challenge in Patalkot and Amarkantak using four key components such as boundary, demography, livelihood and

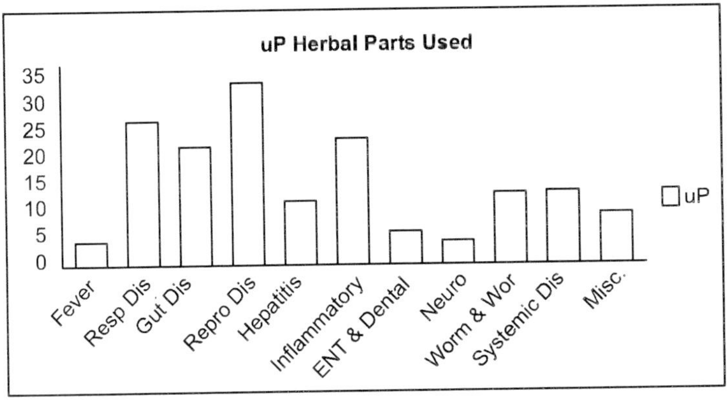

Fig. 3.9: Number of Underground Parts used per Disease Group
Source: Adopted from Pandey and Shukla, 1997.

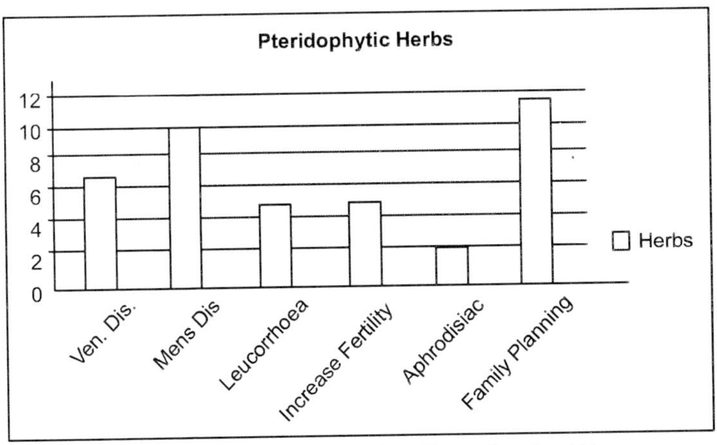

Fig 3.10: Number of Herbal Parts used in Reproductive Diseases
Source: Singh and Singh, 2012.

ecological wisdom to investigate the symmetric balance between GOI's intervention and owner of traditional belief and practice. But, the commonsense designation of a community as tribal is the product of political processes than depending on substantive notions of tribalism as "a level of social organization that pre-dated stratified class society", characterised by "the joint ownership of the natural resources" (Ratnagar, 2004: 32). Hence, in spite of the genesis of pluralistic powerful in emerging market economy of

AKNPT and government initiative in PKV, Baigas-Gonds-Kols-Bharias used to distance from 'mainstream' (Steur, 2009) of fluid nature of urban society, because they think of themselves as tribal through being on the ST list. Government has accepted such reality against the question of development is not just doing a "technological fixes to others" premise (for example, tribes in PKV and AKNPT), (Sillitoe, 1998), by means of inducing, "scientifically validated information" for adoption (Atte, 1992; Barrow; 1992) for those, who have already strengthened their faculty in effective "science" and resource used practice.

The Report of the High-level Committee on Socio-Economic, Health and Educational Status of the Tribals of India by Xaxa Committee, issued by Ministry of Tribal Affairs, Government of India, 2014, proposes a road map to Tribal's vast canvas. It almost covers all basic issues to emancipate them from oppression. This report primarily documents the areas need to be prioritized in which, Prof. Fregenious Xaxa and his colleagues have attempted to dismantle the so called myth of colonial perception. These are family and migration; participation in urban economy, health, use of local knowledge in common ailments. It could, however, be contemplated that the rampant encroachment in the tribal areas in the name of urbanization and development projects needs to be restructured; which does not give any projected growth in the international standard at the cost of tribal, and such attempts to associate recent history with the achievements of the tribal unrest, conflicts prevailed "over time in an unstable pattern" (Damodaran, 2006). Committee obviously feels that some contrast but not all, prevails between colonial times and post-independent scenario.

Dichotomy: The most interesting subject in population dynamics in India is tribes are present in clusters across the country. It has felt its presence quite a long back has been properly addressed during colonial times. Without engaging themselves, their presence is politically felt and going stronger with the growth of Indian economy. Although tribes, irrespective of their identity, slowly get entangled with Indian society—being felt from the labourer to white colour job echoing "dichotomized ethnic statuses" (Fredrik Barth, 1998). This dichotomy is ambiguous in nature. The cash based economy plays a subtle role in transformation from wisdom to so called urban emancipation has been thoroughly dealt in two unique settlements—Patalkot valley, where Bharias and Gonds are embedded in geomorphic architecture and Amarkantak, where Baigas-Gonds-Kols are unevenly tuning with the urban expansion.

Boundary: A general and a naïve feeling is that tribes are living under a sort of "bellicose ignorance of its neighbours" (Ghurye, 1943; Elwin, 1955; Barth, 1969) so, also the negative impact of colonial administration and policies on tribal social life. Nevertheless, like neighbours, tribal individuals maintain certain rights to get insulated in political sense of protection to ensure the state of livelihood in tandem with the interest of total population aggregates and regions too (Corbridge, 1988). It might appear to be logical to discuss with an attempt to answer the question put at the beginning—to what extent the concept of tribal boundaries as a geographical region needs to be revised in order to be applicable to the present day? We were tempted to do these but refrained for two reasons. Firstly, this question is rather outside the scope of this chapter. Secondly, since so many important facts like the future of tribal developments are still in making if not undecided, and so much is still in a state of flux, it would be too soon to give any definition of tribal boundaries as a geographical region today, which would have of more than ephemeral validity. Nevertheless, it seems appropriate to indicate the general direction which the development of tribes has taken. Thus, we may argue that tribal boundaries in terms of cultural units, historically and geographically, a space with certain cultural qualities, is not fixed in particular area, and once it had come into being it tended to expand its modernity with all its temporality and likely to move parallel with the gradual expansion of larger and complex society.

Demography: Central India is supposed to be the synonymous with the oldest inhabitants (Table 3.1) of various tribes such as Baigas, Bharias, Gonds, Kols and cluster of tribes in AKNPT (Table 3.2), which are marked by the ST for enumeration, administration and development projects. The development projects and progress of urbanization likely to influence these oldest inhabitants to earn their livelihood in elsewhere as main, marginal, other workers (Table 3.3), agricultural labourers, household industry and other workers (Table 3.5) for long time. Pertaining to marginal work, the argument of migration comes into being, could be linked with seasonal (Bharias of Gaildubba, Kareyam-Rated, Chimtipur village of Tamia block in PKV used to leave the village in summer time as seasonal migrants).

Fig. 3.11: Bird's eyeview of Karayem Rated, Patalkot. Photo: Daizy Ray

Fig. 3.12: Bharia is seen coming up step by step to sell the agricultural produce to Tamia Tahsil—a daily phenomenon. Photo: Daizy Ray

Because, tribal people suffer predominantly from the phenomenon of poverty-induced migration on account of rain-fed agriculture and urbanization and industry (Baigas-Kol-Gond in AKNPT) (Sundar, 2010; Srivastava *et al.*, 2003 and Misra, 2002). Both Office of the Registrar General and the National Sample Survey Office (NASSO) data do not fully cover seasonal category (Xaxa, 2014) due to the lack of knowledge of the pattern of migration. The latter half of the

Fig. 3.13: Amarkantak Forest approaching Vrigu Kamandal depicting bunches of fuel wood by Baigas for selling it on the road side shops behind the Narmada temple. Photo: Author

Figs. 3.14: Concrete road midway between Sonemura and Mai-ki-Bagicha as per AKNPT development programme. Photo: Author

Fig. 3.15: Fuel NTFP, Amarkantak forest. Photo: Author

Figs. 3.16 and 3.17: Road side Stalls behind the Goddess Narmada temple selling NTFP and herbal parts and 'puja shops' (Vecchione, 2008) of offerings such as coconut, drape, *kumkum, prasaad,* camphor, insence sticks, lamp as the necessary components for the ritual. The road leads to Sonemuda, occupying one side attaching the temple wall by different makeshift shops including tea and snax, herbal shops. Photo: Author

twentieth century has been the plausible time for India emerges as global economic partner in association with the component of globalization, escalating growth of mining and metal, cement and iron industry, digital and electronic industry, dam (Dreze *et al.*, 1996) and real estate. This is reflected in the growing trend of uprooted of which, tribal are primary victims. The displacement has been like an 'endemic phenomenon' associated with modernization of any country (Colson, E., 2003). Such consistent uprooting of such marginalized people, promotes 'loss of trust' in Central and State Governments including political leaders. Uprooted people have a limited choice: either resettlement on their own or live in government aided camps (Mahapatra, 1999; Xaxa, 1999).

Livelihood: While remaining in new configuration of livelihood economy blending with tribal wisdoms in Amarkantak as a case, demands a sheer challenges against predictabilities in growing urban market and negotiating political crevices such as police raid, Panchayat's dictum, administrative vigilance etc. in order to lead an unencumbered life of Kols, Baigas and Gonds and others of said status. Clusters of different informal and formal outlay of stores involve in exhibiting spectrum of items for selling these to pilgrims and tourists against suitable bargain (Figs. 3.16 and 3.17). Nevertheles, there are ample scopes for tribal to enhance their income sources from the forest products (Debnath, 2015). Dozens of *ashramas* centering Goddess Narmada are doing daily religious activities from individual rights to collective performance for maintaining the livelihood.

In case of PKV, Government's point of view is broad, her purpose is being to bring them out from its insularity by virtue of geomorphic positioning of 12 villages in the valley particularly those living in different contours (Fig. 3.4), to get them access to avail modern amenities right from the knowledge to the extent of productive resources for standardizing living pattern. Administratively, Bharias are listed as PVTG are supposed to get Government's aids and amenities has been documented in the Cabinet decision of Madhya Pradesh Government drawing up an action plan for protection-*cum*-development scheme. The action plan has been divided into six sectors, i.e., education, health and nutrition, drinking water, agriculture and irrigation, housing and employment (Malviya, 2008).

Ecological Wisdom: Traditional knowledge is not genetically mapped in every tribal repertoire. Rather, this small but precious "knowledge repository" is prevalent through spontaneous practice and transmitted in a 'habitus' (Sarengapani, 2003) in the form of handing down to subsequent generation through festivals, events in the pretext of birth, marriage, death, sowing of new crops (Richard, 2000). It could be liable, if it is altered in inevitable circumstances (Navarro, 2006) such as forgetting the techniques or shifting to sustainable urban economy lifestyle. So, this invaluable knowledge—"is directly functional in long term survival" (Purcell, 1998) and this knowledge is quite likely to form human ecology [Bennett, 1976, Moran (eds.) 1990]. About 30.48 per cent of Madhya Pradesh geographical area is forest full of precious valuable plants give a forest ecological support to these people as source of energy, income generation (Pandey and Shukla, 2008; Singh and Singh, 2012; Rai and Pandey, 1997) and remedies from ailments (Tables 3.6 and 3.7) (Pandey and Shukla, 2008; Patel, 2012; Lawal *et al.*, 2013; Rekka *et al.*, 2013) which they consume orally, apply on the surface of the wounds and allowed to get dried for processing the parts with respect to the immediate relief in symptomatic situation and prolonged intake for the systematic problems.

Cultivation of wild edible and medicinal plants along with regular crops for consumption is also supposed to increase the food base (Turton, 1977). Tribes of Patalkot explore the soil suitability, codification of seasons, organization of labour, nutrition (Brush, 1980), knowledge of vegetation and staple food and harvesting or plucking the aerial parts (aP), underground parts (uP) (Flatie *et al.*, 2009) —all such information strengthen their cultivable skill which is a stronger argument to face the trade-off between 'being there' with local ecology and engage in Government job. Tribes used to avoid the uprooting of the whole plant (Flatie *et al.*, 2009) to protect the plants. In case of uP, they harvest once in a year, preferably before Lord *Ganesh Chaturthi*.

Reflecting the tribal natural resource practices, the contemporary concept of the conservation is laden with understanding about forestry, plantation, natural recycle, seasonal cultivation, and horticulture are not necessarily needed to understand in exactly the same way in tribal knowledge about nature. Here lies the tussle between throwing off the yoke of top-down approach of modernization *versus* coming from a culture that stems from the fruits of colonization-urbanization-globalization. This is a fault line that the policy has hitherto be formed does not cover the nitty-gritty of tribal state of affair. That does not also mean that GOI does not understand the fault line.

Conclusion

The idea and the understanding of tribe might in the present, be moving towards a time in which the meaning and controversy of nineteenth and twentieth century conceptions of tribe is not on the wane, rather still is valid in India is the foregone conclusion. In spite of political interference in the name of the development, they still have a closer proximity to their own habitus against the questions of conventional wisdom posed by the modern science. Nevertheless, from the revelation of rethinking the ethnographic ways of knowing the tribal social landscape from Bharias and Gonds of Patalkot and Baigas-Gonds-Kols of Amarkantak that the objective of tribal development is a massive one, and it demands a kind of cerebral elasticity to perceive each tribal person of each tribal community in order to meet the vast webs of outcomes. Central to such developments is an attention to multiple predictabilities to look into as a pattern or process, as recurrent inappropriate fulfilment of the project, brought forward as past experience sedimented in future projects, to welcome more questions in uneven path.

Acknowledgements

I would like to thank

(i) Prof. Subir Biswas of the Department of Anthropology, West Bengal State University, for providing me enormous time with a responsible task and supporting morally in every way and at all stages.

(ii) Dr. Pramathes Das Mahapatra, Director, Spectrum Clinic and ERI, Kolkata for his encouragement, and support.

(iii) Dr. Snehasikta Swarnakar, Senior Principal Scientist & Head, Cancer Biology and Inflammatory Disorder Division CSIR-IICB, Kolkata, India for her tremendous support, dedication and wide expertise in very insightful data analysis as well as interaction with excellent suggestions for improving this manuscript.

(iv) My informants Shree Khusil Durbe, Gond by birth in Chhindwara, and respected Dadaji, Kol by birth in Amarkantak for valuable support and co-operation.

(v) My colleagues at Spectrum Clinic and ERI, Kolkata, who took an interest in this paper and debated it with me.

References

Acharya, D., 2016. "Chaitua or beginning of summer Palayan or Migration". Sunday, June 12, 2016. Mera Chhindwara. http://merachhindwara.com/patalkot/

Ahirwar, R.K. and G.S. Sandya, 2013. Multifarious Plant Uses in Various Diseases by Tribes of Amarkantak Plateau District Anuppur (Madhya Pr*adesh). International Journal of Science and Research,* 4(2): 2319-7064.

Alonso, W. and P. Starr, 1987 (Eds.). *The Politics of Numbers*. New York: Russell Sage Publications.

Anderson, B., 1991. *Imagined Communities*. New York: Verso.

Atte, O., 1992. *Indigenous local knowledge as a key to local level development: Possibilities, constraints, and planning issues*. Ames: Iowa State University.

Barrow, E.G.C., 1992. Building on local knowledge: The challenge of agroforestry for pastoral areas. *Agroforestry Today,* 3(4): 4-7.

Barth, F., 1969. 'Introduction'. In Fredrik Barth, (ed.), *Ethnic Groups and Boundaries: The Social Organization of Culture Difference*, pp. 9–38. Oslo: Universitetsforlaget.

Barth, F., 1997. Ethnic Groups and Boundaries. *Journal of Archaeological Research,* Vol. 5, No. 4.

Barth, F., 1998. *Ethnic Groups and Boundaries: The Social Organization of Culture Difference*. Long Grove: Waveland Press.

Bennett, J.W., 1976. *The Ecological Transition: Cultural Anthropology and Human Adaptation*. New York: Pergamon.

Bhattacharyya, P.K., 1977. *Historial Geography of Madhya Pradesh from Earlier Records,* Delhi: Motilal Banarsidass.

Bhattacharya, R. and A. Bhattacharya, 2002. *Resource Utilization Among the Bharias of Patalkot in Central India*. New Delhi: Atlantic Publishers and Distributors.

Brush, S., 1980. "Potato Taxonomies in Andean Agriculture", in D. Brokensha, D. Warren, and O. Werner, (eds.) *Indigenous Knowledge Systems and Development*, pp. 37-47. Lanham: University Press of America.

Corbridge, S., 1988. The Ideology of Tribal Economy and Society: Politics in the Jharkhand, 1950-1980, *Syracuse Modern Asian Studies,* 22, 1, pp. 1-42.

Colson, E., 2003. Forced Migration and the Anthropological Response. *Journal of Refugee Studies,* 16(1): 1-18.

Damodaran, V., 2006. *Colonial Constructions of Tribe in India: the Case of Chotanagpur by Edizioni Plus*—Pisa: Pisa University Press.

Debnath, D., 2015. The Role of Indigenous Knowledge System in Biodiversity Management and Livelihood Securities in the Baigas of Madhya Pradesh: An Anthropological Perspective. In: Vijay

Prakash Sharma (ed.) *Contemporary Indian Society (In the beginning of 21st Century),* Anmol Publications Private Ltd., New Delhi.

Demmer, U., 2008. Contested Modernities in the "Tribal Zone". The Post-Colonial State, Adivasi Politics and the Making of Local Modernity in the Northern Nilgiris (South India). *Zeitschrift fur Ethnologie,* 133, 257-282.

District Census Hand Book, 2011. http://www.censusindia.gov.in/2011census/dchb/DCHB.html.

Dongre, N.L., 2015. Evolution of experimental and natural river basins in view of the Pachmarhi. *Source:*https://scholar.google.co.in/scholar?cluster=176984120890677 12970&hl=en&as_sdt=0,5

Dongre, N.L., 2015. Comprehensive Study of Tectonic Processes in Geomorphologic Perspective. https://scholar.google.co.in/scholar?start=20&q=N.L.+Dongre &hl= en&as _sdt=0,5

Dreze, J. with Samson, M. and Singh, S. (eds.) 1996. *The Dam and the Nation: Displacement and Resettlement in the Narmada Valley.* New Delhi: Oxford University Press.

Elwin, V., 1955. "Do we Really Want to Keep Them in a Zoo?", Chapter 2 in Government of India: *The Adivasis.* New Delhi: Ministry of Information and Broadcasting.

Eriksen, T.H., (Ed.) 2010. *Ethnicity and Nationalism, Anthropological Perspectives* (3rd ed). London: Pluto Press.

Firth, R., 1939. Primitive Polynesian Economy. *The Economic Journal,* 49(196): 729-731.

Flatie, T. with T. Gedif, K. Asres and T. Gebre-Mariam, 2009. Ethnomedical survey of Berta Ethnic group Assosa Zone, Benishangul-Gumuz regional state, mid-west Ethiopia. *Journal of Ethnobiology and Ethnomedicine,* 5:14.

Gaonkar, D., 1999. On Alternative Modernities. *Public Culture,* ll (l): 1 – 18.

Geertz, C., 1973. *The Interpretation of Cultures selected essays.* New Yark: Basic Books, Inc.

Ghurye, G.S., 1943. *The Aborigines—So Called and Their Future.* Delhi: Oxford University Press.

Giddens, A., 1991. *The Consequences of Modernity.* Stanford: Stanford University Press.

MP Trible Museum 2017, Bharia: http://mptribalmuseum.com/tribes-bhariya.html

Ingold, T., 1993. The temporality of the landscape. *World Archaeology,* 25 (2): 152-174.

Kalb, D., 2007. The Path to the Post-Colony: why folklore won't save us in Working Paper No. 90 Anthropology's Multiple. Chris Hann *et al.,* Anthropology's Multiple Temporalities and its Future in Central and Eastern Europe—A Debate. Halle / Saale 2007. Max Planck Institute for Social Anthropology.

Kapale, R. and M. Kumar, 2011. Medicinal Plants of Amarkantak Balco Open Cost Forest Area, India. *Pharmacologyonline,* 3: 1290-1295.

King, B., 2011. Spatialising livelihoods: resource access and livelihood spaces in South Africa, Trans. *Inst. Br. Geogr. NS,* 36 297–313, ISSN 0020-2754 2011. The Author. Transactions of the Institute of British Geographers 2011 Royal Geographical Society (with the Institute of British Geographers).

Lawal, I. with, A. Amao, K. Lawal, T. Alamu, and I.L. Sowunmi, 2013. Phytotherapy approach for the treatment of gynaecological disorder among women in Ido Local Government Area of Ibadan, Oyo State. Nigeria. *J. Adv. Sci. Res.,* 4: 41–44.

Mahapatra L.K., 1999. *Resettlement, Impoverishment and Reconstruction in India, Development for the Deprived.* New Delhi: Vikas Publishing House.

Malviya, D., 2008. Department of Public Relation, Madhya Pradesh. Bhopal : Thursday, February 27.

McSweeney, K., 2004. The Dugout Canoe Trade in Central America's Mosquitia: Approaching Rural Livelihoods Through Systems of Exchange. *Annals of the Association of American Geographers,* 94(3): 638–661.

Merrifield, C. with R.C. Jobson and S. Randle, 2013. *Modernity of this Century: Four Ethnographic Perspectives.* AOTC. Issue 9, Oct. London. http://aotcpress.com/articles/modernity-century-ethnographic-perspectives.

Misra, K.K., 2002. *"Andhra Pradesh, Madhya Pradesh (undivided) and Odisha": A study of land alienation of Tribal Lands in Schedule V Areas.* Hyderabad.

Mitchell, J.C., 1966. "Theoretical orientations in African urban studies". In Michael Banton, (ed.), *The Social Anthropology of Complex Societies,* pp. 37–68. London: Tavistock.

Moran, E. (ed.) 1990. *The Ecosystem Approach in Anthropology: From Concept to Practice.* Ann Arbor: University of Michigan Press.

Navarro, Z., 2006. "In Search of Cultural Intepretation of Power", *IDS Bulletin,* 37(6): 11-22.

Pachauri, S., 2014. Diving deep: The hidden world of Patalkot Madhya Pradesh Published: August 27, *The Indian Express.* http://indianexpress.com/article/lifestyle/diving-deep-the-hidden-world-of-patalkot/

Pandey, A.K., and P.K. Shukla, 2008. Role of Medicinal Plants in Health Care and Rural Economy in the Tribals of Satpura Plateau Region of Central India. *Indian Forester.* 134 (11): 1438-1446.

Patel, M.L. (eds.), *Global Perception of Tribal Research in India,* pp. 47-68.

Patel, P.K., 2012. Ethnogynaecological uses of plants from Gujarat. India. *Bangla. J. Plant Taxon.,* 19: 93–94.

Purcell, T.W., 1998. Indigenous Knowledge and Applied Anthropology: Questions of Definition and Direction. *Human Organization*, 57 (3): 258-272.

Rabinow, P., 2008. *Marking Time: On the Anthropology of the Contemporary*. Princeton, NJ: Princeton Press.

Rai, M.K. and A.K. Pandey, 1997. Folk medicines of Gond tribe of Seoni District, Madhya Pradesh, India. *J. Non-Timber Forest Products*, 4(1/2): 61-69.

Ratnagar, S., 2004. *The Other Indians: Essays on Pastoralists and Prehistoric Tribal People*. Delhi: Three Essays Collective.

Rekka, R. with S. Murugesh and R. Prabakaran, 2013. Plants used by Malayali Tribes in Ethnogynaecological disorders in Yercaud Hills, Southern Eastern Ghats, Salem District. *Tamil Nadu Sci. Res. Reporter*, 3: 190–192.

Richard, J., 2008. *Rethinking Ethnicity* (2nd ed.), London: Sage Publications.

Richard, K.W., 2000. Three Perspectives on Music and the Idea of Tribe in India. *Asian Music*, 32, (1) : 5-34.

Sarangapani, P.M., 2003. Indigenising Curriculum: questions posed by Baiga Vidya. *Comparative Education*, 39 (2) : 199–209.

Schnepel, B., 1990. Corporations, Personhood, and Ritual in Tribal Society: three interconnected topics in the anthropology of Meyer Fortes. *JASO* 21(1): 1-32.

Simon, P. with P. Victor and A.A. Gagnon, 2015. Social Statistics and Ethnic Diversity Cross-National Perspectives in Classifications and Identity Politics. The Making of Racial and Ethnic Categories: Official Statistics Reconsidered, Springer Open. ISSN 2364-4087, ISSN 2364-4095 (electronic) IMISCOE Research Series. ISBN 978-3-319-20094-1, ISBN 978-3-319-20095-8 (eBook) © The Author (s) 2015 1 P. Simon *et al.* (eds.), *Social Statistics and Ethnic Diversity*, IMISCOE Research Series, DOI 10.1007/978-3-319-20095-8_1, pp: 1-16).

Singh, S. and R. Singh, 2012. Ethnomedicinal use of Pteridophytes in Reproductive Health of Tribal Women of Pachmarhi Biosphere Reserve, Madhya Pradesh, India. *IJPSR*, 3(12): 4780-4790.

Srivastava, R., and S.K. Sasikumar, 2003. "*An overview of migration in India. Its impacts and key issues.*" Report Prepared for International Development.

Statistical Profile of Scheduled Tribes in India 2013. Ministry of Tribal Affairs Statistics Division, Government of India. www.tribal.nic.in

Steur, L., 2009. Adivasi Mobilisation: 'Identity' *versus* 'Class' after the Kerala Model of Development? *Journal of South Asian Development*, 4:1: (25-44).

Sundar, N., 2010. Pleading for Justice, Seminar, 607. Available at http://www.india-seminar.com/2010/607/607_nandini_sundar.html

Taylor, C., 1999. Two Theories of Modernity. *Public Culture*, 11 (1):153-174.

Turner, N.J. with M.B. Ignace and R. Ignace, 2000. Traditional Ecological Knowledge and Wisdom of Aboriginal Peoples in British Columbia. *Ecological Applications,* 10(5):1275-1287.

Turton, D., 1977. Response to drought: the Mursi of south-western Ethiopia. *Disasters,* 1: 257-287.

Upadhya, C., 2011. Anthropology, law and adivasi movements in Jharkhand. In: Sujata Patel (ed.), *Doing Sociology in India: Genealogies, Locations and Practices,* pp. 266-289. New Delhi: Oxford University Press.

Vecchione, A., 2008. The Microcosmos of Pilgrimage: Vindhyachala (The Goddess, the Pilgrim, and the Scholar) Comprehensive Exam for Professor Jim Ryan. https://www.academia.edu/25404451/The_Microcosmos_of_Pilgrimage_Vindhyachala_The_Goddess_the_Pilgrim_and_the_Scholar_

Venkatakrishnan, R., 1975 : *Landform Evolution of the Pachmarhi Area.* Unpublished MSS thesis, Department of Applied Geology, University of Delhi, Delhi.

Verma, V.K., 1972. Drainage and slope characteristics of lower Gondwana terrain of Central India, *Not. Geomorfol. Campinas,* 12(24): 39-50.

World Health Organization, 2002. *WHO Traditional Medicine Strategy 2002–2005.* Geneva, Switzerland: WHO.

Worsley P., 1984. *The Three Worlds: Culture and World Development.* Chicago: The University of Chicago Press.

Xaxa, V., 1999. Tribes as indigenous peoples. *Economic and Political Weekly,* 34 (51), 3589–3595.

Xaxa Committee, 2014. *Report of the High Level Committee on Socio-Economic, Health and Educational Status of Tribal Communities of India.* Ministry of Tribal Affairs Government of India, May, pp. 1-431.

4

Socio-Economic Growth Through Women Education

A Case Study on the Santal at Ballipara of Birbhum, West Bengal

Sampa Das

Introduction

Education is a form of learning in which the knowledge, skills, and habits of a group of people are transferred from one generation to the next through teaching, training, or research. The wealth of knowledge acquired by an individual after studying particular subject matters or experiencing life lessons that provide an understanding of something. Education seeks to develop some desirable knowledge, understanding, skills, interests, attitudes and critical thinking. That is an individual acquires knowledge of history, geography, arithmetic, languages and sciences. It develops some understanding about life, the complex human relations, social needs and soon. Education is a key part of strategies to improve individuals' well-being and societies' economic and social development.

Women's education is of greater importance than men's education. Increases in the amount of female education in regions tend to correlate with high levels of development. Educating girls leads to a number of social and economic benefits. Female schooling raises human capital, productivity, and economic growth as much as male schooling does and it also seen that the social benefits from investing in female education are far greater than those from investing in male education. Specifically, female education has powerful effects on the total fertility rate (and hence on population growth), the infant mortality rate, the child survival, and on child health and nutrition. Female education decreases the fertility rate by reducing desired family size and that this, in turn, is because education raises the value of women's economic activities by raising the labour market rewards from going out of the home for work. In other words, the opportunity-cost of staying at home for child bearing and rearing increases as women become more educated and, so, educated women desire smaller families. Education may also change women's preferences about the quantity *versus* the quality of children, with educated women choosing fewer children, but of better "quality". Education of women improves child health because of educated mothers' greater knowledge of the importance of hygiene and of simple remedies. All this lowers infant mortality, which in turn means that a family does not need to have a large number of children in order to hedge against the possibility of premature death of some children. Further, it appears that education of females increases the age at marriage (or at cohabitation) and through this delay, lowers the total fertility rate, i.e., number of children ever born to a woman.

Finally, some studies find that mother's education has a greater impact on the educational attainment and school achievement of children than father's education. This is plausible given the greater interaction between mother and children in most families since, in most countries, fathers are usually the main earners in the household. In this way, education of females contributes more significantly (than the education of males) to increase in human capital, productivity, and economic growth not only in their own generation but also in the next generation.

The tribal population is an integral part of India. Tribals have traditionally lived in about 15 per cent of the country's geographical areas, mainly forests, hills and undulating inaccessible terrain in plateau areas, rich in natural resources. They have lived as isolated entities for centuries, largely untouched by the society around them. This seclusion has been responsible for the slower growth, dissimilar pattern of their socio-economic and cultural development and inability to negotiate and cope with the consequences of their involuntary integration into mainstream society and economy. Tribals continue to be socio-economically backward.

Women in a tribal society play a vital role in their social, cultural, economic and religious ways of life and are considered as an economic asset in their society. But they are still lagging far behind in the various walks of life like education, employment, good health and economic empowerment etc. Development may be understood as enabling weaker sections like poor women, especially tribal women to acquire and to possess power and resources, in order to make decisions on their own. The tribal women being economically poor and socially backward live at a low level of scale of the quality life. Thus, the tribal women often face the problems of food insecurity, malnutrition, lack of access to health care services and education and the victim of domestic violence and rape. Unlike the well organised modern communities, the tribal communities and tribal women lag far behind in social networking. This is the nature and dimension of socio-economic disempowerment problem among the tribal women in India.

The Santals are one of the largest and the indigenous tribal communities in India. They are an agricultural tribe, from time immemorial they have cleared forests, toiled the land and produced food for subsistence. They are also labourers. They domesticate animals. They are practicing hunting gathering and so on. Basically, they belong to economic backward classes. They live mainly in the States of Jharkhand, West Bengal, Bihar, odisha and Assam.

LOCATION OF VILLAGE

In this study, we focused on the Santal village of Ballipara, which situated at Birbhum district in West Bengal. The latitude and longitude of this village are 23°68′ N and 87°68′ E respectively. In Ballipara, total 12 clans are found among the villagers. They are Hansdak, Marndi, Murmu, Besra, Chore, Bedea, Hembrom, Soren, Baske, Kisku, Tudu, and Puria. In this Santal community, we seen that they are much poor and the reason is lack of education. Here educational development is very slowly, still most of the peoples are illiterate and people, who got education, are not highly educated so the standard of living is also low.

Fig. 4.1: Village Road, House Type of Village and Health Centre

Fig. 4.2: Flora and Fauna of the Village

Fig. 4.3: Participating in Local Festival

Fig. 4.4: House Wife, Working at Maid and Practicing Handicraft work

Fig. 4.5: Agricultural Labour Working Under Visva-Bharati

LITERATURE REVIEW

Education is an important factor by which tribal women can be empowered and get well placed in society and it reduces inequality and improving their roll in family and society (Chakraborty & Mandal, 2014).

In general, there is higher female enrolment rate in the developed world and in urban areas than in the developing world and rural areas. Socio-economic factors may create different social and private benefits and costs for female education. This, in turn, might create different private and social rates of return on female education in the world, and therefore, different incentives to invest in female education (Dollar & Gatti, 1999).

Women education in India plays a very important role in the overall development of the country. It not only helps in the development of half of the human resources, but in improving the quality of life at home and outside. Educational women not only tend to promote education of their girls children, but also can provide better guidance to all their children. Moreover, educated women can also help in the reduction of infant mortality rate and growth of population (Suguna, 2011).

The most prevalent relationship between women's education and fertility is negative and this arises from delays in marries, improved labour market opportunities, increased use of contraceptives, and weakening of women's traditional role of child bearing. They also mentioned that strength and the form of this relationship had varied considerably across societies and countries. Some societies exhibited positive associations between women's education and their number of children whereas others showed a non-monotonic pattern (Mare and Maralani, 2005).

The association between women's education and fertility and found that fertility associated with a specific level of female education was much lower compared to women no education (Hill and King, 1993).

India is a patriarchal society which limited the education of females and may be partly to blame for the wage gap between men and women. As widely acknowledge, gender equity can empower women resulting in improved literacy rates, increased employment and lower fertility rates (Sen, 2001).

In addition, educated women are likely to marry educated men who usually have higher income and proper care about their child and nutritional position of those family is better than uneducated family (Brierovia and Duflo, 2002).

The association of women's education with children education or health would be a reflection of the transformation of educational effects passing from one generation to another, this process impacts more or girl's education in successive generations (Ravallion and Wodon, 2000).

Women education in India plays a very important role in the overall development of the country. It not only helps in the development of half of the human resources, but in improving the quality of life at home and outside. Educational women not only tend to promote education of their girls children, but also can provide better guidance to all their children. Moreover, educated women can also help in the reduction of infant mortality rate and growth of population (Suguna, 2011).

The rate of returns to education is in many cases higher for women then men, due to lower participation in the labour market, the overall returns in terms of earned income are lower for women than men (Aslam, 2007).

It since that girls tend to be concentrated at lower levels of education and also the returns are inclined to be higher at those levels, higher investment in women for primary education could provide the higher returns (Psacharopoulos, 1994).

The rate of returns to women's educaton became significantly lower after adjusting their labour force participation (Tilak, 1989).

Economic benefits mostly depend on the behaviour of women's participation in the paid labour force or how they act in that labour market (Carville, 1983).

The profitability of education, according to estimates of private rate of return, is indisputable, universal, and global. The principle holds particularly for women, who can expect a 1.2 per cent higher return than men on the resources they invest in education. Providing one extra year of education to girls increases their wages by 10-20 per cent. This increase is 5 per cent more than the corresponding returns on providing a boy with an extra year of schooling (Patrinos, 2008).

OBJECTIVES

- To examine the educational achievement of the Santal women.
- To analyse the importance of women education for socio-economic growth.

MATERIALS AND METHODS

The qualitative and quantitative research approach are used for collecting the field data. The secondary data which is included journals, books, articles, conferences, published and unpublished research work were conducted from online resources by using electronic search engines Google and PubMed and also from the library resources of Visva-Bharati. A case study method applied for primary data take up, also observation participant and in-depth interview used to conduct the field study. Structure questionnaire has been used as a tool of data collection.

RESULTS AND FINDINGS

The present data has been collected from the Santal village of Ballipara, Birbhum, West Bengal. The all five tables are seen for the research study. These are as follows:

Table 4.1: Distribution of Population According to Age and Sex

Age group (years)	*Male in No.*	*Male in %*	*Female in No.*	*Female in %*	*Total in No.*	*Total in %*
0–5	6	2.55	16	6.81	22	9.36
6–10	12	5.11	12	5.11	24	10.21
11–15	6	2.55	13	5.53	19	8.09
16–20	14	5.96	11	4.68	25	10.64
21–25	6	2.55	16	6.81	22	9.36
26–30	16	6.81	16	6.81	32	13.62
31–35	12	5.11	13	5.53	25	10.64
36–40	14	5.96	14	5.96	28	11.91
41–45	11	4.68	2	0.85	13	5.53
46–50	5	2.13	4	1.70	9	3.83
51–55	3	1.28	6	2.55	9	3.83
56–60	0	0	4	1.70	4	1.70
61–65	0	0	2	0.85	2	0.85
66–70	0	0	1	0.43	1	0.43
Total	**105**	**44.68**	**130**	**55.32**	**235**	**100**

Source: Present fieldwork.

In Table 4.1, we have seen the distribution of population based on the age and sex of the village, where lived 235 individuals in them 105 (44.68%) are males and 130 (55.32%) are females. It is also seen that the highest number (13.62%) of individuals belong to 26-30 age group.

In Table 4.2, we saw that the educational status among the male is very poor. Here 27 (26.21%) are illiterate and 25 (24.27%) are literate. In total 17 (16.50%) are primary and 26 (25.24%) are secondary educated. The Higher Secondary and above are very poor—both are 4 (3.88%).

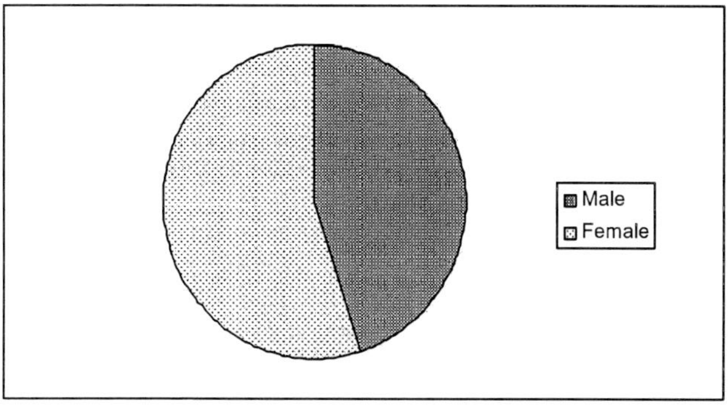

Fig. 4.6: Pie Chart of Distribution of Population
Source: Present fieldwork.

Table 4.2: Distribution of Male by Educational Status

Age Group	*Illi-terate in No.*	*Illi-terate in %*	*Literate in No.*	*Literate in %*	*Primary in No.*	*Primary in %*	*Secon-dary in No.*	*Secon-dary in %*	*H.S in No.*	*H.S. In %*	*Above in No.*	*Above in %*	*Total in No.*	*Total in %*
0–5	2	1.94	3	2.91	1	0.97							6	5.83
6–10					7	6.80	3	2.91					10	9.71
11–15	1	0.97					4	3.88			1	0.97	6	5.83
16–20			1	0.97	2	1.94	6	5.83	2	1.94	1	0.97	12	11.65
21–25	1	0.97	1	0.97	1	0.97	2	1.94	1	0.97			6	5.83
26–30	8	7.77	4	3.88	1	0.97	2	1.94	1	0.97	1	0.97	17	16.50
31–35	3	2.91	5	4.85	2	1.94	2	1.94					12	11.65
36–40	4	3.88	7	6.80	1	0.97	2	1.94					14	13.59
41–45	3	2.91	4	3.88	2	1.94	2	1.94					11	10.68
46–50	3	2.91					3	2.91					6	5.83
51–55	2	1.94									1	0.97	3	2.91
Total	**27**	**26.21**	**25**	**24.27**	**17**	**16.50**	**26**	**25.24**	**4**	**3.88**	**4**	**3.88**	**103**	**100**

Source: Present fieldwork.

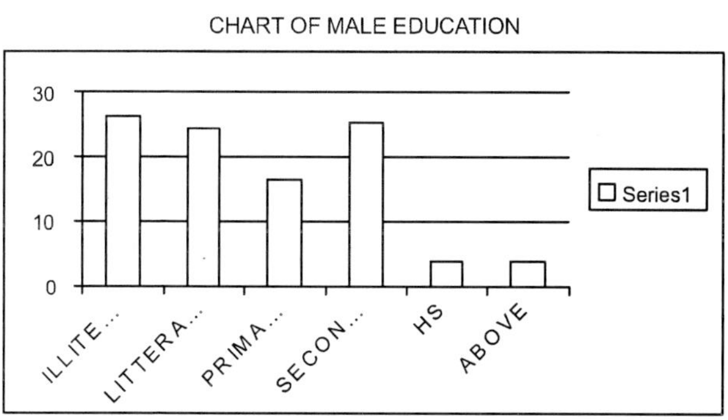

Fig. 4.7: Chart of Male Education
Source: Present fieldwork.

Table 4.3: Distribution of Female by Educational Status

Age Group	*Illi-terate in No.*	*Illi-terate in %*	*Literate in No.*	*Literate in %*	*Primary in No.*	*Prymary in %*	*Secon-dary in No.*	*Secon-dary in %*	*H.S in No.*	*H.S. In %*	*Above in No.*	*Above in %*	*Total in No.*	*Total in %*
0–5	8	6.06	4	3.03	3	2.27							15	11.36
6–10					12	9.09	1	0.76					13	9.85
11–15			1	0.76	4	3.03	8	6.06					13	9.85
16–20	5	3.79	1	0.76			2	1.52	4	3.03	1	0.76	13	9.85
21–25	7	5.30	4	3.03			3	2.27	1	0.76	1	0.76	16	12.12
26–30	7	5.30	3	2.27	3	2.27	4	3.03					17	12.88
31–35	4	3.03	8	6.06			3	2.27					15	11.36
36–40	7	5.30	2	1.52	1	0.76	1	0.76					11	8.33
41–45	2	1.52											2	1.52
46–50	4	3.03											4	3.03
51–55	3	2.27	3	2.27									6	4.55
56–60	4	3.03											4	3.03
61–65	2	1.52											2	1.52
66–70	1	0.76											1	0.76
Total	**54**	**40.91**	**26**	**19.70**	**23**	**17.42**	**22**	**16.67**	**5**	**3.79**	**2**	**1.52**	**132**	**100**

Source: Present fieldwork.

In Table 4.3, we can seen that the educational status among the females are very poor. Here 54 (40.91%) are illiterate and 26 (19.70%) are literate. Out of 132 females, 23 (17.42%) are primary and 22 (16.67%) are secondary educated. The H.S. is 3.79 per cent and only the above of H.S. is 1.52 per cent.

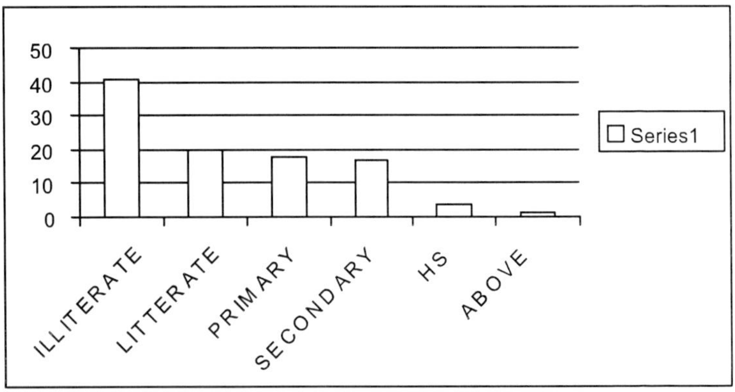

Fig. 4.8: Chart of Female Education
Source: Present fieldwork.

Table 4.4: Health Indicators

Social group	*Infant mortality (%)*	*Under 5 deaths (%)*	*Under nutrition of child*
Santal	74.3	40.8	85.6

Source: Present fieldwork.

In Table 4.4 seen that the infant mortality of the village is 74.3 per cent the percentage of under 5 year age of child death is 40.8 per cent and almost 85.6 per cent child are under nutrition.

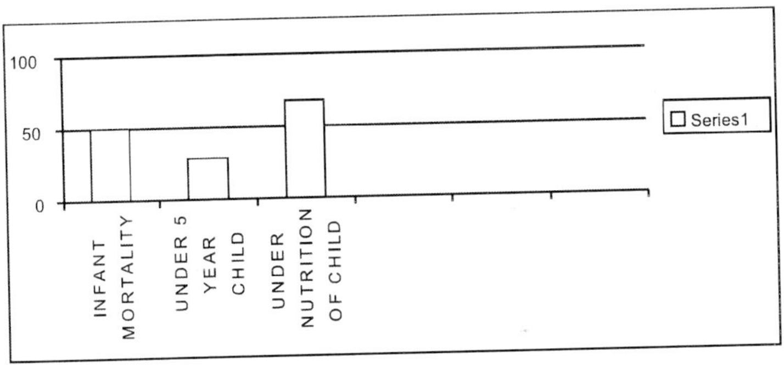

Fig. 4.9: Cylinder Chart of Health Indication
Source: Present fieldwork.

Table 4.5: Occupational Distribution of Santals in Balipara Village

Occupation	*No. of male*	*% of male*	*No. of female*	*% of female*	*Total no.*	*Total in %*
Agricultural labour	10	4.26	5	2.13	15	6.38
Daily labour	25	10.64	15	6.38	40	17.02
Service	2	0.85			2	0.85
Business	4	1.70	2	0.85	6	2.55
Cart pullar	27	11.49			27	11.49
Helper	1	0.43	30	12.77	31	13.19
Handicraft			5	2.13	5	2.13
Priest	1	0.43			1	0.43
Driving	2	0.85			2	0.85
Work under Visva Bharati	9	3.83	35	14.89	44	18.72
Others	24	10.21	38	16.17	62	26.38
Total	**105**	**44.68**	**130**	**55.32**	**235**	**100**

Source: Present fieldwork.

Table 4.5 shows that, in the Balipara out of the total population only 6.38 per cent population depends on agricultural labour. In the total population 17.02 per cent is daily labours, in their 10.64 per cent is male and 6.38 per cent is female. Besides 18.72 per cent is worked under the Visva-Bharati to the different department like security, garden, sanitation department as sweeper, helper in the hospital etc., in their 14.89 per cent is female and only 3.82 per cent is male. Only 2.55 per cent of the total population is businessmen, they have own vegetable shop, tea shop, stationary shop or handicraft shop. There a most important occupation is house servant, in this occupation 13.19 per cent population is engaged, in their 12.77 per cent are females who go and work in the morning and evening to wash dishes, clothes and clean house. In this group 11.49 per cent are cart pullers are who only male. And 2.13 per cent is practicing handicraft like embroidery. Besides this, they practiced driving, priest etc.

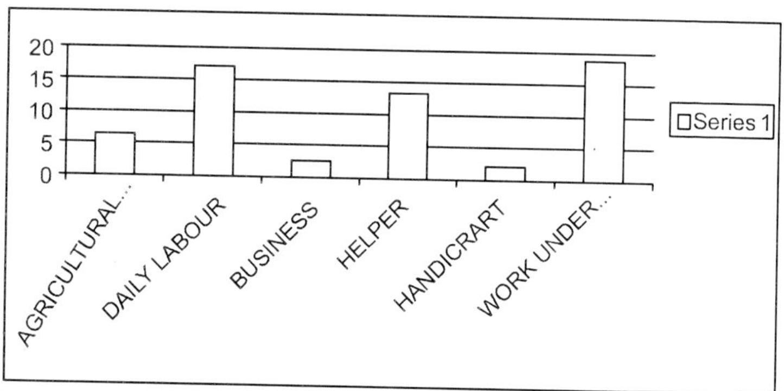

Fig. 4.10: Cone Chart of Occupational Distribution
Source: Present fieldwork.

Table 4.6: Monthly Earning

Monthly earning (Rs.)	*Percentage*
Below 3000	42.55
3000–4500	29.78
4500–6000	14.89
Above 6000	12.77

Source: Present fieldwork.

Table 4.6 shows that the monthly income below Rs. 3000 is 42.55 per cent, they are mainly house servant, daily labour, priest and some cart puller. In the Rs. 3000—Rs. 4500 is 29.78 per cent mainly belong to the agriculturalists, cart puller, businessman, driver, some worker of the Visva-Bharati. In the Rs. 4500–Rs. 6000 is 14.89 per cent mainly the staff of the Visva-Bharati. Above 6000 is 12.77 per cent, some of them are staff of Visva-Bharati and others are employees of government sector.

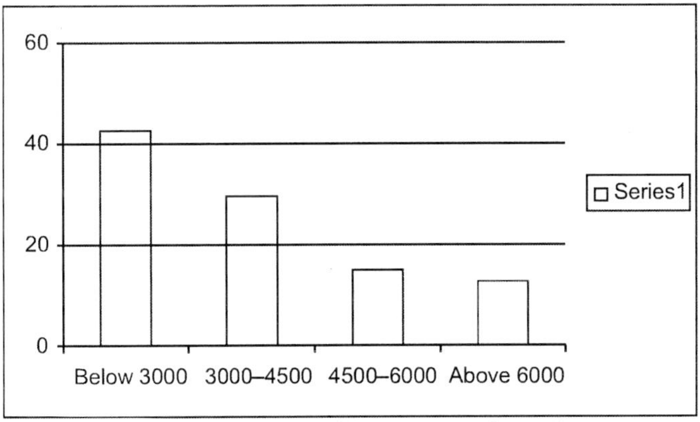

Fig. 4.11: Pyramid Chart of Mamthly Earning of Family
Source: Present fieldwork.

Conclusion

The social gains from female schooling are generally far greater than those from male schooling. From this study it concludes that Santal women play a major role in their family. They are backward due to traditional values, illiteracy, dominant roles in decision-making and social evils.

From above findings it is seen that the health status of this village is very low. The infant mortality among them are high but the under 5 year's of child death is no more high. The nutritional status of the children is also low. But, I have seen that during time there are decrease in all those problems which are the effects of women education. Mothers, who are primarily or secondarily educated, take better care of her child than illiterate mothers. The H.S. passed or graduated women are married latter and they take good care of their child and parity status decreased. Educated women are taken good care of their family and also take decision for their family which is a part of social growth of a developed country.

In the Ballipara village, the Santal women are not developed economically due to lack of education. Women, who have education, joined the Visva-Bharati for different works and earned money. They also worked as agricultural labour, daily labour and helper of house. In this Santal village, some women are practicing handicraft work like making ornaments by fruit's seed, *katha* stitching and weaving mat etc. and sold that things at the market in a low price and earned money through those work and helped their family economically. For lack of education, they don't get better job and they have no idea about the marketing so, they are economically very week.

Education is the first stage of development if Santal women will be educated then they may be get good job and earned sufficient money. If they have sufficient money, they will be able to fulfil their all needs.

After education economy is the most important part of development, if the backward peoples are economically developed then they can develop their social position also.

References

Aslam, M., 2007, "*Rates of Return to Education by Gender in Pakistan*". Research Consortium on Educational outcomes and Poverty, University of Oxford, pp. 2-24.

Breierova, L. & Duflo, E., 2004, "*The Impact of Education on Fertility and Child Mortality: Do Fathers Really Matter Less Than Mothers?*", National Bureau of Ecinimic Research, Cambridge, pp. 1-17.

Carville, L.W., 1983, "*Barriers to educational attainment for rural women exiting welfare*", B.S. Nichols State University, Louisiana, pp. 1-37.

Chakraborty, D. & Mondal, D., 2014, "Roll of education in women empowerment: A case study on the social development of the 'Santal' of Birbhum district, West Bengal", *New man International Journal of Multidisciplinay Studies,* Vol. 1, Issue 12, ISSN: 2348-1390, pp. 315-320.

Dollar, D. & Gatti, R., 1999, "Gender inequality, income and growth. Are good times good for women?" *The World bank development research group/poverty reduction and economic management network,* Vol.1, pp. 1-42.

Hill, E.M. & King, M.A. (ed.) 1993, "*Women education in developing countries, Barriers, Benefits & Policies*", The John Hopkins University Press, Washington. pp. 6-20.

Mare, R. & V. Maralani, 2005, "*How do Women's Educational Attainment Affect the Educational Attainment of the Next Generation?*" California

Centre for Population Research, University of California, Los Angeles, pp. 5-7.

Patrinos, H. (2008) *"Return to Education: The Gendar Perspective in Girls"*, The World Bank, Washington, pp. 53-66.

Psacharopoulos, G., 1994, "Returns to Investment in Education: A Global Update", *The World Bank,* Vol. 22, Issue 9. pp.1325-1343.

Ravallion, M. & Wodon, Q., 2000, "Does Child Labour Displac Schooling? Evidence on Behavioural Response to an enrollment Subsidy", *The Economic Journal,* Vol. 110, Issue 462, pp. C158-C175.

Sen, A., 2001, "Population & Gender Equity", *Journal of Public Health Policy,* Vol. 22, Issue 2, pp. 169-174.

Suguna, M., 2011, "Education and Women Empowerment in India", *International Journal of Multidisciplinary Research,* Vol. 1, Issu. 8, ISSN 2231-5780. pp. 198-204.

Tilak, J., 1989, "Education and Its Relation to Economic Growth, Poverty, and Income Distribution, Past Evidence and Further Analysis", *The World Bank,* Vol. 46. Issue 3. pp. 10-13.

5

Occupational Change and Its Influence on the Cultural Tradition of the Lohras in West Bengal

Suman Das and *Suchismita Sen Chowdhury*

Introduction

The Lohras are a little-known community of West Bengal. Risley (1891) stated that they are a sect of Mundas in Chotanagpur and their name is a synonym for *Asur*. The name of the community has been derived from the word *'Loha'*, meaning iron, as they were traditionally blacksmiths. They were the artisan tribe. They used to supply iron implements to the neighbouring agricultural tribes. Lohras used to live in the villages surrounded by hill ranges covered with thick forests. So, their locality also leads them to practice hunting and gathering seasonal fruits and woods from the jungle. Hunting is not practiced as an occupation but rather as a recreation by Lohra community (Prasad, 1961). According to 1941 census, the Lohras were concentrated in various districts of Bihar like Ranchi, Singhbhum, Palamau and Hazaribagh. At present these districts are located at Jharkhand State. Lohra are one of the major tribes of Jharkhand.

According to K.S. Singh (1994), Lohra people were bought from the Western districts like Bankura and Chotanagpur of Bengal during British period for working in Indigo plantations at Nadia district. They stayed there for about four to five generations. According to 1981 Census, most of the Lohra population was settled in West Dinajpur district. Again in the same time period the Lohra community migrated to the Tea Gardens of North Bengal as Tea garden worker. They are living in Jalpaiguri district since many generations. A major portion of the Lohra tribe of the state is also concentrated in Purulia district and they also have migrated from Jharkhand.

The Lohras speak in Bengali at home and outside, since they have forgotten their own language. They sometimes speak a corrupt form of Hindi in Jalpaiguri. Language presently is not a barrier among Lohras and the school teachers as the Lohras of Purulia speak *Panch Pargania* that is an admixture of the following languages, i.e., Bengali, Kurmali, Tamariya, Santali and Mundari. They do not have any script for the language. They use Bengali script. Mainly, the Lohras tend to speak in the same language where they reside, like the Lohras residing in Bagmundi speak in Santali and Lohras in Jharkhand speak in Mundari.

Objectives

1. To understand the present occupational status of the Lohras in two districts of West Bengal with a focus on change from tradition.
2. To find out the difference in cultural tradition of the Lohras in two districts of West Bengal.

Studied Area and Population

As per 2011 Census the population of the Lohra tribe was 24,783 in the State including 12,413 males and 12,370 females. The Lohra formed only 0.47 per cent of the State's tribal population. They were concentrated mainly in Jalpaiguri district (7,360) followed by Purulia districts (3,664). Most of them are settled in the Tea Gardens of Jalpaiguri. They are mainly concentrated in two blocks of Purulia, namely Jhalda-I and Baghmundi. In Baghmundi they are inhabited some villages on hill top of Ayodhya.

Description of the Studied Areas

The present study on the Lohra community was done in Nagaisuri Tea Garden of Matiali Block in Jalpaiguri district and also in Jhalda-I and Baghmundi blocks of Purulia district. Both of these areas have the oldest settlements with high concentration of the Lohra people.

The Nagaisuri Tea Garden of Matiali block is inhabited by a number of tribal and non tribal communities having 1080 families. This tea garden is surrounded by Chalauni tea garden in the north, Matiali bazar in the east, Aibhil tea garden in the south and Jhuranti tea garden and Engo tea garden in the west.

In Purulia district the detailed study was done in two villages, namely Ona and Jojohatu of Jhalda-I Block, while the village Bagandih of Baghmundi block was also visited.

The Bagandih village is situated at the top of the Ayodhya hills and there were 25 Lohra house in the village. This village is important as the remnant of the iron smelting works of the Lohras is still found in this area.

The village of Ona is situated in Jhalda-I block near the Torhar forest where 17 houses of Lohra community are found. Other community people like Mundas, Modi (the Oraons), Rajput and Gop also resides in this village. The Lohra male population of the village is 42 and female Lohras are 36 here.

Jojohatu is a multi-ethnic village. A number of communities live there along with Lohra community. People belonging to the Nayak (Machu), Modak, Singhdeu (Rajputs), Kotal (Rajputs), Mundha and Mahato community live in this village. There are 16 households inhabited by the Lohra community in this village. The village Jojohatu is situated at the side of the Sidhruliya Pahar surrounded by Hurlung village in the north, Barakdih in the east, Khamar in the South-eastern border, Burudi in the south and Keotia in the west. The eastern part of the village is under Ayodhya Hill zone.

About the Studied Population

The 81 Lohra households of Nagaisuri Tea Garden are inhabited by the 331 individuals. There are 160 males and 171 females and the sex-ratio is 1069 which is higher than the sex-ratio of the State's Lohra population (982) in 2011 Census. In two villages of Purulia district total studied population of the Lohras was 169 covering 91 males and 71 females. The sex-ratio of the population is 857, which is much lower than the sex-ratio of the Lohras of Nagaisuri TG and also lower than the state's Lohra sex-ratio.

It is interesting to find that in Jalpaiguri Lohra males constitute 48 per cent of the total studied population, while in case of Purulia males constitute 54 per cent of the studied population.

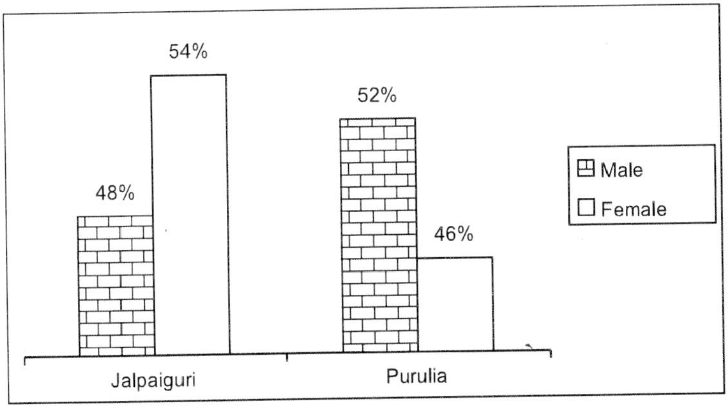

Fig. 5.1: Sex-wise Distribution of Lohra Population in Jalpaiguri and Purulia

Source: Present Fieldwork.

The literacy rate of the Lohra population in the State is 55.27 per cent as per 2011 Census. Among the studied population of Nagaisuri Tea Garden of Jalpaiguri District, the literacy rate is higher (57%) than State level. In Purulia the literacy rate is 33 per cent which is lower than state's literacy rate and even lower than the literacy rate of the Nagaisuri TG. The female literacy rate is lower than male in both the areas, but in Purulia it is alarming as only 21.31 per cent of the Lohra females are literate in the studied areas. In Nagaisuri TG female literacy rate (50.97%) is better than States Lohra female literacy rate (45.18%). In Purulia the lack of interest among the family members for sending the girl child to school has been observed. In Nagaisuri TG the education of the Lohra girls is given importance.

The gender-wise difference among the Lohras of Jalpaiguri and Purulia is also found in case of their age at first marriage. Majority of the Lohra females in Nagaisuri TG are getting married above 18 years (42.55%). In both the studied areas males are mostly getting married above 21 years. In Purulia most of the Lohra women are married at the age between 15 to 17 years. In both the districts a few females got married below 14 years of age. Males

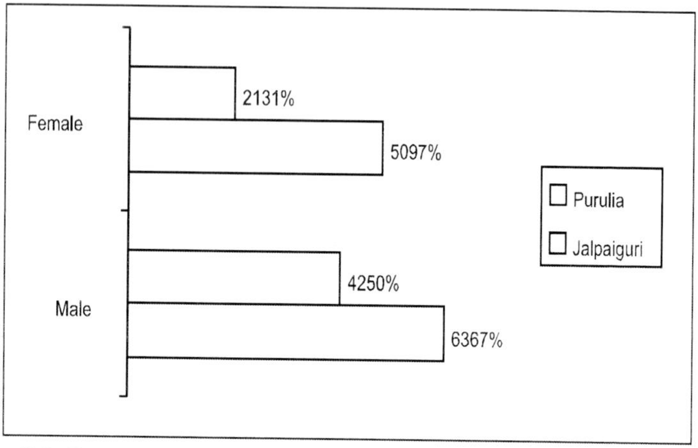

Fig. 5.2: Comparative Literacy Rate of the Lohras in Two Districts
Source: Present fieldwork.

getting married within 15 to 20 years are not uncommon. The reason behind early age at marriage for the female is mainly economic. The backwardness in education and early dropout also leads to early marriage among the Lohra population. Men and women getting higher education are more common in Nagaisuri TG than in the studied villages of Purulia district.

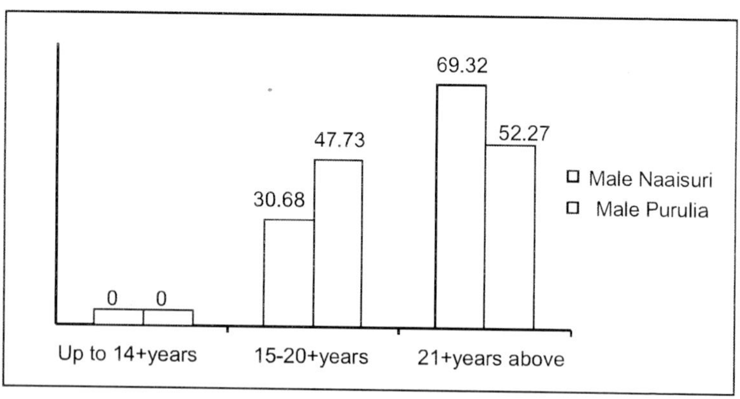

Fig. 5.3(a) Comparative Age of First Marriage of the Lohras in Two Districts
Source: Present fieldwork.

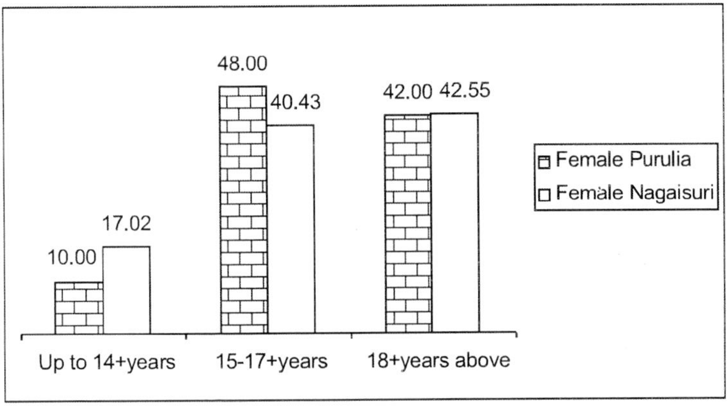

Fig. 5.3(b): Comparative Age of First Marriage of the Lohras in Two Districts

Source: Present fieldwork.

Economists believe that education has direct influence on economic growth. The Lohras of two districts have taken up different economic pursuit for their livelihood. Educated people get opportunity for choosing different occupations outside the village, while the others remain confined within the village. Once the villages were self-sufficient economically, but now such villages could hardly be found. The reason for this is economic diversification.

Settlement Pattern

The houses in the tea garden are linear in pattern. The Lohra families were distributed in all the tea garden lines. In Purulia, the linear type of settlement pattern is observed in Jojohatu village and Ona village shows the clustered pattern. The houses built by the tea garden authority are semi-*pucca* in type as the floor is cemented, the wall is built with brick and the roof is of tin. There are 39 such houses at Nagaisuri TG. The only one house was found to be concrete at the TG (Tea Garden) area. The people who practice iron smelting in Purulia built a separate room for the purpose and keep all the implements there. They also have separate kitchen at the house. Some of the Lohra houses in Nagaisuri TG were constructed by the tea garden authorities. But now the tea garden labourers construct their houses by themselves. In both the studied areas they have small quantity of homestead land.

Land Holding

The primary and secondary occupation of the studied population suggested that there are a few people dependent on agriculture as most of the families do not possess land of their own. In the tea garden areas the tea garden authority provides land for making house, but there is no agricultural land. Only a few individuals got land from the garden. In Purulia the region is hilly and surrounded by jungle. There is no land for the people living there.

Table 5.1: Agricultural Land Holding Pattern of the Lohras in Two Districts

Amount	Jalpaiguri District		Purulia District	
	Number of family	Percentage	Number of family	Percentage
Below 3 decimal	1	25.00	–	–
7–10 decimal	1	25.00	–	–
11–14 decimal	–	–	1	20.00
Above 15 decimal	2	50.00	4	80.00
Total	**4**	**100.00**	**5**	**100.00**

Source: Present fieldwork.

In Nagaisuri only 4.9 per cent (among 81 families) of the Lohra families possess agricultural land, while in Purulia 15.2 per cent (among 31 families) of the families possess land. Only 2 Lohra families possess more than 15 decimal lands (50%) in Nagaisuri TG. These lands are mostly rain-fed and non-irrigated. Majority of the land owners got land in lease from the Tea Estate. Some contractual tea garden labourers cultivate in the land shared by others. Four Lohra families possess more than 15 decimal lands (80%) in Purulia. These lands are mostly rain-fed and non-irrigated.

Table 5.2: Ownership of Agricultural Land in the Studied Areas

Land Ownership Pattern	Jalpaiguri District		Purulia District	
	No. of families	Percentage	No. of families	Percent
Own	1	25.0	4	80.0
Shared	1	25.0	–	–
Lease	2	50.0	–	–
Vested land (Khas)	–	–	1	20.0
Total	**4**	**100.0**	**5**	**100.**

Source: Present fieldwork.

In Nagaisuri TG only one family has own land while in Purulia 4 families possess own land. One family in Purulia got Khas land. Two families have land under TG which has been given in lease. The families in Purulia cultivate once in their land, but the land owner families of Jalpaiguri TG areas do not depend on cultivation.

Economic Pattern of the Lohras

Fig. 5.4: Traditional iron smelting process (PC-Karamcand Lohra)

The traditional occupation of the Lohras was iron smelting. The Lohras of Nagaisuri TG do not practice this occupation any more. They are mostly dependent on the tea garden labour works. But in Purulia some of them still retained their traditional occupation. The Ayodhya Bagandihi village under Ayodhya GP is one of the oldest settlements of the Lohras in Purulia. This fact is established by them as they showed us the factory site where their forefathers used to extract iron from the iron ore. The reminiscent of the iron smelting procedure are dispersed at the end of the village. Still the roughage of the iron work could be seen beneath an old fig tree. In this village two males are found to work for iron smelting. In these villages two individuals are found to work with irons. They are gradually shifting their occupation from iron smelting to others.

According to them in a village one or two persons are enough to carry on this occupation as there is no need for involvement of many people in the same. Due to non-availability of work they have shifted to other occupations. The persons who are still involved in iron smelting get work of repairing or making iron implements from neighbouring communities or even outside. In a day they hardly earn Rs. 100 to 200. In a week a day may remain without work also. Their neighbours in all these villages belong to other tribal communities like Santal, Munda and others. They are agriculture dependent. They use different iron implements for agriculture purpose. In case of repairing work they come to the Lohra people. Earlier there was system of exchange between the communities. Not they mostly take money for iron work. In Ona village one of the informant said that during *Kali Puja* they earn little more. The Lohras wear iron ring on the date of *Kali Puja.* They believe that this ring protect them from evil eyes. The iron smelters of the village get orders for making such rings from the villagers and even outsiders. They sale a ring at Rs. 20. This day brings prosperity to them. The room specially made for doing iron smelting is called *Sal Ghar*. The wooden material required for iron smelting is made by them. The wood is collected from the jungle. The other things required are purchased from the market.

Present Occupational Status of the Lohras

The Scheduled Tribes of the tea garden were brought from Jharkhand. They have left their traditional occupation during migration. Through time the importance of the tea garden labour has decreased due to present non-profitable condition of the tea gardens. But the old settlers of tea garden are still found to be involved as tea garden labourers, either as permanent or temporary labour.

Division of Labour among the Studied Population

Both men and women of the Lohra families are involved in work. Females are found to be active longer than males in both the districts, where aged females are also engage in work. The children are encouraged to study in Jalpaiguri where as they work in Purulia district.

Table 5.3: Distribution of Workers and Non-workers among the Lohras

Age Group	*Jalpaiguri*		*Purulia*	
	Male	*Female*	*Male*	*Female*
Workers (0–14)	0.00	0.00	6.90	4.35
Workers (15–19)	36.79	43.70	81.13	87.76
Non-workers (15–19)	63.21	56.30	18.87	12.24
Workers (60 & above)	44.44	55.56	0.00	85.71
Non-workers (60 & above)	55.56	44.44	0.00	14.29

Source: Present fieldwork.

It needs to be mentioned that there are more non-workers than workers among the labour force in Nagaisuri TG. Workers have been found above 60 years. But the general trend shows that there are many people between 15 to 59 years of age are workless whereas in Purulia 84.31 per cent Lohras are working under labour force. At the age above 60 years working men was not found as the aged people cannot do laborious work but women at this age are still found to be active in household works. Two males and 1 female under the age of 14 years have been found.

In Nagaisuri tea garden 39.75 per cent of the workers are primarily dependent on the tea garden including majority of the males and females. A number of males are presently involved in day labour work. Business and service is rare. Among them migrant labours are also included. Due to economic problem in the Nagaisuri tea garden many males and females are working out of the State like Bangalore, Delhi, Kerala, Punjab, Rajasthan, Tamil Nadu etc. They work as agricultural labour, day labour or other manual labour, mason etc. One man and a woman are working as ICDS Sahayika. Others are involved in private service. At the age within labour force 10 males are found to be unemployed. Apart from tea garden labour women are mostly involved in household work. In Purulia the Lohras are not land owners. They work in the land owned by the Santal, Munda or Rajputs.

Table 5.4(a): Primary Occupation of the Studied Population of Jalpaiguri District

Primary Occupation	Male		Female		Total	
	No.	%	No.	%	No.	%
Agricultural labour	0	0.00	1	0.60	1	0.32
Animal husbandry	1	0.67	0	0.00	1	0.32
Business	0	0.00	1	0.60	1	0.32
Day labour	16	10.67	7	4.19	23	7.26
Household Work	2	1.33	30	17.96	32	10.09
Mason	1	0.67	0	0.00	1	0.32
Other	3	2.00	1	0.60	4	1.26
Pension holders	3	2.00	3	1.80	6	1.89
Service	5	3.33	1	0.60	6	1.89
Student	44	29.33	59	35.33	103	32.49
Tea garden labour	65	43.33	61	36.53	126	39.75
Unemployed	10	6.67	3	1.80	13	4.10
Total	**150**	**100.00**	**167**	**100.00**	**317**	**100.00**

Source: Present fieldwork.

The economic condition of the Lohras of Purulia is different from Nagaisuri TG. Since iron smelting is gradually decreasing, the Lohras are becoming dependent on other works. In the studied areas of Purulia they work as day labour in the brick kiln or work as manual labour. The land in this region is not suitable for agriculture.

Most of the studied population are day labourers in Purulia. As most of the agricultural lands are rain-fed, they work in the fields during rainy season and work in the brick kiln for the rest of the year. Some of the labourers go out in other States like Andhra Pradesh, Goa, Kerala, Uttar Pradesh etc. to work as labourer.

There are two men working as migrational labour. The villagers are also dependent in the jungles around. They bring dry sticks from the jungle and sale them in the market and shops. Besides dry wood, they collect leaves, twigs, herbs, roots and fruits. They have acquired the rain-fed land, where they cultivate, forcibly to themselves. The people who have land can cultivate once in a year and, i.e., in monsoon. The land is rain-fed. Those who work in brick kilns earn Rs. 400 for seven days. The workers have to reach factory by 6 a.m. and they can work till 11 a.m. such work needs hard labour. They become very tired after working for 5 hours. After 11 a.m. they stay at home and take rest. The men and women go to the forest for collection of fire wood. Although forest product collection is not allowed by the Forest Department, they

Table 5.4(b): Primary Occupation of the Studied Population of Purulia District

Primary Occupation	*Male*		*Female*		*Total*	
	No.	*%*	*No.*	*%*	*No.*	*%*
Agriculture	2	2.33	0	0.00	2	1.28
Agriculture labour	6	6.98	3	4.29	9	5.77
Bidi Maker	0	0.00	1	1.43	1	0.64
Day labour	29	33.72	12	17.14	41	26.28
Forest dependent	13	15.12	12	17.14	25	16.03
Household Work	1	1.16	20	28.57	21	13.46
Iron smelting	1	1.16	0	0.00	1	0.64
Service	1	1.16	0	0.00	1	0.64
Student	22	25.58	16	22.86	38	24.36
Unemployed	11	12.79	6	8.57	17.	10.90
Total	**86**	**100.00**	**70**	**100.00**	**156**	**100.00**

Source: Present fieldwork.

do not have option other than going to the forest. In Purulia there is one man who works as district level reporter of a news channel.

Case Study from Jalpaiguri

Phainnath Lohra is 61 years old a tea garden labour in Nagaisuri Tea Garden of Jalpaiguri District. About of 45 years age, he with his wife, Budain Lohra (56 years) have migrated from Ranchi to Nagaisuri Tea Garden in Jalpaiguri. In Ranchi, his father was a blacksmith. Though he also had helped his father in the job, it was not his regular job. According to the informant, there was a lack of working facilities in Ranchi. So, his parents had sent him with his wife to Jalpaiguri to work as tea garden labour. After coming here he got a permanent job in the tea garden. As the availability of other jobs are more than working as a blacksmith, so in Matiali he never done such works that he used to do in Ranchi.

Case Study from Purulia

Renuka Lohra (28 years) and her husband, Santil Lohra (34 years) from Purulia district, work as a day labourers in agricultural fields and in a brick manufacturing factory.

They have two children who have been admitted in primary school. Their working hours are from 9:00 a.m. to 5:00 p.m. Sometimes, they also work in Ranchi migrating there temporarily for 2 to 3 months when there is no work in Purulia. There they work as agricultural labourers. There they earn Rs. 500 to Rs. 600 a week. These two months Renuka's father-in-law and mother-in-law take care of the children. They work in the brick manufacturing factory for 5 to 6 months during the winter and spring season. They receive Rs. 800 as payment of a week. They have to work 6 days in a week there.

Secondary Occupation

As primary occupation for the workers is not enough for better livelihood, many males and females are also engaged in other economic activities as secondary source of income. In the tea garden areas the people mostly engage in household works as they primarily engage as tea garden labourers.

Table 5.5: Secondary Occupation of Lohras of the Jalpaiguri District

(In per cent)

Secondary Occupation	*Jalpaiguri*			*Purulia*		
	Male	*Female*	*Total*	*Male*	*Female*	*Total*
Agricultural labour	11.11	1.37	3.30	3.30	3.85	3.55
Day labour	27.78	4.11	8.79	7.69	5.13	6.51
Forest Dependent	5.56	0.00	1.10	13.19	15.38	14.20
Household Work	44.44	90.41	81.32	0.00	8.97	4.14
Painter	5.56	0.00	1.10	0.00	0.00	0.00
Tea garden labour	5.56	4.11	4.40	0.00	0.00	0.00

Source: Present fieldwork.

Since last one year, the Nagaisuri Tea Garden was closed due to some internal problem. So, the Tea Garden labours did not received their payments from three months. Due to this reason, most of them are suffered from economical problem. For livelihood, both the permanent and contractual workers of Tea Garden are now working in Jhuranti Tea Garden as contractual labours and some of them migrate to other places like Gangtok, Darjiling, to work in hotels and lodges. Some children also migrate to other places to earn and also to study with working. In that case some outsiders take them after conveying their parents and other family members. Livestock is an important asset of every tribal family. Among the Lohras of both the studied areas livestock has been found. They do not generally do business with the live stocks, they mainly utilize the cattle products for household purpose.

Table 5.6: Family-wise Income and Expenditure of the Lohras

Income Group (In Rs.)	*Jalpaiguri District*				*Purulia District*			
	Income		*Expenditure*		*Income*		*Expenditure*	
	No. of family	*%*	*No. of family*	*%*	*No. of family*	*%*	*No. of family*	*%*
Below Rs. 1000	1	1.23	1	1.23	–	–	–	–
Rs. 1000–Rs. 3000	32	39.51	32	39.51	21	63.64	21	63.64
Rs. 3001–Rs. 5000	36	44.44	37	45.68	10	30.30	10	30.30
Rs. 5001–Rs. 10000	9	11.11	8	9.88	1	3.03	1	3.03
Above 10000	3	3.70	3	3.70	1	3.03	1	3.03
Total	**81**	**100**	**81**	**100**	**33**	**100**	**33**	**100**

Source: Present fieldwork.

In the studied villages of Purulia the absentee land lord was a *Zamindar* of the area. The house of *Zamindar* is present. The *Zamindar* does not live there. He lives in Jhalda town with his family. He occasionally visits here especially during payment of wages to the labourer of his agricultural land, or during the sorting out of any disagreements. At present, his *Munshi,* who lives next door to the house of *Zamindar,* takes care of his land. On asking about the *Zamindar,* Mr. Govind Lohra said that this lineage of *Zamindars* cheated them, took all their land and sold them elsewhere.

The Lohras of the both the studied areas in two districts mostly earn within Rs. 5000 per month depending on the type of earning. The people working in tea garden have fixed income, but the labours' incomes depend on the number of days they get job. At Nagaisuri TG the labours get Rs. 130 per day. They work for 6 days a week from 7 a.m. to 3 p.m. They get payment after every 15 days. The permanent labour get certain facilities which the temporary labours are not entitled to. The service holder in Nagaisuri TG earn more than Rs. 5000. A man working in private sector earns more than Rs. 10000 per month. There is also a Government servant working as CRPF posted in Kolkata. His family income is more than Rs. 10,000. In most cases the family expenditure remained same as they earned. But only in one case who earned more than Rs. 10,000 spent within Rs. 5,000. That means they can save money. The only service holder of Purulia earn more than Rs. 10,000. His father is agriculturist. So, their family income is much higher than others.

The Lohras are now giving preference on moving to labour work outside West Bengal rather than holding on to their traditional occupation. The highest paid work in Purulia was *chowkidari*. Now-a-days, the highest paid Lohras are the ones who got a permanent job, by selection or inheritance, in Panchayats and earning Rs. 7000 to Rs. 10,000 a month. Due to problem of land they cannot even practice agriculture in Purulia. They generally studied till Class VIII to Madhyamik. In case of tea garden the Lohras have left the traditional occupation long back. They started working as garden labour and still doing so, although due to weakening of tea garden they have to shift to other sort of labour works. They are even migrating to other states and Bhutan. Reflection of ecology is clear on the occupation of the Lohras and difference in cultural tradition could also be found in two areas.

Rituals and Practices among the Lohras of Two Districts

The Lohras are divided into different clans like Tirki, Beliar, Kaithya, Santiar, Hapor, Baguar, Induar, Minz etc. They use Lohra, Lohar, Karmakar, Karmali, Kamar etc. as their surnames. The Lohras living in two different areas have been influenced by the cultural tradition of that locality. The Lohras living in tea garden depict a mixed culture which is followed by other tribal and non tribal communities of that area. On the other hand the Lohras of Purulia still retained their cultural tradition which is reflected in their ritual practices. The comparative portrayal of the life cycle rituals and religious practices prove that fact.

Birth Rituals

Among the Lohras of Purulia, a pregnant woman does not observed any food restriction. But she is not allowed to go alone either to fetch water or to collect firewood and fruits from the jungle. Suppose a woman enters a house and after she leaves, the baby of the house starts crying continuously. Then the older men who are capable of healing traditionally were summoned. They pray and chant spells and the baby stops crying. That woman will be treated as a witch.

On the day of delivery, a mid-wife (*Dhai*) who belongs to other caste is asked to come and after child's birth, she cuts the umbilical cord (*Nabhi*) with knife which is buried on the back of the house. On 9th day, the mother and newborn have to take a ritual bath after cuts the nail by barber. After bath, the maternal uncle or grandmother select a name for the baby. Birth pollution is observed for 20 days. A feast is given to the kinsmen on this occasion. On the 21st day, a bath in a pond is essential, before worship at the *ghat* (bank of the pond). Red spots are drawn on cow dung with vermilion, while praying to *Dharmaraj* (their supreme deity).

In Jalpaiguri restrictions for pregnant woman is not strictly followed. In the studied areas hospital delivery is more common as the inhabitants of tea garden can avail the facility of tea garden hospital. During pregnancy they consult doctor of garden hospital. The tradition of keeping mother and child in a separate room after delivery is practiced and only mother-in-law is allowed to enter the room. First five days are maintained as pollution period. This time healthy food has been served to the mother. *Chhatti* is observed on the sixth day which is a common tradition of all the communities living in tea garden. On that day, in the morning after removing the hair of the baby the wasted hair were thrown to the jungle. Then the mother and the baby take bath in nearby river. This is known as *Chooth Kam.* The term suggests that this ritual is also adopted from other communities. In absence of *Daima* mother-in-law performs all the rituals. On that day a new *saree,* Rs. 1000, sweet and *Haria* (a local liquor) were presented to her. On 12th day morning name giving ceremony is performed. On this occasion relatives and neighbours are invited. They sacrifice chickens in the name of god and the cooked meat is served to the invitees.

Marriage

The Lohras are endogamous tribe. They follow clan exogamy in both the studied areas. But in the tea gardens inter-caste marriage is common. Widow re-marriage is permitted among them and it is called *Sangha*. In case of marriage rules Lohras of Purulia are stricter than the Lohras of Jalpaiguri. Marriages are mostly monogamous, but polygyny is not unknown. *Sankha, Sindur* and *Loha* are the symbol of a married woman. It is observed that the Lohras of both areas perform elaborate marriage rituals and there is many common elements in marriage practice.

The middleman generally brings the news of any available girl to the boy's house. Then after repeated visit by both the parties at both the house date of marriage is fixed. The ritual of considering a perfect match is called *Chhipa chal* which is executed by *Parganat* or any older person of the house. In this ritual three rice grains dedicated to groom, bride and their religious *guru* are left to float on a big bell-metal made bowl (*chhipa*) full of water. The rice grains are smeared with vermillion and *kajal*. If the grains touch together, the couple is considered as perfect.

After some days, the bride's parents along with several relatives and invitees (*kutum*) visit the groom's house for a feast. The occasion continues whole night and everyone from the bride's side returns next morning. This occasion is called *Jongmari*. Everyone from the bride's side gifts something to the groom and blesses him. This occasion is performed in both the houses.

The system of paying bride price has become ceremonial and it is called *Chadda-Sikhas* and *bhaita-selami* (fourteen coins each worth on-fourth of a rupee). After finalization of the date of marriage, *Ashirbaad* or *bandhuni* (blessing / binding) is performed at the bride's place. Actual marriage rituals include *gayeholud* (performed before 3-5 days), *satpak-ghora, malabadal* and *ashtamangala*. On day of marriage groom's relatives goes to bride's house where they are served with food and drink. After taking rice-beer they dance and sing. Bridegroom sits parallel to each other in the *Marwa* (marriage platform). The groom applies vermillion on the forehead of the girl three times with the little finger of his right hand. The bride repeats the same thing. The *Chumawan* ritual is performed after that.

In Purulia the bride and groom are first made to marry a banana tree (*Kayra biye*) before actually marrying each other. Another ritual is performed in Purulia only which is called *beti-gur-kha*. This ceremony is performed when the bride elopes towards her parent's home with a basket and a grinding stone (*shil nora*) on her shoulders.

Everyone shouts that the bride is running away. The groom then runs after her and beats her twice with a stick after catching. The bride then throws the basket with the *shil nora* in it. When the *nora* falls down, the older women jokingly starts crying that the groom is hurt and may die. Then the bride and groom enter the groom's house. Before entering groom's house, the bride offers water to *Bura Buri than*. This ritual is uncommon is Jalpaiguri.

Death

In Purulia the Lohras bury their dead in the graveyard called *Mansa*. Those who die of small pox, cholera, pregnancy are not buried in the *Mansa*. They are carried to the river and buried there. The corpse is carried on a cot by four persons. The women do not go to the *Mansa*. At the time of burying the corpse the head is placed towards north.

During pollution period which continues till 10 days after death the family members eat vegetarian food without spices. After the pollution period *Shraddha* rituals are performed on, on the eleventh day. The priest called *Naikha* (caste-panchayat member) performs the rituals. The ritual *ghate-tola* is observed in which all men of the dead person's lineage and also the corpse-bearers shaved their heads and pare their nails. After that they take bath and wear new clothes which are gifted by affinal kins. The houses are cleaned with cow dung. On twelfth day, a *kush* (a kind of grass) idol of the dead person is made and placed on a banana leaf. The members of the bereaved family then anoint the idol with turmeric paste and mustard oil. The eldest member carries it to a water body and throws it. Finally, a feast is given to kinsmen and this brings an end of the death pollution.

In Jalpaiguri also pollution period continues till 10 days after death, but the family members eat milk and rice along with fruits during this period. A Brahmin comes everyday and read *Garuda Purana*. The Brahmin is paid money everyday for this purpose. On the 10th day, they go to river and a barber cut their hair and nail in presence of the Brahmin priest. Rice powder, 5 bananas, 250 g jaggery, 100 g batasa, 100 g sesame, incensed sticks, 500 g milk, 11 pieces of beetel leaf, 11 pieces of beetel nut, and white string were used in this process (the quantity of the items may vary). *Pinda* is prepared with these. Rituals are performed by the priest as they do in case of the Hindus. After completing the rituals these *Pindas* are thrown into the river by the deceased's son. On the eleventh day, the Brahmin came again. One *pind* is made and kept with flowers over a stone or tree in the house for the peace of soul. On twelfth day, *Ganesh Puja* was organized and only the Brahmin along with 5 children was fed at first and then, all the invitees attend a feast. Calf, utensils set, cot, set of new clothes, set of accessories along with money are gifted to the Brahmin.

It may be noted that the death ritual followed in Jalpaiguri is totally Hinduaised. But in Purulia they still follow the tradition.

Religion and Festival

The religion of the Lohras is Sarna and they worship nature through hills, trees and other natural objects. During the occasion of *Sarul* and others, they worship three or four hens and name them as Bagur, Pudra etc. On the day of *Nabami* of *Durga Puja,* they worship the place of iron smelting by sacrificing a red cock and drinking *haria*. This is called *Sal puja*. During *Sarul puja,* the whole village worships nature together as well as the individual families doing the same in their respective houses. Any one member of the family would fast that day and he will worship and sacrifice. Women can also participate in this *puja*. They also perform *Bura Burir puja* when there is an eldest son in the house. They are now assimilated with Santals and Mundas.

Festivals and other Religious Occasion

Traditionally, the main family deity of the Lohras is *Dharmaraj* and *Dharmaraj Puja* which is held in month of *Magh*. They also have other community or village festivals such as *Dal Puja* or *Karam* in *Shavan* or *Bhadra, Panchabhut Puja* in *Kartik, Makar* in *Poush* and the annual hunting festival on *Magh-Purnima* day. In Purulia they have started worshiping *Biswakarma* which is actually the deity of the *Lohar* (a Scheduled Caste Community). They also perform *Fagua* (festival of colour observed during *Holi*) and *Shorai* (celebrated in moth of *Kartik*). This is done by those *Lohras* who own cattle. A fowl is sacrificed in the cattle-shed and in the evening, the houses are lighted.

Traditional Panchayat

The Lohras have their own traditional Panchayat found only in Purulia headed by *Parganats*. It is a hereditary post. *Parganats* solve the village level problems. In case of major problem Lohras from 22 villages (called *Baishi Kutum*) are called to solve it. A meeting is arranged and variable numbers of individuals from every invited villages attend it. When a girl of Lohra community elopes with a boy of other castes or tribes, this meeting with Lohras of 22 villages will be held. Generally, the decision was to arrange a feast called *mrito vhoj* that marks the non-acceptance of the girl in Lohra community in the future. When a Lohra boy marries a girl of other tribes and castes, the girl will never get her identity as Lohra.

General Observation and Conclusion

When people face difficulty in continuing traditional occupation, they shift to available occupations of that locality. The Lohras of Purulia tried to keep traditional occupation in the village under mutual adjustment among themselves. Only one family in every studied village continuing iron smelting work as more than one involved in such occupation creating financial problem. Naturally, others have taken up works like manual labour or agricultural labour etc. educated people get job, although this is a rare scenario.

On the other hand tea garden people have left traditional occupation long back and none of them continuing the same. From many generations they are working as tea garden Labours. Recently, Nagaisuri Tea Garden has stopped operating and the labours lost permanent jobs. Most of them are facing economical problem. Either the permanent and contractual labours are working in Jhuranti Tea Garden as contractual labours or they are migrating to other areas for working in hotels and/or other labour works. Some children also migrate to other places for economic purpose and continue study while working.

The trend of education is found to be better in the tea garden due to influence of Christianity and availability of school in nearby areas. In Purulia the Lohras are comparatively backward in terms of education. Some of the families in tea garden have converted to Christianity and follow Christian rituals and festivals. In Purulia they profess Hinduism and still practice traditional rituals and festivals. Even the life cycle rituals have been influenced by the local tradition of the Nepalies and other tribes. In Purulia influence of traditional Panchayat is still found.

Therefore, it may be concluded that occupational change not only influence the economic life of a group, but it also influences their culture.

References

Prasad, Narmadeswar (1961), *Land and People of Tribal Bihar*, Ranchi: Bihar Tribal Research Institute.

Risley, H.H., (1981), "The Tribe and Caste of Bengal." *Ethnographic Glossary*, Vols. I & II, KLM Firma Mukhopadhyay, Calcutta, India.

Singh, K.S. (1994), *The Scheduled Tribes*, Vol. II, Oxford University, Delhi, Mumbai, Culcutta, Madras.

Singh, K.S. (1998), *India's Communites*, Vol.VI, Oxford University.

Singh, K.S. (ed.) 2008, *People of India: West Bengal*, Vol. XXXXIII (Part II), Seagull Books, Calcutta.

6

Development of Thrifting Habit Among the Tribes of West Bengal

A Study on the Tribal SHGs under LAMPS

Ananya Chanda and *Sanjay Basu*

Introduction

A total of 52,96,953 persons belonging to different tribal communities constitute approximately 5.8 per cent of the total population of West Bengal according to the 2011 Census Report. There are 40 communities enlisted as Scheduled Tribes as per the Scheduled Castes and Scheduled Tribes Orders (Amendment) Act, 2002 (Act 10 of 2003) in the State. Many of these tribes have their cultural uniqueness in different aspects despite being continuously influenced by the surrounding change factors, especially experienced by those living near the urban areas. It is often seen that though they have a rich traditional heritage, most of them continue to remain backward in many ways for which they face numerous problems including a strikingly low literacy level or total illiteracy leading to non-awareness about many development opportunities, low economic status, migration stress, frequent displacement and re-habilitation in search of work or earning resources, health and nutrition related problems and moreover lack of interest in creation of a thrifting habit for future necessity.

To upgrade the livelihood of these backward classes of tribal people and to increase their knowledge about thrifting the West Bengal Tribal Development Cooperative Corporation Ltd. (WBTDCCL) established a co-operative society, namely Large-sized Agricultural Multi Purpose Co-operative Societies (LAMPS) under Backward Welfare Department, Government of West Bengal. At present among the 154 LAMPS of West Bengal the Deposit Mobilization Scheme (DMS) or *Adivasi Sanchao 'O' Dadan Arah* is operating in 82 LAMPS situated in different districts of West Bengal to develop the savings habit of the tribal people.

About the TDCC

The West Bengal Tribal Development Cooperative Corporation Ltd. (WBTDCCL) was formed in 1976 under West Bengal Co-operative Societies Act, 1973 (currently revised, amended and updated and known as the WBCS Act, 2006). WBTDCC is the apex body of the Large-sized Agricultural Multi Purpose Co-operative Societies (LAMPS) project of the Backward Classes Welfare Department, Government of West Bengal. WBTDCC has different development programmes for the tribals which are implemented through the LAMPS at the grass roots level. Deposit Mobilization Scheme (DMS) or *Adivasi Sanchao 'O' Dadan Arah* which aims at developing a savings habit among the tribal people was started during 2001.

The LAMPS in West Bengal remarked that —strategically, the LAMPS were the suitable agency to satisfy the needs of the tribes in the rural areas.

About SHGs

A Self-Help Group (SHG) is a non-professional group formed by people with a common problem or situation for the purpose of pooling resources, gathering information and offering mutual support and services. It is also a method of organizing the poor people and the marginalized to come together to solve their individual problems (Sen Chowdhury, 2013). The SHG method is now a well-known concept used by the Governments, NGOs and others worldwide. Members of the tribal SHGs in this study under reference have mainly been found to be women. This has led to improvement of the process of women empowerment. Today many of these Self-help groups have become an effective vehicle of change for the poor and the marginalized tribals.

The Ninth Five Year Plan of the Government of India had given due recognition to the importance and relevance of the Self-Help Group Approach to implement developmental schemes at the grassroots level (Sen Chowdhury & Bhattacharya, 2015). The economically backward STs collect their savings and save it in DMS and also get easy access to loans at a nominal rate of interest which helps them to build their houses, to grow their businesses and promptly attend to emergency financial needs of their families without getting entangled in the lucrative traps of local unscrupulous money-lenders. The total number of SHGs in the studied 82 LAMPS is about 10,799 among whom 9080 SHGs have already opened their accounts in DMS.

Objective of the Present Study

The objective of the present study, conducted from 2014 to 2016 is to explore the mechanism of involvement of the tribal SHGs under LAMPS in developing their thrifting habit and their proactive impact in improvement of the economic status of the Scheduled Tribes.

Methodology

The present study is both analytical and descriptive in nature and is based on primary and secondary data. Some of the secondary data have been collected from the census reports and also from the previous studies on the tribal SHGs and the Co-operative Corporations as well. In-depth interviews were conducted with the LAMPS staff, WBTDCC Regional Managers, Branch Managers and Board of Directors of all LAMPS concerned. Information was also collected from the SHG beneficiaries having accounts in DMS under 82 LAMPS units, covering 53.25 per cent of the total LAMPS in West Bengal, through structured schedules. Special Case Studies are also documented to understand the benefits of DMS and also the problems faced by them.

Data Collection

Primary data was collected from the LAMPS as well as from the Account Holder Beneficiaries. A total of 177 SHG members were interviewed through the Structured Schedule and many of them have been found to be operating individual accounts apart from affiliation to the collective SHG Accounts thereby demonstrating an encouraging trend of responsible decision-making through creation of a money-saving aspect into their otherwise gloomy economic scenario.

The Area of the Present Study

The State of West Bengal is divided into three Administrative Divisions, namely—Jalpaiguri Division, Barddhaman Division and Presidency Division respectively. Among the 20 districts of West Bengal the present study was conducted between 2014 and 2016 in 13 districts that belong to three major Administrative Divisions of West Bengal, namely Jalpaiguri division, Barddhaman division and Presidency division. Under Barddhaman division 5 districts, under Jalpaiguri division 6 districts and under Presidency division 2 districts have been covered under the present study. WBTDCC is also operating in 3 other districts of the State. There are 154 LAMPS in total 16 districts managed by 4 Regional Offices (RO), 1 Head Office and 4 Branch Offices (BO).

The Deposit Mobilization Scheme (DMS) or *Adibasi Sancha O Dadan Arah* is currently operating in 82 LAMPS across the State. There are 51 LAMPS under four Regional Offices and 30 LAMPS under four Branch Offices and 1 LAMPS under Head Office of WBTDCC. The study was done in all the DMS approved LAMPS.

Status of Deposit Mobilization Scheme (DMS)

Deposit Mobilization Scheme (DMS) or *Adibasi Sancha 'O' Dadan Arah* is an effort towards at introducing a customer friendly localized banking system in remote tribal areas. It is a new initiative undertaken since 2001 promoting saving habit among many of the tribes who were totally unaware about saving money for future benefits. Whatever they earned was utilized immediately for livelihood. The tribal people had lack of access to fair and safe financial services, which may also be regarded as a sort of financial exclusion of the tribes from the economic mainstream. Lack of awareness, illiteracy and poverty contributed to this process of exclusion. At the same time distance of the nearest Bank Branch, Bank timings, 'cumbersome' documentation, 'alien' language, 'attitude' of the bank staff etc. augmented the trend of financial exclusion in the rural areas.

Before initiation of DMS in the LAMPS, the tribal SHGs had to transact and also received almost all schemes or subsidies through other Nationalized or Private Banks where they faced many such problems as discussed above. Thus, with the aim of bringing the tribal people within the framework of easy banking system, DMS was started by the WBTDCC. This scheme, popularly known as Mini Bank was opened in different LAMPS for depositing money by the tribal people and also for making transaction of loans and subsidy under different financial schemes for them through their own accounts. The savings of the SHGs under the respective LAMPS were also deposited in the Mini Bank. Till date, 82 such DMS-enabled LAMPS branches have been approved in 13 Districts of the State.

The DMS system thus opened up a secure option to invoke thriftiness among the members of LAMPS by promoting Micro-Savings. Here separate Registers for each Micro-Deposit and Micro- Loan of the SHG are maintained and everything relating to this are listed in it at the end of each Financial Year both by the official staff alongside the Account Holder SHGs.

Besides these 82 WBTDCC approved DMS operating LAMPS as seen in Table 6.1, there are 17 other LAMPS which have initiated DMS, but, as on date, these are yet to get approval from WBTDCC.

Status of the Self-Help Groups (SHGs)

According to the rules of DMS, SHG accounts are required to be formed such that the deposit programme for the tribes can be extended to cater to maximum number of ST people. All official documents i.e., Separate Ledger Books, Passbooks, and Resolution Books for individual SHGs, Specimen Cards etc. for each SHG account are separately prepared so that it may be easier to access the various schemes and the Mini Banking System as well.

In total, the 82 LAMPS have 10,799 SHGs, majority of which are formed by tribal Women, while male-based and Combined or Mixed Sex SHGs are comparatively less in number. This situation can be best observed from Table 6.2 where majority of the studied LAMPS are found to have more Female SHGs than Male SHGs. It highly indicates the growing interest of the tribal women in their

Table 6.1: District-wise Distribution of DMS in the LAMPS

Districts	*Head Office/ Regional Office/ Branch Office*	*Number of LAMPS*	*Number of Approved DMS*	*Percentage of LAMPS having DMS*	*SHG Accounts*
North 24 Parganas	Head Office	3	1	33.33	547
Bankura	Bankura RO	20	10	50.00	1128
Darjeeling	Jalpaiguri RO	7	4	57.14	239
Alipurduar		11	4	36.36	558
Jalpaiguri		7	4	57.14	663
Paschim Medinipur	Jhargram RO	21	11	52.38	844
Purulia	Purulia RO	23	18	78.26	1680
Dakshin Dinajpur	Dakshin Dinajpur BO	16	10	62.50	1927
Barddhaman	Barddhaman BO	8	4	50.00	236
Malda	Malda BO	10	7	70.00	1415
Uttar Dinajpur		3	1	33.33	244
Murshidabad		3	1	33.33	94
Birbhum	Suri BO	12	7	58.33	408
13 Districts	**Total**	**154**	**82**	**53.25**	**9983**

Source: Data collected from WBTDCC.

all over development and it also highly signifies the empowerment of the tribal women.

Dakshin Dinajpur has the highest number of Male SHGs (276), but if LAMPS to SHG ratio is considered, Alipurduar gets the highest number of Male SHGs (200) in four LAMPS, while in Sandeshkhali of North 24-Parganas District there are 94.88 per cent Female SHGs which is highest among all the studied areas. In Dakshin Dinajpur 10 LAMPS units have 2070 SHGs which is the highest among the studied districts. Only two districts, namely Murshidabad with 19 and Purulia with 10 have Combined or Mixed SHGs where both male and female are part of single Self-Help Groups.

It is interesting to note in correlation with Table 6.1 that a total of 9983 SHGs among these 10799 SHGs under the LAMPS have already have opened their accounts in DMS. After initiation of DMS within the LAMPS, at humb-rule was made that the SHGs under the LAMPS will not only have to open their own separate SHG accounts but would also help in opening individual

Table 6.2: Numbers of SHGs Present in the Studied LAMPS

cSl. No.	District	No. of LAMPS	SHG Categories						
			Male		Female		Combined		Total
			No.	%	No.	%	No.	%	No.
1.	Alipurduar	4	200	30.12	464	69.88	0	0.00	664
2.	Bankura	10	185	15.55	1005	84.45	0	0.00	1190
3.	Barddhaman	4	32	13.01	214	86.99	0	0.00	246
4.	Birbhum	7	69	11.98	507	88.02	0	0.00	576
5.	Dakshin Dinajpur	10	276	13.33	1794	86.67	0	0.00	2070
6.	Darjeeling	4	24	8.66	253	91.34	0	0.00	277
7.	Jalpaiguri	4	127	19.16	536	80.84	0	0.00	663
8.	Malda	7	137	9.68	1278	90.32	0	0.00	1415
9.	Murshidabad	1	0	0.00	85	81.73	19	18.27	104
10.	North 24 Parganas	1	28	5.12	519	94.88	0	0.00	547
11.	Paschim Medinipur	11	99	10.68	828	89.32	0	0.00	927
12.	Purulia	18	102	5.44	1764	94.03	10	0.53	1876
13.	Uttar Dinajpur	1	23	9.43	221	90.57	0	0.00	244
	Total	**82**	**1302**	**12.06**	**9468**	**87.67**	**29**	**0.27**	**10799**

Source: Data collected from Branch Offices and Regional Offices of the Districts.

beneficiary accounts for their members which they can access by themselves. Since transacting with these accounts by the tribals *via* DMS proved to be far easier than through any other banks the interest of the tribals in opening their respective accounts in the DMS pattern is increasing day by day. Table 6.3 is given below to support the above findings. Table 6.3 also shows numerically that among the total SHG Accounts, Female SHG Accounts (87.45%) are higher than Male and the Combined as well. It can be observed here that Dakshin Dinajpur has the highest number of Male SHG accounts as well as Female SHG accounts. Alipurduar, on the other hand has the lowest percentage of Female SHG accounts, i.e. 72.94 per cent in total.

It is interesting to find that among the studied LAMPS of 13 Districts 92.44 per cent of all the SHGs have accounts in DMS. More than 90 per cent male and female SHGs in the studied LAMPS have accounts in DMS. In Jalpaiguri and Malda districts 100 per cent of the SHGs have accounts with the LAMPS (Table 6.4). Rest of the SHGs still have their accounts in Nationalized Banks.

SHG accounts have been started to be opened since 2001 or earlier in some of the studied LAMPS from each district. Considering the districts, the highest numbers of SHG accounts were opened in Purulia during 2012-13, when the number reached around 400. Special efforts have been exerted by all the LAMPS regarding opening of SHG accounts because it is easy to motivate people for opening group accounts and initiate group activities rather than to open individual accounts. Every district has seen a boom in the number of SHG Accounts opened during 2009-10 which amply reflects the thrust put forth by the WBTDCC to make the tribal members of LAMPS aware of DMS through its staff. Again, a sudden downfall in the number of opening of SHG Accounts is observed during 2013-14 which may be a result of a saturation effect caused by the reasons mentioned earlier. Among the three districts under Jalpaiguri Regional Office, a significant growth has been observed in Darjeeling and Jalpaiguri districts while a steep growth is observed in the Alipurduar district only during 2010-11. A more or less steady growth is found in case of Dakshin Dinajpur district (Graph 6.1).

Table 6.3: SHG Accounts in Details of the Studied DMS

Sl. No.	Districts	No. of LAMPS	SHG Account Details						
			Male		Female		Combined		Total
			No.	%	No.	%	No.	%	Nos.
1.	Alipurduar	4	151	27.06	407	72.94	0	0.00	558
2.	Bankura	10	199	17.64	918	81.38	11	0.98	1128
3.	Barddhaman	4	31	13.14	205	86.86	0	0.00	236
4.	Birbhum	7	57	13.97	351	86.03	0	0.00	408
5.	Dakshin Dinajpur	10	237	12.30	1690	87.70	0	0.00	1927
6.	Darjeeling	4	24	10.04	215	89.96	0	0.00	239
7.	Jalpaiguri	4	127	19.16	536	80.84	0	0.00	663
8.	Malda	7	137	9.68	1278	90.32	0	0.00	1415
9.	Murshidabad	1	0	0.00	75	79.79	19	20.21	94
10.	North 24 Parganas	1	28	5.12	519	94.88	0	0.00	547
11.	Paschim Medinipur	11	99	11.73	745	88.27	0	0.00	844
12.	Purulia	18	100	5.95	1570	93.45	10	0.60	1680
13.	Uttar Dinajpur	1	23	9.43	221	90.57	0	0.00	244
	Total	**82**	**1213**	**12.15**	**8730**	**87.45**	**40**	**0.40**	**9983**

Source: Primary Data collected from the studied LAMPS.

Table 6.4: Percentage of SHGs of LAMPS having Accounts in DMS

Sl. No.	Districts	No. of Lamps	Male			Female			Combined/Mixed			Total Shgs in Lamps	Total SHG Account in DMS	Percentage on Total Members & Accounts
			Male SHGs in Lamps	Male SHG Account in DMS	Percentage of SHGs having Accounts	Female SHGs in Lamps	Female SHG account in DMS	Percentage of SHGs having Accounts	Combined SHGs in Lamps	Combined SHG Account in DMS	Percentage of SHGs having Accounts			
1.	Alipurduar	4	200	151	75.5	464	407	87.72	0	0	0	664	558	**84.04**
2.	Bankura	10	199	199	100	1005	918	91.34	0	0	0	1190	1128	**94.79**
3.	Barddhaman	4	32	31	96.88	214	205	95.79	0	0	0	246	236	**95.93**
4.	Birbhum	7	69	57	82.61	507	351	69.23	0	0	0	576	408	**70.83**
5.	Dakshin Dinajpur	10	276	237	85.87	1794	1690	94.2	0	0	0	2070	1927	**93.09**
6.	Darjeeling	4	10	24	240	253	215	84.98	0	0	0	277	239	**86.28**
7.	Jalpaiguri	4	127	127	100	536	536	100	0	0	0	663	663	**100.00**
8.	Malda	7	137	137	100	1278	1278	100	0	0	0	1415	1415	**100.00**
9.	Murshidabad	1	0	0	0	85	75	88.24	19	19	100	104	94	**90.38**
10.	North 24 Parganas	1	28	28	100	519	519	100	0	0	0	547	547	**100.00**
11.	Paschim Medinipur	11	99	99	100	828	745	89.98	0	0	0	927	844	**91.05**
12.	Purulia	18	102	100	98.04	1764	1570	89	10	10	100	1876	1680	**89.55**
13.	Uttar Dinajpur	1	23	23	100	221	221	100	0	0	0	244	244	**100.00**
	Total	**82**	**1302**	**1213**	**93.16**	**9468**	**8730**	**92.21**	**29**	**29**	**100**	**10799**	**9983**	**92.44%**

Source: Primary Data collected from the studied LAMPS.

Graph 6.1: Graphical Representation of Year Wise Account Opening Status

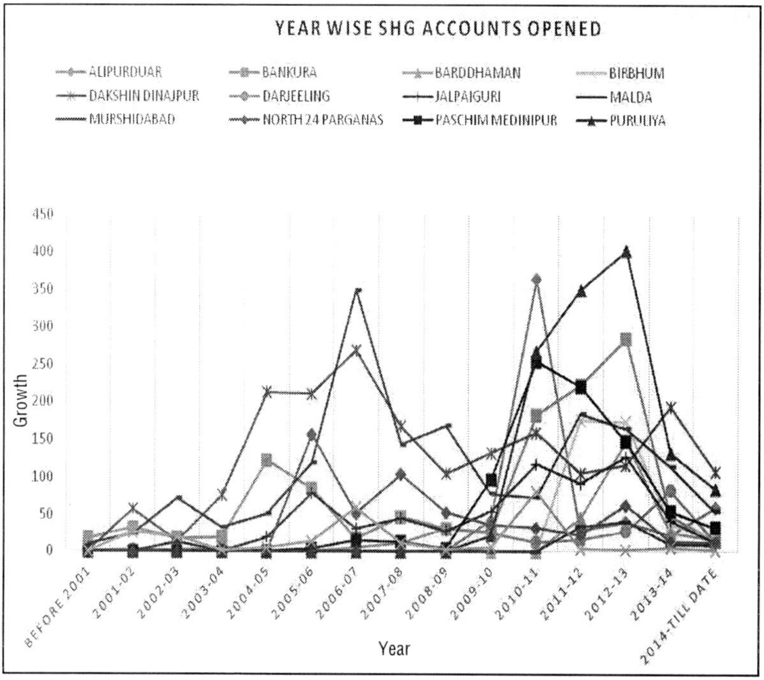

Source: Primary Data collected from the studied Lamps.

The SHGs are encouraged to take loan from the DMS. Among 82 LAMPS in 13 Districts of West Bengal, 38 LAMPS invested their money by giving loan to SHGs. All of the 10 LAMPS in Dakshin Dinajpur gave loan to the SHGs whereas Malda stands at the second position in facilitating loans to the SHG members (6 out of 7 LAMPS are providing loans to the Groups). LAMPS of Jalpaiguri, Murshidabad, North 24-Parganas and Uttar Dinajpur are also giving loan. On the reverse side of the scale, a very small amount has been invested by giving loan to SHGs in one LAMPS unit each in the districts of Purulia followed by Barddhaman, Paschim Medinipur, Birbhum, and Bankura respectively. It has been found that out of a fear of non-recovery of loan, not only are the SHGs under these LAMPS units avoiding to take a loan, but also in some of the cases the LAMPS staffs are showing minimal interest to encourage them in this regard.

There is no provision for taking mortgage while disbursement of loans to the tribals and so it has been found that in many places the LAMPS staff have faced problems regarding the repayment of the loans from some of these SHGs.

Table 6.5: Loan Distributed to SHG in DMS

Sl. No.	*District*	*No. of LAMPS*	*Loans to SHG*			
			Given		*Not Given*	
			Nos.	*%*	*Nos.*	*%*
1.	Alipurduar	4	2	50.00	2	50.00
2.	Bankura	10	4	40.00	6	60.00
3.	Barddhaman	4	1	25.00	3	75.00
4.	Birbhum	7	2	28.57	5	71.43
5.	Dakshin Dinajpur	10	10	100.00	0	0.00
6.	Darjeeling	4	2	50.00	2	50.00
7.	Jalpaiguri	4	4	100.00	0	0.00
8.	Malda	7	6	85.71	1	14.29
9.	Murshidabad	1	1	100.00	0	0.00
10.	North 24 Parganas	1	1	100.00	0	0.00
11.	Paschim Medinipur	11	3	27.27	8	72.73
12.	Purulia	18	1	5.56	17	94.44
13.	Uttar Dinajpur	1	1	100.00	0	0.00
	Total	**82**	**38**	**46.34**	**44**	**53.66**

Source: Primary Data collected from the studied LAMPS.

Profile of the Studied Self-Help Groups in DMS

Leaders and members from 177 SHGs were interviewed. Among them 161 (90.96%) are female and 15 (8.47%) are male. A rare scenario of a mixed SHG is found in only one LAMPS. It is clear from this distribution that females are more prone to form SHGs than males. It also proves that females are encouraged more than males for forming group in LAMPS. In Kashipur Dakshin LAMPS of Purulia district, besides LAMPS staff, a NGO also encourage females to make groups and suggests them to get affiliation with the local LAMPS.

The SHGs were mostly formed during 2011 to 2013, when 40 per cent of the total male SHGs and 46.58 per cent of the total female SHGs were formed. This is due to the fact that most of the LAMPS got their sanction of DMS from WBTDCC during this time. The low percentage during 2014 and above is because it has been a year only (Table 6.6).

Table 6.6: Year of Formation of the SHGs

Year of Formation	Male		Female		Mixed		Total	
	No.	%	No.	%	No.	%	No.	%
Before 2005	1	6.67	16	9.94	0	0.00	17	9.60
2005 to 2007	2	13.33	22	13.66	0	0.00	24	13.56
2008 to 2010	4	26.67	39	24.22	1	100.00	44	24.86
2011 to 2013	6	40.00	75	46.58	0	0.00	81	45.76
2014 and Later	2	13.33	9	5.59	0	0.00	11	6.21
Total	**15**	**100.00**	**161**	**100.00**	**1**	**100.00**	**177**	**100.00**

Source: Present fieldwork.

Though there is no specific rule regarding the number of members in a SHG, a general trend of making a SHG with minimum 10 members has been found all along the study and so is found in Table 6.7, which depicts that 53.33 per cent of Male SHGs and 62.11 per cent of Female SHGs are comprised 10 to 12 members. These members are generally found to belong to one particular community. Mixed groups are rare (Table 6.7).

Table 6.7: Number of Members in SHGs

No. of Members in SHG	Male		Female		Mixed		Total	
	No.	%	No.	%	No.	%	No.	%
Below 10	4	26.67	42	26.09	1	100.00	47	26.55
10 to 12	8	53.33	100	62.11	0	0.00	108	61.02
13 to 15	1	6.67	15	9.32	0	0.00	16	9.04
16 and above	2	13.33	4	2.48	0	0.00	6	3.39
Total	**15**	**100.00**	**161**	**100.00**	**1**	**100.00**	**177**	**100.00**

Source: Present fieldwork.

As the Santals form the major concentration among tribal population in West Bengal, the members in each LAMPS are mostly the Santals and so also in the SHGs. Hence, 46.67 per cent of the total Male SHGs and 75.78 per cent of total Female SHGs interviewed are the Santals. Striking enough, among 15 male SHGs interviewed, 6 (40%) are from Oraon community. Five Mixed Female groups have also been found. Among the studied SHGs a few belong to other communities like Mahali, Mech, Lohra etc. Four female SHGs consisting of members of the two PVTGs are also found (Table 6.8).

Table 6.8: Community-wise Distribution of the SHGs

Sl. No.	*Community of the SHG*	*Male*		*Female*		*Mixed*		*Total*	
		No.	*%*	*No.*	*%*	*No.*	*%*	*No.*	*%*
1.	Bedia	0	0.00	2	1.24	0	0	2	1.13
2.	Bhumij	0	0.00	3	1.86	0	0	3	1.69
3.	Kora	0	0.00	2	1.24	0	0	2	1.13
4.	Lodha	0	0.00	2	1.24	0	0	2	1.13
5.	Lohra	0	0.00	1	0.62	0	0	1	0.56
6.	Mahali	1	6.67	5	3.11	0	0	6	3.39
7.	Mech	1	6.67	1	0.62	0	0	2	1.13
8.	Munda	0	0.00	7	4.35	0	0	7	3.95
9.	Oraon	6	40.00	11	6.83	1	100	18	10.17
10.	Santal	7	46.67	122	75.78	0	0	129	72.88
11.	Mixed	0	0.00	5	3.11	0	0	5	2.82
	Total	**15**	**100**	**161**	**100**	**1**	**100**	**177**	**100**

Source: Present fieldwork.

Case study: Swarnalata Besra is the Group leader of Dolderia Muluk Mahila Swanirvar Dal — One of the oldest SHG in the Manbazar-I LAMPS, Purulia. After knowing about LAMPS from local people 10 female members of the Santal community of Dolderia village opened their account in Manbazar-I LAMPS in 2010. In the group, only the group leader (Informant) is literate. Every month each member of the group deposits Rs. 50 in DMS. On 10th February 2015 their balance was more than Rs. 30,000 in DMS. They donot know about the interest rate of Savings Account in DMS. The group has one more savings account in State Bank of India, Manbazar-I branch having balance of Rs. 14,505. The group members took loan from their savings at the rate of 2 per cent interest. Now, they only save money for their personal purpose. The group members donot face any problem in transaction with LAMPS. Easy availability of loan is the prime cause of the continuation of the accounts.

Case study: An interview was taken from Ramala Sardar, leader of the Sundarban Adivasi SHG under Sandeshkhali LAMPS. The informant has said that they have a group of eight Bedia persons where all of the members are co-operative and active. They hold 24 meetings annually where they regularly maintain the resolution book and details of transaction in bank. The group includes six literate members. The rest can only sign. Each member deposits Rs. 20 monthly. The SHG has opened their account on 25/02/2010. The group has done a fishery business together with the money of Micro-Credit Loan (MCL). According to the informant, the staff of the LAMPS announced about DMS in the villages. Thereafter she, with her neighbours organized a meeting and decided to open a group account here. On 2011 the group has received Rs. 80,000 as MCL at 5 per cent rate of interest where they have recovered Rs. 31,000 through 7 installments. This group also received DISHA @ Rs. 10,000 each. They have not yet utilized the money of Disha (a subsidy under Tribal Sub-Plan). This group mostly utilizes the deposited amount in their fishing business. According to the leader, it is easier for them to operate their account from the LAMPS as they are providing them loan more easily than any other bank at a low amount of interest. This group has also received training twice for DMS and Fishery schemes from the LAMPS.

Table 6.9: Frequency of Literate Members in the Self-Help Groups

No. of Literate Members	*Male*		*Female*		*Mixed*		*Total*	
	No.	*%*	*No.*	*%*	*No.*	*%*	*No.*	*%*
Below 4	3	20.00	93	57.76	1	100.00	97	54.80
4 to 7	6	40.00	53	32.92	0	0.00	59	33.33
8 to 11	4	26.67	14	8.70	0	0.00	18	10.17
11 and above	2	13.33	1	0.62	0	0.00	3	1.69
Total	**15**	**100.00**	**161**	**100.00**	**1**	**100.00**	**177**	**100.00**

Source: Present fieldwork.

Most of the female SHGs have less than 4 literate members in each group. In contrast, most of the male SHGs have at least 4 to 7 literate members. In some cases, almost all the members of the group are found to be literate, 13.33 per cent among male SHGs and a negligible 0.62 per cent among female SHGs. If total number of SHG is taken into account, 54.80 per cent have less than 4 literate members. In case of DMS literate members of the SHG operates the account and keeps the record and they are helped by the LAMPS' staff (Table 6.9).

Case study: Suchitra Mura (40 years) not only has an SHG accountant Baredi Adivasi Mahila SHG under Bagmundi UFS LAMPS in Purulia, but after a few years she has also opened her individual account in DMS. Suchitra was illiterate till she started working with the other group members. She is a forest product collector and even her family economy is depended on the same activity. At first she was taught to sign in the resolution copy, later with time she learnt how to calculate the balance and keep record of other group accounts details. Now, she operates her account and even the group account herself. She also has received DISHA subsidy with which she has made a small animal husbandry unit. At this moment DMS is not only the way of developing her economic condition, but also a path of grooming herself with holistic perfection where education plays an important part.

Table 6.10 clearly shows the presence of a Micro-Savings habit among the studied population where most of the studied SHGs have been found to save albeit majority of them vary from less than Rs. 50 (46.67% among male SHGs and 65.22% among female SHGs) up to Rs. 150 per head per month. This means that the SHG members have started acquiring a thrifting habit irrespective of the amount deposited. It is also interesting to find that 28.25 per cent among the total interviewed groups are also depositing above 50, but less than Rs. 100 per month per head. This is also a good indication of their growing interest in the thrifting process.

Table 6.10: Per Capita Savings in the Self-Help Groups

Savings per Head per Month	*Male*		*Female*		*Mixed*		*Total*	
	No.	*%*	*No.*	*%*	*No.*	*%*	*No.*	*%*
Below 50	7	46.67	105	65.22	1	100.00	113	63.84
50 to 99	4	26.67	46	28.57	0	0.00	50	28.25
100 to 149	3	20.00	9	5.59	0	0.00	12	6.78
150 to 199	1	6.67	0	0.00	0	0.00	1	0.56
200 and above	0	0.00	1	0.62	0	0.00	1	0.56
Total	**15**	**100.00**	**161**	**100.00**	**1**	**100.00**	**177**	**100.00**

Source: Present fieldwork.

Case study: Baldev Tudu (30 years) is the leader of Aligarh Adivasi SHG under Rajnagar LAMPS in Birbhum. This is a group operated by 12 ST male members. During the formation of the group in 2012 each group member deposited Rs. 30 per month. Later through the group account they have applied for Micro Credit Loan with which they could buy seeds for agriculture. Now, with the profit they have made from cultivation, they have also developed an interest in Savings which encouraged them to deposit more for future need. Now, the members of the group are depositing Rs. 50 per month per head from 2014.

Table 6.11: Details of Group Activities

Group Activity	*Male*		*Female*		*Mixed*		*Total*	
	No.	*%*	*No.*	*%*	*No.*	*%*	*No.*	*%*
Agriculture and allied activities	0	0.00	6	3.73	0	0.00	6	3.39
Animal Husbandry	3	20.00	7	4.35	0	0.00	10	5.65
Business	1	6.67	5	3.11	0	0.00	6	3.39
Other Activities	0	0.00	4	2.48	0	0.00	4	2.26
Working under Govt. Contract	2	13.33	7	4.35	0	0.00	9	5.08
No Activity	9	60.00	132	81.99	1	100.00	142	80.23
Total	**15**	**100.00**	**161**	**100.00**	**1**	**100.00**	**177**	**100.00**

Source: Present fieldwork.

All the group activities start after training is provided to the SHG members through Block, Gram Panchayat or LAMPS regarding the activities. According to Table 6.11, most of the studied SHGs (80.23%) show no activity in groups and among all group activities found, most of them were preferred Animal Husbandry.

Case study: Kundimeru Mohila SHG of Kabiguru LAMPS in Birbhum was formed with DMS in the year of 2011. According to the informant, named Putul Hansda (leader), there are 14 members and all of them belong to Santal ST community. The group includes only two literate members and the remaining 12 members can sign only. Every month the group arranges a meeting where they maintain the resolution book and review the transaction system. Monthly each of the member deposits Rs. 30. The SHG has opened their account on 27/12/2011. In the year of 2014, the group members received a subsidy of Rs. 5000 each from DISHA, which they have utilized for the purpose of goatery. She believed that it is safe and easier to operate their account from the LAMPS. They also said that, in DMS of LAMPS, the transaction of small amount is possible that is very much helpful for them.

Case study: Palashkura Adibasi Rilamala Mahila Samity group was formed on 2010 after a meeting with LAMPS staff in Palashkura Village of Para in Purulia. The total member strength is 10 and all are female. Among all the members only four are literate. The pass book is handled by the Dalanetri and Saha-Dalanetri. The Informants group leader (Dalanetri) Ajanta Hembram said that the group holds12 meetings in a year. They don't have any other account except DMS. They don't have any group activity for lack of proper planning. Each member deposits Rs. 80 per month. The members don't take loan from the group account. The withdrawal tendency among the group is not prevalent. The group got training and subsidy for making of *Agarbatti* (Incense stick) in the year 2014. They individually utilize their money for goatery. But they could not make much profit as maximum no. of goats died prematurely due to lack of proper vaccination or care. Like other groups, this group also wants training for business especially on animal husbandry and *Agarbatti* (Incense stick) making and selling to improve their income.

Table 6.12: Knowledge about Rate of Interest

Knowledge about Rate of Interest	*Male*		*Female*		*Mixed*		*Total*	
	No.	*%*	*No.*	*%*	*No.*	*%*	*No.*	*%*
Yes	3	20.00	29	18.01	0	0.00	32	18.08
No	12	80.00	132	81.99	1	100.00	145	81.92
Total	**15**	**100.00**	**161**	**100.00**	**1**	**100.00**	**177**	**100.00**

Source: Present fieldwork.

Most of the members among studied SHGs do not know the rate of interest for their savings account. It is obvious from this fact that the members of SHGs trust the LAMPS staff and do not feel the need of keeping it on their own. Furthermore, since many of them are not much educated, they are not concerned about it yet properly. For this matter they still depend either on the LAMPS staff or sometimes even on outsiders.

It is very interesting to note in Table 6.13 that most of the SHGs did not have any deposit before DMS, which means LAMPS and its DMS facility has been successful in bringing people under a

Savings Scheme through SHG formation and that too within the LAMPS itself. 86.87 per cent among male SHGs and 73.91 per cent among female SHGs did not have any kinds of accounts to save their money before.

Table 6.13: History of Deposit before Starting DMS Account

Had Deposits before DMS	Male		Female		Mixed		Total	
	No.	%	No.	%	No.	%	No.	%
Yes	2	13.33	42	26.09	0	0.00	44	24.86
No	13	86.67	119	73.91	1	100.00	133	75.14
Total	**15**	**100.00**	**161**	**100.00**	**1**	**100.00**	**177**	**100.00**

Source: Present fieldwork.

Table 6.14: Presently having Other Deposit Accounts in Other Banks

Other Types of Deposit Present	Male		Female		Mixed		Total	
	No.	%	No.	%	No.	%	No.	%
Yes	0	0	38	23.60	0	0.00	38	21.47
No	15	100	123	76.40	1	100.00	139	78.53
Total	**15**	**100.00**	**161**	**100.00**	**1**	**100.00**	**177**	**100.00**

Source: Present fieldwork.

In total, 78.53 per cent of the total studied SHGs do not have any kind of deposits other than DMS savings account. Though some instances of SHG disintegration were also found, in most of the LAMPS, the staffs were still able to re-develop the SHGs to keep their accounts active. It is also interesting to find out that 21.47 per cent among the interviewees also have accounts in other banks as well. This highly signifies their increasing interest in the thrifting process.

Table 6.15: History of Borrowing Loans

Taken Loan from DMS	Male		Female		Mixed		Total	
	No.	%	No.	%	No.	%	No.	%
Yes	5	33.33	43	26.71	0	0.00	48	27.12
No	10	66.67	118	73.29	1	100.00	129	72.88
Total	**15**	**100.00**	**161**	**100.00**	**1**	**100.00**	**177**	**100.00**

Source: Present fieldwork.

It has been revealed from this study that the SHGs maintain their savings account in order to get subsidies as explained to them by the loan providers. Taking money and giving it back with interest has a lower acceptance level among the studied SHGs as could be seen from Table 6.15. Only 48 (27.2%) out of 177 studied SHGs took the advantage of taking loans at a rate of 6 per cent 12 per cent interest per annum and many loans from DMS were found to have already been repaid with interest. Still it is better to encourage the tribal SHGs to receive loans from the DMS system which they can then utilize for getting involved into profitable business ventures.

Case study: Sohagi Murmu, the group leader of Govindapur Lakshmibai SHG under Balarampur LAMPS was interviewed. The informant told that at UBI bank 11 Santal neighbours of Govindapur village including the informant have opened a savings account forming a group in 2008. Till date they have deposited Rs. 31,338. In 2011 they came to know about DMS in the LAMPS and opened an SHG account. The group includes 7 literate and 4 illiterate members. All of them deposit Rs. 10 monthly to their account. Yearly they organize 24 meetings where they regularly maintain the resolution book and the transaction system. According to the informant, the staff of the LAMPS informed them about the DMS. In 2011 the group has taken a loan from UBI bank amounting to Rs. 25,000 at 24 per cent rate of interest and they have fully recovered the amount through 8 installments. They have mainly invested the loan amount in their personal business or formedical treatment of their family members. This group has also received DISHA subsidy which they have not utilized yet. The group has not received any training from the LAMPS. Once each of the members of the groups were provided with 5 goats for goatery, but unfortunately all of them died in some unknown disease. According to the leader, the concerned UBI Bank Branch always remains congested and transactions are a long time taking matter, whereas at DMS under the LAMPS, transaction is much easier as they do not need to waste their time standing on a queue. From DMS they have also received subsidies easily and did not face any linguistic problem. But the only problem they identified inthissystem is that they have to travel a long way to reach the LAMPS. The group is now planning to engage in animal husbandry later with proper training.

Table 6.16: Utilization of Loan Taken from DMS

Utilization of DMS Loan	*Male*		*Female*		*Mixed*		*Total*	
	No.	*%*	*No.*	*%*	*No.*	*%*	*No.*	*%*
Agriculture	2	40.00	13	30.23	0	0.00	15	31.25
Animal Husbandry and Fishery	3	60.00	2	4.65	0	0.00	5	10.41
Family Purpose	0	0.00	9	20.93	0	0.00	9	18.75
No Plan	0	0.00	19	44.18	0	0.00	19	39.58
Total	**5**	**100**	**43**	**100**	**0**	**0.00**	**48**	**100**

Source: Present fieldwork.

Considering the total number of SHGs who had taken loan from DMS as seen in Table 6.16, around half of them either had no definite plan about what they intended to do with the money or they could not clearly tell what exactly they did with it. 31.25 per cent of the total SHGs who had taken loan utilized the money on agricultural purposes. On the other hand, among 5 male SHGs who had taken loan, 3 of them used the money on animal husbandry and fishery purposes.

Case study: Kalpana Hembram, group leader of Anita Mayabhar SHG under Balarampur LAMPS, Purulia stated that in 2003, she with her 9 neighbours started the group and became members of the LAMPS. Thereafter on 2nd January, 2004 they have opened their SHG account at the DMS. All the members can sign only and are depositing an amount of Rs. 20 per month per head at the group account. They saved total monthly deposit of the group in DMS account. Yearly they organize 12 meetings. They maintain regular transaction which is mainly done by the leader. They have not received any training from the LAMPS yet. In 2014, the group has taken loan of Rs. 15,000 from DMS at 11 per cent rate of interest, but they could not repay any amount till date. They had taken the loan for buying a Power-Tiller. The group also received Rs. 50,000 as loan in 2013 at 5 per cent rate of interest which they fully recovered through 48 installments. They invested the money for buying mustard seeds. The group has now planned to take up agricultural activities separately with the deposited amount.

Table 6.17: Utilization of Micro-Credit Loan (MCL) received from LAMPS

Utilization of MCL Loan	*Male*		*Female*		*Mixed*		*Total*	
	No.	*%*	*No.*	*%*	*No.*	*%*	*No.*	*%*
Agricultural Activities	1	25.00	9	20.00	0	0.00	10	20.41
Animal Husbandry & Fishery	2	50.00	33	73.33	0	0.00	35	71.43
Family Purpose	0	0.00	1	2.22	0	0.00	1	2.04
Others	1	25.00	2	4.44	0	0.00	3	6.12
Total	**4**	**100.00**	**45**	**100.00**	**0**	**0.00**	**49**	**100.00**

Source: Present fieldwork.

Micro-Credit Loan (MCL) is a kind of loan in which half of the sanctioned money is provided for an activity upon the completion of which rest of the amount is disbursed and these activities mostly include Animal Husbandry because it is quite convenient to purchase animal calves with the amount of money provided in the first phase. According to the data collected and displayed in Table 6.17, it is seen that 49 out of 177 studied SHGs got MCL. Several cases were found where SHGs are very keen to get MCL and has already applied for the same but LAMPS are unable to provide them with the same due to some technical reasons. 71.43 per cent of total SHGs who got MCL used their loan money for Animal Husbandry and Fishery projects. Though, it is neither recommended nor encouraged to let the SHGs use the MCL money on any other purposes except those that will help in uplifting their economic status, 2.04 per cent of the total SHGs who got loan, used the money for family purpose satisfying their personal needs having no outcome or yield as required by the Scheme guidelines.

Case study: Lakshmi SHG under the Raiganj LAMPS in Uttar Dinajpur was formed in 2008 with 8 Santal women and opened an account in DMS. Here they are depositing Rs. 25 per head per month. Each month the group holds 4 meetings. It is also found that for 1 year they stopped all group activities due to internal disharmony. At first the neighbours and thereafter, the staff of the LAMPS informed them about the DMS. In 2010 the group has taken MCL of Rs. 35,000 which they have fully recovered on time. They have invested the money of the MCL in Agriculture, Business purposes and to tide over family crisis. This group has also received the first phase of DISHA in 2014. Each member received Rs. 5000 which they invested in Agriculture. The money of the second phase have not yet been provided by the WBTDCC till the date of survey. All the group members also took loan of Rs. 5800 six times at 5 per cent rate of interest from the Group Account. The group has not yet received any training from the LAMPS. According to the leader, it is easy to transact at DMS under the LAMPS. Here the staff are very friendly and from the DMS they could receive loan at a low rate of interest. They mostly utilize the deposit money for their urgent family needs or for agricultural purposes.

Case study: Asha Minj is a member of Sapna SHG of Nagrakata LAMPS, Jalpaiguri. All the ten members of this SHG belong to the Oraon community and most of them are very active and co-operative. It is a very old SHG, formed in the year 2004. The group includes three literate members and the rest can sign only. Although they do not meet regularly, but each member deposits Rs. 20 every month. The SHG had opened the account on 4-7-2004. There were no group based economic activities performed by this group. According to the informant, the staff of the LAMPS and BOD (Board of Directors) members announced about DMS in the villages. Thereafter, she with her neighbours organized a meeting and decided to open a group Account here. In the year 2013, the group members have received a subsidy of Rs. 10,000 individually from DISHA, but they have utilized the money for meeting their personal needs. According to the informant, it is easier for them to operate their account from the LAMPS as they are providing them loan more easily than any other bank at a low amount of interest also giving them subsidies. They have now applied for MCL, but did not get it till the date of Survey. *(Contd.)*

Case study: Sibrani Besra, a 48 years old widow Santal woman is an account holder of Rajnagar LAMPS in Birbhum. She has passed Class IV and now works as a cook at the ICDS along with farming in her own land. She earns Rs. 4000 monthly and her family expenditure is around Rs. 3500/month. She is also a member of Gudmandi Piljuburi SHG which also supports her economically. The supervisor of the LAMPS had informed her about DMS system and thereafter she has opened her account here on 2-5-2012. The present balance in her account is Rs. 2580. During the last 3 years she has deposited Rs. 14,265 through 8 transactions while Rs. 12,000 have been withdrawn through 2 transactions. It has been found that she has received yearly interest properly and she is also aware about the rate of interest provided by the LAMPS. She has already received the total amount of DISHA through her SHG Account which she has utilized to recover the loan taken from a local money lender. The Informant told that, she has a Savings Account at the local UBI Branch where she has kept Rs. 2000, but does not transact there regularly. She has opened the account previously while she had no idea about DMS of the LAMPS. She took loan from a money lender at high rate of interest before starting her account at DMS. UBI bank could not help her in this regard. According to the informant, unlike the other Nationalized Banks she does not face any problem here with DMS and all the staff of the LAMPS are quite friendly. She utilizes most of her savings for family purpose.

The SHG members took loan from the group account as well as from the DMS. The rate of interest varies from group to group. Generally, the interest rate varies from 2 per cent to 4 per cent. Most members of the SHGs took loan for meeting sudden urgent family needs like medical treatment, education or marriage. The repayment status of the loan also varies substantially across the SHGs. While in some cases, the loan amount has been totally recovered and in most other cases the group could not pay any amount to DMS as interest since their members did not repay anything.

Table 6.18: Perception of the SHGs Regarding Benefits of DMS

Benefits of DMS	*Male*		*Female*		*Mixed*		*Total*	
	No.	*%*	*No.*	*%*	*No.*	*%*	*No.*	*%*
Easy Local Transaction	4	26.67	44	27.33	0	0.00	48	27.12
Family Purpose	0	0.00	8	4.97	0	0.00	8	4.52
Getting Loan and Subsidy	4	26.67	54	33.54	0	0.00	58	32.77
Others	1	6.67	3	1.86	1	100.00	5	2.82
No Benefit	4	26.67	36	22.36	0	0.00	40	22.60
Small Savings	2	13.33	16	9.94	0	0.00	18	10.16
Total	**15**	**100.00**	**161**	**100.00**	**1**	**100.00**	**177**	**100.00**

Source: Present fieldwork.

As already discussed earlier, beneficiaries of DMS have a pre-conceived notion that DMS provides subsidies and also loans at lower interest rates simply on maintaining a Savings Account in DMS. This fact is clear from Table 6.18 that shows 32.77 per cent of the total studied SHGs think the benefit of DMS is to get loan and subsidies. Another issue that came out from this Table is that the location of LAMPS being inside the villages itself and the staff being STs, mostly of the same community as the beneficiaries themselves, were of great importance because 27.12 per cent of the total studied SHGs mentioned "Easy Local Transaction" as a major benefit of DMS.

Case study: Subhadra Sardar, a 42 years old married woman belonging to the Bedia ST community, is a member of Sandeshkhali LAMPS (North 24 Parganas). She is also a member of the Sundarban Adivasi Self-Help Group since 2010. She has opened her savings account at DMS on 9th February, 2007. Since then she is closely associated with the LAMPS. She has passed Madhyamik and operates the account by herself. She is doing fishing business in collaboration with her other group members. She also owns a small poultry farm and has agricultural land. From this she fulfils her family needs and also maintains a regular transaction in the DMS. It is found that during last three years she has deposited a total of Rs. 41,600 through 9 transactions where each year she has received the interest properly. During the last three years she has withdrawn Rs. 79,100 through 23 transactions for business. Though she is not fully aware about the interest, but she keeps record of her account through the Passbook. She has also opened a Savings Account in SBI. Here she has Rs. 3000 and she rarely transacts here. She has also received DISHA through her savings account. According to her, it is easier for her to transact through DMS than any other nationalized bank.

Case studies of Account holders, who are mainly females, suggest that they have been immensely benefited by the DMS. It has helped in easy transaction. They can deposit a small amount anytime. Although many of them do not understand the rate of interest and transaction process in detail, but they admitted that they get loan at times of necessity and also get Scheme subsidies through this account. They do not have communication problem with LAMPS Staff, which they experienced in other Nationalized Banks. The only problem found was the distance of the LAMPS from some villages resulting in transportation related problems between the beneficiaries and staff and this also has a latent bearing upon the repayment and loan recovery scenario. But a closer look at the overall perspective reveals a gradual development of a thrifting habit among these tribal people which ushers in a radiant glimmer of hope in the lives of these marginalized ST people of this State.

Conclusion

Deposit Mobilization Scheme (DMS) or *Adibasi Sancha 'O' Dadan Arah* of the LAMPS under WBTDCC is an effort to develop the habit of thrift among the Scheduled Tribes. The scheme started operating since 2001. In 13 districts of West Bengal 82 LAMPS got formal sanction for operating DMS. It is a great effort on the part of the LAMPS to bring the poor tribal people under a simple banking system. For the tribal people, language is a bar for communicating with the wider mainstream society. Even if some of them could open an account in a Nationalized or Co-operative Bank they faced problems of communication. Primarily this problem was solved through opening an account in LAMPS as the staff of LAMPS who deal with the DMS mostly belong to their own community. Moreover, the tribal people with a meagre income can deposit small amount of money anytime they desire and they can similarly withdraw the same without any hassles. The staff help them in all respects during the transaction. At times of necessity they can even take loan from the DMS easily. The problem of borrowing loan from the money lenders at high rate of interest and mortgaging the assets like land have definitely been minimized with the formation of the DMS.

There are more female Accounts than male Accounts. The tribal women have been found to be economically very active and they save small amounts from their earning so that they can utilize this amount at times of necessity. SHGs are found to be pretty regular in depositing money in the DMS Group Accounts and they also borrow loan for different purposes starting from economic to social needs. The individual accounts holders are still not very confident about taking loan. The beneficiaries have a fear of not being able to return the loan (For example, Balarampur LAMPS, P.R. Murmu LAMPS, Kanksha LAMPS etc.). Many of them got DISHA subsidy and *MCL* through LAMPS and utilized the amount for developing business. It has also been observed that the SHG members take loan frequently for various family needs like education, house construction, medical treatment, marriage etc. and the rate of interest in the group is also very low which helps them to repay the loan in time. SHGs taking loan from DMS is also common. In most cases they repay the loan with a few exceptions of delayed repayment.

The tribal people who used to save money in chit funds have identified the problem and are desperately trying to come out from their traps. They have also come out of the gruesome clutches of the 'friendly' local money lenders. In some cases, the LAMPS staff and BOD members have even saved the land of the poor tribals from the grasp of such money lenders (For example, in Banshihari LAMPS of Dakshin Dinajpur).

The problem of distance between the village and the LAMPS is the only major cause of concern for the beneficiaries of those LAMPS which cover large areas. They are unable to maintain regular transactions at the DMS of the LAMPS. For this reason, the Manager of Bagmundi UFS LAMPS of Purulia has proposed formation of a separate LAMPS in the Ayodhya Hills area as the distance of his LAMPS unit is so far from the villages adjacent to the Ayodhya Hills to the LAMPS that the beneficiaries are not able to deposit their money here nor are the staff in a position to keep regular contact with those villages. DRMS LAMPS in Bankura has opened a separate branch in this region for this same reason. Similar initiatives are the need of the hour and if properly implemented and monitored closely, the progressive generation of this thrifting habit could definitely have a lasting influence in improving the quality of life of the society in general and that of the Scheduled Tribes of West Bengal in particular.

A PHOTO-PROFILEOF DMS, SHG & THEIR ST BENEFICIARIES

Plate 6.1: Sainthia LAMPS, a LAMPS effectively operating DMS with the SHGs situated in a remote village with a huge concentration of tribals.

Plate 6.2: Madpur S.K. LAMPS, a LAMPS that influences the forest product collectors to assemble themselves aiming to develop their status.

Plate 6.3: The DMS operating section of Banshihari LAMPS in Dakshin Dinajpur.

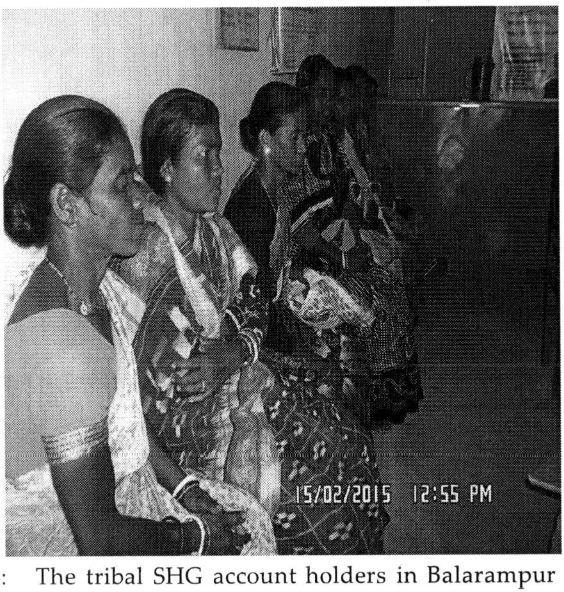

Plate 6.4: The tribal SHG account holders in Balarampur LAMPS, Purulia.

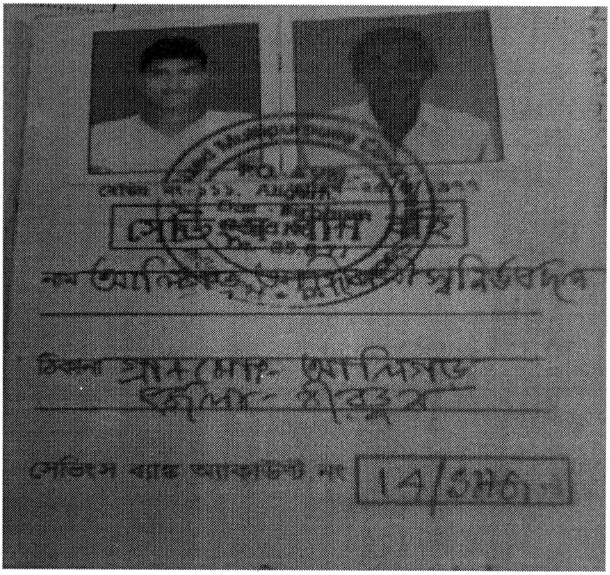

Plate 6.5: A passbook of a male Self-Help Group in the DMS of Rajnagar Adivasi LAMPS, Birbhum.

Plate 6.6: A passbook operated by a female Self-Help Group in the DMS.

Plate 6.7: Business of Clothes by the SHGs at Rajnagar Adivasi LAMPS, Birbhum.

Plate 6.8: Business of Kendu leaves by the LAMPS; these leaves are gathered and supplied by the local tribes in Jhargram, Paschim Medinipur.

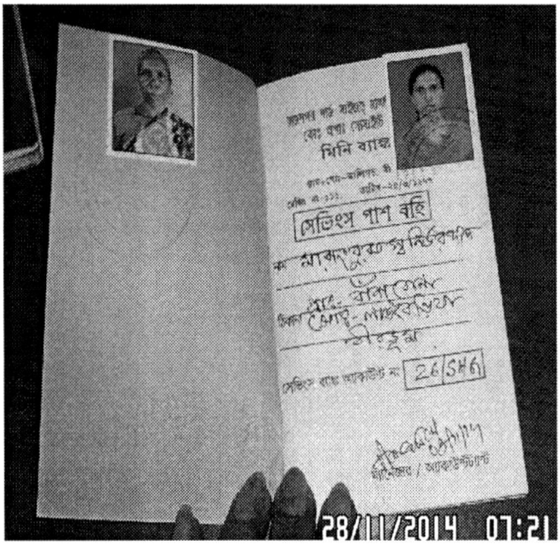

Plate 6.9: An SHG Account of a young woman Santal (ST) woman Rajani Hembram who also had an individual account previously in DMS at Rajnagar Adivasi LAMPS, Birbhum.

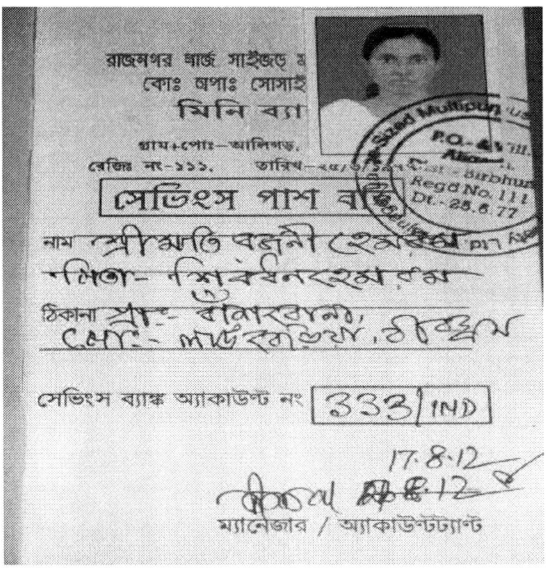

Plate 6.10: The individual Passbook of Rajani Hembram.

Plate 6.11: A tribal woman (from the left) working in Rajnagar LAMPS as a Supervisor is standing with Rajani Hembram, Rajnagar Adivasi LAMPS, Birbhum.

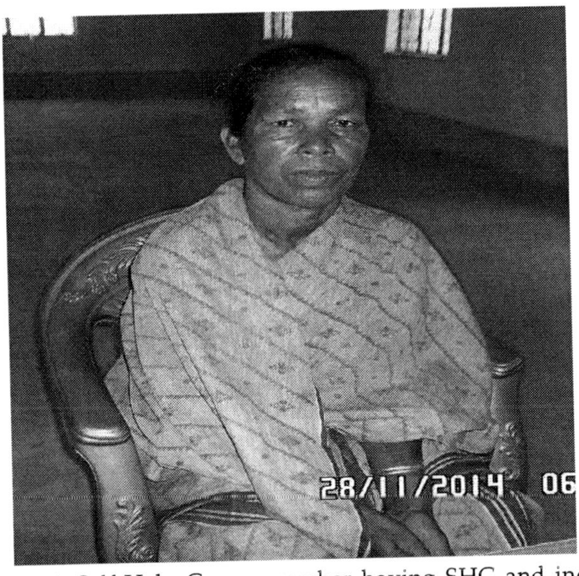

Plate 6.12: A Self-Help Group member having SHG and individual accounts in DMS who became literate with the influence of the educated members of the group, Rajnagar Adivasi LAMPS, Birbhum.

References

Mahalingam, S. (1987). Poverty Reducing Potential of Tribal Co-operatives in North-East India. *NFLC Labour Coops,* Vol. 9(1), No. 1, 8-13.

Registrar General & Census Commissioner, India I. (2011). *Area, population, decennial growth rate and density for 2001 and 2011 at a glance for West Bengal and the districts.* Retrieved from Census of India: accessed from <http://www.censusindia.gov.in/2011-prov-results/prov_ data_products_ wb.html>

Sen Chowdhury, Suchismita & Supratim Bhattacharya, 2015. The Role of Co-operative in Empowerment of Tribal Women: A Study of West Bengal, *Man in India: An International Journal of Anthropology,* Vol. 95, (No. 3), 2015, Serials Publications (P) Ltd., pp. 515–29.

Sen Chowdhury, Suchismita, 2013. *The Santal Women: A Study in Eastern India and Bangladesh,* R.N. Bhattacharya Publishers & Exporters, Kolkata.

7

Indigenous Communities, Livelihoods and Displacement

A Socio-Ecological Approach

Biswajit Parida

Introduction

Indigenous communities in India are largely referred to as '*adivasis*' (aborigine) meaning original inhabitants. They are also referred to as tribals. The territories dominated by these people in India are often rich in hydrologic, mineral, oil, gas, forest and other resources and these sites are the most attractive to locate large projects of various kinds in India. Thus, it is not surprising that a number of development projects undertaken in India in the years since independence are located in areas largely inhabited by the tribal people. For multinational companies, looking for investment opportunities, these areas are fast becoming the most favoured destinations (Mathur, 2006). The tribals, in many parts of India, who were once from time immemorial practicing forest-based biodiversity management for sustainable livelihoods and living in harmony with nature, are now, have lost their livelihoods, medicinal plants, drinking water and other basic requirements due to large scale mining projects.

Besides livelihood issues, the other emerging problem that makes the situation worse has been the issue of mining caused displacements and resulting conflicts with tribal populations in India is not a new phenomena. Studies have witnessed of how for several decades, development projects in India have expropriated and forcibly displaced scores of people without giving them the protection that a formal policy on development-caused displacement should give to these vulnerable communities (Fernandes, 2008).

Odisha is the second poorest state in India and nearly 22 per cent of its total population belongs to tribal peoples (Census of India, 2011). Ecological degradation, erratic rainfall and a high risk of drought have resulted in food insecurity, increasing out-migration and periodic famines. Ecological imbalances are seriously undermining livelihood patterns and vulnerability is rising. A small land base, low agricultural productivity and low incomes have led to rising indebtedness and exploitation. The life of the ethnic tribal people, in particular, is increasingly vulnerable as they have been deprived of their land and forest legislation has turned them into encroachers on land they have always used. They have also been disproportionately affected by displacements for mining operations, irrigation projects, even wildlife sanctuaries.

This chapter was originally prepared as a background chapter to a proposed ethnographic study of development and displacement among the tribal of Jajpur district of Odisha. Anthropology is generally characterized as a 'holistic' discipline which emphasizes the total social and cultural context in the explanation of the structure and the behavioural patterns of human groups. Anthropological concerns include the study of dialectical relationship between individual society and culture.

Developments refer to the change in quality of life towards betterment, to growth, progress, improvement and expansion of a complex process involving the social, cultural, political and economic betterment of people and of society. Development projects not only bring changes in country's economy, but also alter the lives of millions of people by displacing them from their natural habitat. Government of India has been implementing many development projects in the tribal areas and they were literally chased away from their own traditional land and turned into displaced, landless, migrant people in search of a livelihood.

Rehabilitation and Resettlement Policy

The rehabilitation and resettlement policy of the governments is yet to be successful and women are suffering both by state machineries and customary practices. The present setting of tribal livelihood is changing from its traditional root due to the growth of urbanization, industrialization, cash economy etc. which are promoted by the state with the influence of economic liberalization-privatization-globalization which is called as LPG model also. In the name of developing the backward regions, the present model of development is focuses on such as industry, mining, hydropower projects, big dams etc. in the natural resource regions. These projects require huge land acquisition, deforestation and depletion natural resources for their establishment. As a result, livelihood of the tribal is now under threat because they are becoming the victims of land alienation, poverty and bonded labour. Generally, disputes associated with these tribal communities are less support, insufficient compensation, loss of livelihood, increase in stress and health problem as well as loss of their identities (Sarath, 2013). Each year, approximately fifteen million people are displaced as a consequence of large development projects (Cernea, 2006).

Development Induced Displaced in Odisha

After Independence Project based development began in tribal regions of Odisha to encroach on tribal people's age-old lands and thereby displaced them register speedy economic growth. These projects have an immense impact on their live and livelihood. The major projects set up in Odisha were the Rourkela Steel Plant (1950), Hirakud Dam (1948), Hindustan Aeronautics Limited (1965), Talcher Power Station (1995), National Aluminium Company (NALCO) at Angul (1985) and Balimela Dam Project (1963). During Seventies several multi-purpose dam projects, like, Hindustan Aeronautics Ltd. (1962), the Bauxite Mining Project at Koraput (1985), Mandira, Rengali (1973), Upper Indravati (1978) and Subarnarekha Irrigation Project (1978) were started in the State. These projects were established in resource rich Tribal areas and other marginalized sections of the society, which estimates more than 10 lakh people have been displaced and 50 lakh have been affected by these projects in the State. Similarly, out of 71,794 people displaced by industrial projects in Odisha, only 27,300 (38.03%) have been rehabilitated mining projects have displaced around 1,00,000 people, of whom almost 60 per cent have been rehabilitated and around 50,000 people have been displaced through declaration of sanctuary, of which only 15,540 (31.08%) have been rehabilitated (Mohapatra, 1999). All these projects have had an immense impact on tribal village economics, family life and village power structures, as has been documented through various empirical studies in the State (Panda and Panigrahi, 1989; Behura and Nayak, 1993; Mohapatra, 1998; Swain and Panigrahi, 1999; Patnaik, 2000; Behura and Panighrahi, 2001, 2002). The following Tables 7.1 and 7.2 explain the extent of displacement of households according to decadal variations in different sectors.

Table 7.1: Extent of Displacement of Households in Different Development Projects in Odisha

Sectors	*No. of Families Displaced*				*Total*
	1950-60	*1961-70*	*1971-80*	*1981-90*	
Power project	22,144	1357	19,769	443	43,713
Irrigation project	1015	578	2883	3607	8083
Industrial project	4251	468	---	5794	10513
Total	**27,410**	**2403**	**22,652**	**9844**	**62,309**

Source: Pane, 1998; Swain and Panigraghi, 1999.

Table 7.2: Displacement Caused by Development Projects in Odisha from 1950 to 1990

Categories of Projects	*No. of Families*	*Percentage of Total Displacement*
Mines	3134	3.37
Industries	10,704	11.47
Thermal power	2426	2.60
Dams	64,903	69.55
Wildlife sanctuary	142	0.15
Urban Slums	12000	12.86
Total	**93,319**	**100.00**

Source: Pane, 1998; Swain and Panigraghi, 1999.

Objectives of the Study

With this background the chapter has the following objectives:

1. It gives an over view of Kalinga Nagar industrial Estate in Odisha.
2. To documents the impact of the industrial Estate on the socio-cultural live of the tribal people.
3. It analyses the changes in the livelihood basket of tribal people due to the Kalinga Nagar, Tata Steel plant.

Review of Literatures

Various literature are done for preparing this chapter deals with the issue of development and displacement which is caused by industrial projects, which affects large number of people and the resistance offered by people to this development induced displacement. It also tries to analyse the role of government in the process.

Tanmay (2014) in his paper clearly concluded that, all over India industrial projects are facing resistance from displaced or potentially displaced people. The displacement has given rise to a wide range of protest movements all over the country. Through struggles in Nandigram and Singur of West Bengal, Kalinga Nagar and Paradip of Odisha or the Bastar region of Chhattisgarh people are asserting the need to both democratize the model as well as to seek alternative to them. According to Smitu Kothari (1995), since independence of the country, development projects of the Five-Year Plans have displaced 0.5 million persons each year primarily as a direct consequences of administrative land acquisition which does not include displacement by non-Plan projects, changes in land-use, acquisition for urban growth, and loss of livelihood caused by environmental degradation and pollution. Another path breaking work in displacement and resettlement is of Michael Cernea (2000) who points out that forced displacement and being ousted from one's land and habitat carries with it the risk of becoming poorer than before. Cernea impoverishment risk and reconstruction model proposes that the onset of impoverishment can be represented through a model of eight interlinked potential risks intrinsic to displacement. These are identified as landlessness, joblessness, homelessness, marginalization, food insecurity, increased morbidity and mortality, loss of access to common property and social integration. Prof. Sen (1999) rightly compared development with freedom which may cross the limit of enjoyment especially for human being in using various facilities as instruments. But today, we are on the board of such development where the fruits are reaching too few people or segment the people. They are none peasants who are missing vehicle which carries fruit of development thereby they remain in the lower strata in the society being socially excluded and marginalized. Dwivedi (2002) argues that the displacement discourse falls into two categories—the reformist managerial and the radical movements. The managerial approach treats displacement as a consequence of past and future development and focuses on how to manage the inadequacies and failures of resettlement to minimize negative effects. The radical movement's position holds that development results in unequal distribution, and cost and benefits are borne disproportionately. They challenge the notion of development that is equated with economic growth. Growth or development that cannot be just, fair and equitable cannot bring social or economic justice for men and women. They raise concerns of fundamental political nature like rights and governance. They advocate for a paradigm shift to poverty reduction, environmental protection, social justice and human rights. Muggah (2000) and Downing (2002) add loss of access to community services and violation of human rights. In 2007, violent protests broke out in 100 villages near Nandigram in the East Midnapur district of West Bengal when the Communist Party of India CPI (M) lead Government attempted to acquire 10,000 acres of land for a Special Economic Zones (SEZs) to be developed by the Indonesian Real Estate Gaints, the Salim Group, on March 14, 2007, 2500 police men were send to capture the land. According to the police records, the farmers were killed in the firing while over 100 were declared missing. The State Government fenced off the land on December 6, 2006. As a result, TMC leader Mamata Banerjee called for a state-wide bandh and later went on a 25th day hunger strike, villages continued to attack on the fences to disrupt the functioning of the project. In the year 2008, Tata group decided to shift the manufacturing bar to Sanard in Gujurat. In case of Niyamsiri of Odisha, the Supreme Court has strongly endorsed the role of Gram Sabha as democratic decision-making forum on issues of individual, community and cultural rights of tribals and traditional forest dwellers (*The Hindu*, 2013).

Location and the People

The proposed steel plant of Tata Steel at Kalinga Nagar is one of the five mega steel plants that are to be set up in the State. This steel plant of Tata's will be located in Kalinga Nagar Integrated Industrial Complex developed by IDCO in Jajpur district of Odisha. Kalinga Nagar area is situated at 20° 56′58″ North latitudes and 86° 02′17″ East longitudes. The area falls within Danagadi and Sukinda block of Jajpur district. For the purpose of setting up of the plant, IDCO allotted a total of 3471.808 acres of land to Tata Steel located in six revenue villages.

The study has been undertaken among the displaced people, residing in four rehabilitation Colonies, which is one of the industrial estate rehabilitation colonies, Jajpur district of Odisha.

Methodology of the Study

For the present study both primary as well as secondary sources were referred to for obtaining the required information for the study. Secondary date collected through various sources like journals, published works and web sites etc. and supplemented by in depth-observation, memory recall, interviews, and focused group discussion. A range of anthropological techniques of data collection were employed for purpose of the study. The study interviewed 200 households from the four rehabilitation colonies of Tata Steel, namely, Gabaraghati Birsa-Munda rehabilitation colony, B.R. Ambedkar Trijanga rehabilitation colony, Sansailo rehabilitation colony and New Champakoila rehabilitation colonies. The data was also collected from local ADM office of Jajpur district. The random sampling was chosen for the study. Some unstructured interviews and focus group discussions were also conducted.

Major Findings of the Study

As seen there are 12 plants are surrounds the Kalinga Nagar area industrial complex prior to 1st January, 2006 is only 5318 acres. The acquisition of land by IDCO for Kalinga Nagar Industrial Complex began in early 90s in different phases. By 1st of January, 2006, about 13,000 acres of land had been acquired by IDCO. Of

Table 7.3: List of Plants and Land Allotted in Kalinga Nagar

Sl No.	*Name of the Plants*	*Land Allotted (in acres)*
1.	Middeast (MESCO)	530
2.	Orion	150
3.	Maithan Ispat	100
4.	Uttam Gala	370
5.	NINL	1500
6.	Mahara Stra Seamless	500
7.	Tata Steel	2400
8.	Rohit Ferrontech	50
9.	JINDAL	678
10.	Visa Industries	390
11.	Dinabandhu	100
12.	K.J. Ispat	50

Source: ADM Office Kalinga Nagar, 2015.

these, 6900 acres were private land and the rest was said to be 'government land'. However in, reality people were cultivating most of these 'government land' for generations. The land survey and settlement in the area was not done since 1928, no Patta over the land they cultivated. The Tata Steel plant's construction work is going on over a massive area of 2400 acres of land, and will begin operation by the end of this study (i.e. in November 2015). All villagers are being displaced from their homestead land. There are six villages are being affected by the Tata Steel plant. These villages are Chandia, Gabraghaty, Gadapur, Baragadia, Khurunti and Nuagaon.

Table 7.4: Compensation Details: Displaced Family and the Rehabilitation Assistance

Sl. No.	*Compensation of Different Things*	*In Rs. per Acre*
1.	Land Compensation	1,00,000
2.	House Building Assistance	1,50,000
3.	Temporary Accommodation Assistance	10,000
4.	Transportation Allowance	2,000
5.	Cash in lieu of Job	2,00,000
6.	Maintenance Allowance	2,300
7.	Training and Employment	Training and employment to nominated person

Source: ADM Office Kalinga Nagar, 22-12-2014.

Table 7.5: Monthly Income Before and After Displacement

Households monthly Income	*Before displacement Average monthly income in Rs.*	*After displacement Average monthly income in Rs.*
	2,500–4,000	8,000–10,000

Source: Primary data, 12-4-2015.

Agriculture was the primary source of income for the majority of the people of the area. People are primarily agriculturalists and some of them earn their livelihood as daily-wage labourer. They collect forest products, like cooking wood, wood for the house making, leaf for the leaf plate. This is their one of their subsidiary occupations. Because forest was very near to their home. Their average monthly income was Rs. 2500–4000 which they were getting from the agricultural land. After the displacement by the Tata Steel their households' average monthly income is increased that is Rs. 8,000–10,000. Because instead of their agricultural land they got job in the Tata Steel Plant. Previously, their economic condition was very bad, due to the Tata Steel Plant their economic condition is strengthening. They are also getting different good facilities from the Tata Steel Plant like Health Centre in B.R. Ambedkar Trijanga Rehabilitation Colony and Tata Steel Gobarghati Hospital, he also cited that company had promised to give free medical facilities to all, but hospital is for first-aid treatment. For serious patient they are referring to Hitech and Som Hospitals of Bhubaneswar which is 120 kms away from our village. There two delivery patients died when they shifted to Bhubaneswar.

The Tata-Kalinga Nagar case has again highlighted that livelihoods of the tribals, poor farmers, agricultural labourers, have been threatened and they have to wait for support from the government or the R&R scheme of the company. Instead of mainstreaming the poor and the marginalized the industrial project is like other industrial projects, SEZs is further marginalizing them. Their poverty is increasing where a new elite is created who is reaping the benefits of this process while the poor farmers or tribals have to now wait for company dole outs, thus increasing their poverty. Thus, as claimed by the government that the mega industries would generate wealth and remove inequality stands challenged.

Forest Resources

The relationship of tribal people and forest resources has been symbiotic in nature. The life-way processes of Odisha's tribal people are reflected in their economy, religion, polity and social institutions, which cannot be understood without understanding various aspects of the forest surrounding them (Behura, 1990, 1996; Mallik and Panigrahi, 1998). Until the intervention of the British, tribal people believed that they were the owners of the forest and forest resources that surround them. Their attitude towards forest resources as a source of food did not change much until Independence. They were more forest friendly and were not exploiting forest resources randomly. Almost all the tribal communities in Odisha observe various forms of social sanctions related to undertaking or not undertaking certain forest related activities: eating or not eating certain products, when and how to eat forest produce, and performance of rituals on a community basis before the first intake of forest food items. The customary laws of various tribal communities have become the guiding force for binding them closely with the forest. This can be seen when one examines the folk taxonomies given by tribal communities to flora and fauna, and from their classification of plants as more and less useful, edible and non-edible, hygienic and poisonous, ritualistic and non-ritualistic, medicinal and non-medicinal (Behura, 1982). A large extent of land in tribal areas is categorised as forest, hence the laws related to forests also have a major impact on access to land for tribals. The Odisha Forest Act, 1972, the Forest Conservation Act, 1980 and the Odisha Forest (Grazing of Cattle) Rules, 1980, Sections 5 and 6, all have an immense impact on the livelihood resources of the tribals. The State's forest can be classified as reserve forests, demarcated protected forests unclassified forests and other forests. *Prima facie* the forest laws provide protection for settlement of the rights of local people and communities before land is declared forest land, but this does not always hold because some reserve and protected forests are so deemed without any settlement taking place, and there is often non-recognition of rights on land used for shifting cultivation, and a lack of settlement of rights and family settlements. This implies that once an area has been classified as forest of any sort, it cannot be used for cultivation or any other purpose without the permission of the Ministry of

Environment and Forest (MOEF) and ownership rights cannot be given without the Supreme Court's permission. In this process the regional variations of customary practices are not taken into consideration. In most cases the rights of the tribal people, which were prescribed in the FA. 1947 Amendment in 1954, were not followed and forests were created in *ad hoc* survey and settlement processes. The reservation of forests has often been made with little consideration of the interests of cultivation. The areas declared as forest very often carry tribal villages where no settlement has in fact taken place. In this context Saxena (1995) points out that "Protected forest (demarcated or un-demarcated) is invariably classified as non-forest area in the Record of Rights (ROR) prepared and maintained under the Odisha Survey and Settlement Act and in function issued by Revenue Department (G.O. No-4898 of 1966) for reservation of Government land for specific purposes in tribal areas."

Impact on Social and Cultural Life

The economic conditions of the people improved in the transit camp after displacement. This is because they get better economic and livelihood opportunities from the Tata company, which they never got before displacement; moreover, they are also getting a chance to come into contact with the non-tribal or the main stream population. On the other hand, they lose their social co-operation; this is because after displacement, they start living an individualistic life. As it was states in the R & R policy, major sons and the unmarried daughters are regarded as a different family. This, to some extent hampers their social and group lives in the main village, because they do not want to leave their traditional land. Hence, after displacement families got fragmented. In hope of a better life and future, they left their close kin, and became isolated from their social as well as cultural life.

Impact on Ecology

Before displacement, the tribal community had access to all the nearby green hills (namely, Kiajhara, Sunajhara, Badasundi, Mahagir), from where they collected the firewood needed for their own use. In other words, the access was within the hands of the local people and the forest committee was formed jointly by the villagers and the *Athagarha* forest range. Loss of forest land causes the loss of grazing land, burial ground, traditional herbal medicines, and also the common land, earmarked for different community activities and other common places they used for social and cultural gatherings. These forests were also taken care of and watched by the community. But after displacement, most of the people stopped going to these forests for firewood and other forest produce. They also lost their grazing lands.

Conclusion

The displacement has multidimensional effect on the people. The social exclusion, alienation, higher growth in poverty, pressure on land and resources in nearby areas where development projects started, rise of anti-nationalistic feeling compelled government to see that less and less people are getting affected by the governmental projects, that displaced people will get proper compensation, and very few cultivable land being used for the development projects. It needs to be mentioned here that whatever kind of compensation is given by government, but losing of home is very much a sentimental issue. Every home says something. When this home is lost that means losing of everything for a person. In every occasion they remember their home. It also leads to the loss of culture; families become defunct, suspiciousness, heatedness, unfaithfulness become more among them. The feeling of alienation and dejectedness is very common among them. The nation is now making it very clear that development projects should affect less and less people. Inclusive education is the need of the hour for PAPs. It became a paradigm shift for India's developmental programme from only development to becoming humanitarian development projects. The present study found that after much trials and tribulations the government is now going to accept the present Land Acquisition, Rehabilitation and Resettlement Act, 2012. However, the success of the Act will be possible only after its real implementation in the field.

Development-Induced Displacement and Resettlement (DIDR) are largely involuntary and permanent. This has led to a wide range of economic, social and environmental changes including loss of livelihood and the means of production and the impoverishment of the displaced people. The most widespread effect of involuntary displacement is the impoverishments of a considerable number of people, which lack social justice and equity. These issues involve complex interrelationships between economic, environmental, social, technical, political and cultural factors. To bring good life to the people is the purpose of development projects in general and to make a better life for all people is not easy to be foreseen in reality. It is extremely difficult in most developing countries with weak policies, low awareness, poor knowledge base and limited financial resources to support sustainable development. The policy did not recognize the displaced people's right to compensation on their loss of access to Common Property Resources (CPRs). The policies also did not mention the needs of exploring the impoverishment risks and risks mitigating mechanism for proper rehabilitation and resettlement of the oustees. The roles of academicians, NGOs and civil societies are not made mandatory in the policy. The policy also does not have any mandatory provision to take the village committees, civil societies, intellectuals, displacement specialists and concerned social activists for the selection of resettlement sites. Instead the rehabilitation and periphery development advisory committee made by the government would select the site for the resettles. Thus, the implementation of the policy is not viable.

References

Arundhati, R., 1999. "The Greater Common Good". *Frontline*, June 4.

Behura, N.K. and Panigrahi, Nilakantha, 2001. *Functioning of the Fifth Schedule of the Constitution of India: The role of the welfare agencies in the state of Odisha*, Report submitted to ICSSR, New Delhi. Bhubaneswar: NKC Centre for the Development Studies.

Behura, N.K. and Nayak, P.K., 1993. "Involuntary Displacement and the Changing Frontiers of Kinship: A Study of Resettlement in Odisha, In: Cernea, M.M. and Guggenheim, S.E. (eds.). *Anthropological Approaches to Involuntary Resettlement: Policy, Practice and Theory*, Boulder: Westview Press.

Bhengara, Ratnakar, 1996. "Coal Mining Displacement". *Economic and Political Weekly*, 31(11): 647-649.

Census of India, 2001. Office of the Registrar General & Census Commissioner, Government of India.

Cernea, Michael, 1991, "*Putting People First: Sociological Variables in Rural Development*". Oxford: World Bank and Oxford University Press.

Cernea, Michael, 2000. "Risks, Safeguard and Reconstruction: A Model for Population Displacement and Resettlement, In: M. Cernea and Christopher McDowell (eds.). *Risks and Reconstrction Experiences of Resettlers and Refugees*. The World Bank: Washington. pp. 11-56.

Dwevedi, R., 1999. "Development, Risks and Resistance: Local Perceptions and Actions in the Sardar Sarwar". *Development and Change*, 33:43-78.

Fernandes, Walter, 2007. "Singur and the Displacement Scenario". *Economic and Political Weekly*. January, 20: 203-205.

Fernandes, Walter. 2008. "Displacement and Alienation from Common Property Resources", In: Lyla Mehta (ed.) *Displaced by Development: Confronting Marginalisation and Gender Injustice*. New Delhi: Sage Publications, pp. 105-129.

Gogoi, Rakhi Moni and Lahon, Thaneshswar, 2014. Paradigm Shift: The Situation of Development Induced Displacement in India. *Asian Journal of Socila Sciences and Humanities*. 3 (1): 132-136.

Human Development Report 2010, UNDP, accessed from <hdr.undp.org>

Mohapatra, L.K., 1999. "Tribal's rights to land and the State in Odisha", In: Behera, D.K. and Pfeffer, G. (eds.), *Contemporary Society Tribal Societies*. New Delhi: Concept Publishing Company.

Ota, Anil, 2010. "Displacement and Rehabilitation Issues in Tribal areas: A Diagnostic Analysis". New Delhi: Inter-India Publication.

Padhi, Sakti and Panigrahi, Nilakantha, 2011. "Tribal Movements and Livelihoods: Recent Developments in Odisha." *Working Paper 51*. Chronic Poverty Research Centre.

Panda, P. and Panigrahi, N., 1989. "The Problem of Displacement of a Displaced People: A Study in the Coal Mines of Brajaraj Nagar, Odisha". In Pati, R.N. and Jena, B. (eds.), *Tribal Development in India*, New Delhi: Ashish Publishing House.

Pande, B., 1998. "*Depriving the Underprivileged for Development*", Bhubaneswar: Institute for Social and Economic Development.

Reddy, Muthyyam, 2006. Development and Displacement. R & R Policies during 1920-2005. Fifty years of Andhra Pradesh 1956-2006.

Sen, Amartya, 1999. *Development as Freedom*, New York: Oxford University Press.

Smitu Kothari, 1996. "Whose Nation? The Displaced as Victims of Development," *Economic and Political Weekly*, 31(24) : 1476-84.

Swain, M. and Panigrahi, Nilakantha, 1999. "Development, Displacement and Rehabilitation in Odisha: An Overview", *Man in Life*. 25 (3-4): 163-179.

Swain, Tanmay, 2014, Development and Displacement in Odisha: A Study of Anti-POSCO Movement in Jagatsinghpur District. *Odisha Review*, February-March: 90-97.

The Hindu, 2013, The Significance of Niyamgiri, Editorial page, p. 3, dated May 03, 2013.

8

Life Style of the Dukpas

A Little Known Ethnic Group of West Bengal

Soumyajit Das and *Suchismita Sen Chowdhury*

Introduction

The Dukpas or the Drukpas are a small tribe of India mainly living in Sikkim and West Bengal. They are mainly concentrated in Bhutan. The Dukpas identify their place of origin in Druk-yul (Bhutan), the "land of the thunder dragon". They are also called Druku and Yul-Mi. The Dukpas are one of the offshoots of the Bhutias. The Bhutia tribe of West Bengal has been accorded Scheduled Tribe status *vide* the Constitution (Scheduled Tribe) Order, 1950. However, since there was no elaboration in the Order as to who all comprised the Bhutia, the Tribes Advisory Council of West Bengal, constituted under Rule 4 of the Fifth Schedule of the Constitution, Part B, during its First meeting held in March 1954 adopted a resolution to seek an explanatory note in the President's Order specifying the Scheduled Tribes to the effect that the word "Bhutia" included Denzongpas, Dukpas, Kagateys, Sherpas, Tibetans, Yolmos and Toto. The name 'Bhutiya' is a generic term used for several groups of people of Tibetan origin inhabiting the ranges south of the Himalayas extending from Jammu & Kashmir in the North-west and extending all the way across to Arunachal Pradesh in the North-east. Dukpas in West Bengal are residing in hills of Darjiling district and Alipurduar district. It may be said that the Dukpas living in Buxa region of Alipurduar district have oldest settlement in West Bengal. The Dukpa settlement in Darjiling is comparatively new.

Objective

To find out the difference in living style of the Dukpa communities residing on two entirely different geographical setting in two districts of North Bengal.

Methodology

We stayed in or close to our studied areas as long as the time required for a detailed ethnography of the studied ethnic group. The populations being small, we tried to cover all the households of these areas considering the availability of families during our study. Scheduled questionnaires, that included household census and questions on basic amenities, were made and filled up while visiting all the households. Audio recorders were used to record long conversations. Videography was done when any religious customs were found to be executed.

Studied Area and Population

Our study was based on two populations of Dukpa communities residing on two entirely different geographical setting. The Lamahatta bustee is a big village located on Darjeeling hills inhabited by several tribal and non-tribal communities and Lepchakha is a small village on Buxa hills chiefly inhabited by the Dukpas. Thirty households from Lamahatta and twenty-four households from Lepchakha were visited. In Lamahatta, we found some empty households, members of which have migrated (seasonal) to Siliguri because it gets cold enough over here during winter. They get two and a half months holidays in schools during the month of December to February. No seasonal migration was noticed in Lepchakha though it is also situated high up in the mountains and gets colder in winters.

The Dukpas are one of the many migrant communities of Tibetan region. There have been several migrations of this ethnic group on to West Bengal in different periods. The two populations we studied belong to two different times of migration. The Dukpas residing in Lamahatta bustee is relatively newer migrants than those residing in Lepchakha.

The Dukpas of Lepchakha trace their time of migration to the first half of seventh century when they came to Buxa hills with the invading Bhutanese armies, while the Dukpas of Lamahatta believes their migration in Darjiling hills to be more recent, i.e., in the 15th and 16th century, an era where religious persecution of the Red hats (Ningmapa sect) forced them to move to safer havens.

Lepchakha is a hilly terrain covered with thin forests, situated at a height of about 5000 feet, where the climate is cold. Lamahatta is located at an altitude of about 5,700 feet and at a distance of 23 kms from Darjeeling hill town. Lamahatta is well connected by the Darjeeling-Kalimpong state highway.

The Dukpas are settled in different areas of West Bengal, but their major concentration is found in Lepchakha of Buxa region and different pockets of Darjiling hills. Lamahatta is one of the pockets in Darjiling hills. Our study on the Dukpas tries to emphasise on the Dukpas living in these two regions.

Studied Area and Population at a Glance

District	*Villages*	*Gram Panchayat*	*Block*	*Police Station*
Alipurduar	Lepchakha	Rajabhatkhawa	Kalchini	Kalchini
Darjeeling	Lamahatta Bustee	Lamahatta	Rongli Rongliot	Darjeeling Sad[illegible]

Name of Villages	*No. of Households*	*Male*	*Female*	*Total*
Lepchakha	24	66	53	119
Lamahatta Bustee	30	64	70	134
Total	**54**	**130**	**123**	**253**

Source: Present fieldwork.

Lamahatta Bustee, located in Takdah block of Darjeeling district, is quite a big village. People belonging to different ethnic groups live here. Among them, Dukpa, Yolmo, Sherpa, Tamang, Chhetri and Mangar are more in number. Lepchakha, located in the Buxa hills under Kalchini block of Alipurduar district, is a very small village with only Dukpas residing there. Among the population of 134 Dukpas in Lamahatta, 70 are females and 64 are males having sex-ratio of 1094. Among 119 Dukpas in Lepchakha, 66 are males and 53 are females having a sex-ratio of 803 (Tables 8.1 and 8.2).

Settlement Pattern

The Dukpas of Lepchaka remained almost isolated till now though means of communication like *kuch* roads, telephonic connection are now being brought into the area. They still could maintain their original language, i.e. Dzhongkha to speak among themselves. Even the children are taught this language in their homes.

Table 8.1: Age and Sex-wise Distribution of Lamahatta Bustee

Age-group (in years)	Sex				Total		Sex-ratio
	Male	%	Female	%	No.	%	
0–4	0	0.00	1	1.43	1	0.75	1094
5–9	3	4.69	4	5.71	7	5.22	
10–14	8	12.50	4	5.71	12	8.96	
15–19	3	4.69	4	5.71	7	5.22	
20–24	6	9.38	9	12.86	15	11.19	
25–29	6	9.38	1	1.43	7	5.22	
30–34	6	9.38	10	14.29	16	11.94	
35–39	4	6.25	2	2.86	6	4.48	
40–44	6	9.38	8	11.43	14	10.45	
45–49	4	6.25	4	5.71	8	5.97	
50–54	3	4.69	8	11.43	11	8.21	
55–59	8	12.50	2	2.86	10	7.46	
60–64	3	4.69	1	1.43	4	2.99	
65–69	1	1.56	4	5.71	5	3.73	
70+	3	4.69	8	11.43	11	8.21	
Total	**64**	**100.00**	**70**	**100.00**	**134**	**100.00**	

Source: Present fieldwork.

Table 8.2: Age and Sex-wise Distribution of Lepchakha

Age-group (in years)	Sex				Total		Sex-ratio
	Male	%	Female	%	No.	%	
0–4	2	3.03	5	9.43	7	5.88	803
5–9	7	10.61	8	15.09	15	12.61	
10–14	12	18.18	3	5.66	15	12.61	
15–19	5	7.58	8	15.09	13	10.92	
20–24	6	9.09	3	5.66	9	7.56	
25–29	7	10.61	6	11.32	13	10.92	
30–34	5	7.58	4	7.55	9	7.56	
35–39	4	6.06	7	13.21	11	9.24	
40–44	6	9.09	5	9.43	11	9.24	
45–49	7	10.61	0	0.00	7	5.88	
50–54	0	0.00	1	1.89	1	0.84	
55–59	1	1.52	2	3.77	3	2.52	
60–64	2	3.03	0	0.00	2	1.68	
65–69	1	1.52	1	1.89	2	1.68	
70+	1	1.52	0	0.00	1	0.84	
Total	**66**	**100.00**	**53**	**100.00**	**119**	**100.00**	

Source: Present fieldwork.

The Dukpas of Lamahatta shows a different picture. They migrated here during British period. At the beginning there were only 2-3 families who supplied milk and egg to the Military camp of Takdah. The number of families increased gradually. All the land of Lamahatta was in the name of Wakil Raje. Nobody could recall his community or other details about him in Lamahatta. Animal husbandry was their traditional occupation which could be still found in Lamahatta region.

Lamahatta, being on the way between Darjeeling and Kalimpong, has a good communication system whereas Lepchakha is on the top of Buxa hill having no communication at all. Lepchakha was once considered to be a part of Bhutan. The area in Lamahatta Bustee where Dukpas live are well connected with stoned roads. This is also due to the fact that a resort has recently been built in that area. All the houses in Lepchakha are semi-*pucca* with floors made of stones, walls and roof of wood and tin respectively. There are several *pucca* houses in Lamahatta. The communication being well developed in Lamahatta makes it easy for the Dukpas residing there to carry the raw-materials for building a *pucca* house. Even if the Dukpas make some money to build a *pucca* house, the carrying cost for the raw-materials from the base of the hill to the top will make them think otherwise (Tables 8.3 and 8.4).

Table 8.3: House Type found in Lamahatta Bustee

House Type	*Households*	
	No.	*%*
Kaccha	9	30.00
Semi-*pucca*	13	43.33
Pucca	8	26.67
Total	**30**	**100.00**

Source: Present fieldwork.

Basic amenities: Almost all the houses in Lamahatta have electricity connections. All the connections of electricity in Lepchakha are solar cell ignited. A negligible number of houses have toilet as well as bathroom in Lepchakha while most of the houses in Lamahatta have them. Though a number of houses have piped water supply in both the areas, those who do not have use the nearest communal tap for water. The families living up the hill has access to water more than those living down the hill because the water is provided to them through gravity from the spring sources above the village (Tables 8.5 and 8.6).

Table 8.4: House Type found in Lepchakha

House Type	*Households*	
	No.	*%*
Kaccha	0	0
Semi-*pucca*	24	100.00
Pucca	0	0
Total	**24**	**100.00**

Source: Present fieldwork.

Table 8.5: Basic Amenities Available in Lamahatta Bustee

Basic Amenities	*Households*			
	Yes	%	No	%
Electricity	29	96.67	1	3.33
Toilet	22	73.33	8	26.67
Bathroom	20	66.67	10	33.33
Tube well	0	0.00	30	100.00
Well	0	0.00	30	100.00
Piped water supply	18	60.00	12	40.00

Source: Present fieldwork.

Table 8.6: Basic Amenities Available in Lepchakha

Basic Amenities	*Households*			
	Yes	*%*	*No*	*%*
Electricity	19	79.17	5	20.83
Toilet	3	12.50	21	87.50
Bathroom	1	4.17	23	95.83
Tube-well	0	0.00	24	100.00
Well	0	0.00	24	100.00
Piped water supply	15	62.50	9	37.50

Source: Present fieldwork.

Family: The family pattern of the community is patriarchal by nature, but mothers have a dominating presence in the family. The members of the family share mutual respect and love for one another. Confrontations, however, take place over inheritance of property. The younger brother is responsible for the maintenance of his elder brother's widow, but is not required to marry her. The dominance of nuclear families is observed at both the areas under study (Tables 8.7 and 8.8).

Table 8.7: Type of Family among the Dukpas in Lamahatta Bustee

Family Type	*Households*	
	No.	%
Nuclear	21	70.00
Joint	7	23.33
Extended	2	6.67
Total	**30**	**100.00**

Source: Present fieldwork.

Table 8.8: Type of Family among the Dukpas in Lepchakha

Family Type	*Households*	
	No.	%
Nuclear	21	87.50
Joint	3	12.50
Extended	0	0.00
Total	**24**	**100.00**

Source: Present fieldwork.

Marriage: The Dukpas are endogamous. They follow clan exogamy. In Lamahatta, Dukpas marrying with other communities is common. Exchange of bride with the Yolmo, Tamang, Sherpa and Bhutia are found. This trend is lacking in Lepchakha. They practice monogamy in both the areas. Divorce is not too difficult. Grounds for divorce include infidelity or a mutual desire to be separated. Both the divorcees can remarry. Cases of divorce are more in Lamahatta than in Lepchakha (Tables 8.9 and 8.10).

Table 8.9: Marital Status-wise Distribution Lamahatta Bustee

Marital Status	*Sex*				*Total*	
	Male	*%*	*Female*	*%*	*No*	*%*
Married	34	53.13	34	48.57	68	50.75
Unmarried	28	43.75	23	32.86	51	38.06
Widow/Widower	1	1.56	11	15.71	12	8.95
Divorce/Separated	1	1.56	2	2.86	3	2.23
Total	64	100	70	100	134	100

Source: Present fieldwork.

Marriage at minor age is not found in Lamahatta. The traditional custom of making a girl marry at younger age is found to exist in Lepchakha. The age at marriage for females tends to be more than 21 years in Lamahatta Bustee and less than 21 years in Lepchakha (Tables 8.11 and 8.12).

Table 8.10: Marital Status-wise Distribution in Lepchakha

Marital Status	*Sex*				*Total*	
	Male	*%*	*Female*	*%*	*No.*	*%*
Married	26	39.39	26	49.06	52	43.70
Unmarried	38	57.58	26	49.06	64	53.78
Widow/ Widower	1	1.52	1	1.89	2	1.68
Divorce/ Separated	1	1.52	0	0.00	1	0.84
Total	**66**	**100.00**	**53**	**100.00**	**119**	**100.00**

Source: Present fieldwork.

Table 8.11: Age at First Marriage in Lamahatta Bustee

Age group	*Male*		*Female*	
	No.	*%*	*No.*	*%*
Up to 14+ years	0	0.00	1	2.13
15-20+ years	4	11.11	20	42.55
21+ years above	32	88.89	26	55.32
Total	**36**	**100.00**	**47**	**100.00**

Source: Present fieldwork.

Table 8.12: Age at First Marriage in Lepchakha

Age group	*Male*		*Female*	
	No.	*%*	*No.*	*%*
Up to 14+ years	0	0.00	4	14.81
15-20+ years	6	21.42	14	51.85
21+ years above	22	78.58	9	33.33
Total	**28**	**100.00**	**27**	**100.00**

Source: Present fieldwork.

Education: All the basic educational facilities except colleges are present inside the Lamahatta Bustee. The nearest main road to Lepchakha is Santalabari, i.e., 10 kms. away. Though a primary school is present in the village, the Dukpas of Lepchakha has to go 3 kms away for studying in a Junior High School and to Alipurduar, i.e. 40 kms. away for high school and college. The literacy rate of people above 7 years is more in Lamahatta (79.23%), than in Lepchakha (64.49%). There are more people in Lepchakha who cannot even sign (31.93%) in comparison to the Dukpas of Lamahatta (14.93%).

Most of the Dukpas of Lepchakha studied till Class VIII as reflected in the Table but we found a lot of graduate Dukpas in Lamahatta Bustee. This, in fact, is the result of good communication system in Lamahatta (Tables 8.13 and 8.14).

Table 8.13: Educational Status of Lamahatta Bustee

Educational Status	Sex				Total	
	Male	%	Female	%	No.	%
Below 7 years age group	3	4.69	7	10.00	10	7.46
Cannot Sign	7	10.94	13	18.57	20	14.93
Can Sign only	1	1.56	2	2.86	3	2.24
Primary (I-IV)	10	15.63	11	15.71	21	15.67
Middle School (V-VIII)	13	20.31	9	12.86	22	16.42
Matriculation (IX-X)	11	17.19	10	14.29	21	15.67
Higher Secondary (XI-XII)	12	18.75	10	14.29	22	16.42
Graduate	6	9.38	7	10.00	13	9.70
Masters	1	1.56	1	1.43	2	1.49
Total	**64**	**100.00**	**70**	**100.00**	**134**	**100.00**

Source: Present fieldwork.

Table 8.14: Educational Status of Lepchakha

Educational Status	Sex				Total	
	Male	%	Female	%	No.	%
Below 7 years age group	3	4.55	7	13.21	10	8.40
Cannot sign	21	31.82	17	32.08	38	31.93
Can Sign only	1	1.52	0	0.00	1	0.84
Primary (I-IV)	16	24.24	10	18.87	26	21.85
Middle School (V-VIII)	13	19.70	11	20.75	24	20.17
Matriculation (IX-X)	6	9.09	6	11.32	12	10.08
Higher Secondary (XI-XII)	5	7.58	1	1.89	6	5.04
Graduate	1	1.52	1	1.89	2	1.68
Masters	0	0.00	0	0.00	0	0.00
Total	**66**	**100.00**	**53**	**100.00**	**119**	**100.00**

Source: Present fieldwork.

Economic Activities

Traditionally they practiced animal husbandry. They also practiced small scale agriculture. Terrace hill cultivation is still practiced in a small piece of land. Land is an asset to them. In Lamahatta 46 per cent of the families do not have agricultural land, but they have small land attached to their home. In Lepchakha all the families have agricultural land and 58.33 per cent of the families have received *patta,* while in Lamahatta 33.33 per cent of the families received *patta* (Tables 8.15 and 8.16).

Table 8.15: Ownership of Agricultural Land in Lamahatta Bustee

Ownership	*Households*	
	No.	%
Own	4	13.33
Patta	10	33.33
Not have agricultural land	16	53.33
Total	**30**	**100**

Source: Present fieldwork.

Table 8.16: Ownership of Agricultural Land in Lepchakha

Ownership	*Households*	
	No.	%
Own	10	41.67
Patta	14	58.33
Total	**24**	**100**

Source: Present fieldwork.

The inhabitants of both the areas are mainly engaged in agriculture, the chief crops being rice, gin, cardamom, maize and millets. Almost all Dukpas own land which serves for their primary resource. The head of the family controls the land. It is mainly a land-owning community with individual proprietors. The occupation of the community is mainly agriculture and farming. Animal husbandry is secondary source of income for most of the households in Lamahatta. However, with educational attainments, some of them have white collar jobs in government and semi-government offices (Tables 8.17, 8.18, 8.19 and 8.20).

Small scale farming in the kitchen garden is found in both the studied areas. The products are marketed, either directly or through middlemen. There is nothing in the kind of bonded labourers. There is also nothing like child labourers, as most of the children go to school. Payment of wages to labourers is made in cash. No significant changes have taken place in primary and

Table 8.17: Primary Occupation in the Lamahatta Bustee

Primary Occupation	*Sex*				*Total*	
	Male	*%*	*Female*	*%*	*No.*	*%*
Agriculture	11	28.20	5	29.41	16	28.57
Business	5	12.82	1	5.88	6	10.71
Pension holder	4	10.25	3	17.64	7	12.50
Service	12	30.76	7	41.17	19	33.92
Animal Husbandry	7	17.94	1	5.88	8	14.28
Total	**39**	**100.00**	**17**	**100.00**	**56**	**100.00**

Source: Present fieldwork.

Table 8.18: Primary Occupation in the Lepchakha

Primary Occupation	*Sex*				*Total*	
	Male	*%*	*Female*	*%*	*No.*	*%*
Agriculture	16	57.14	4	80.00	20	60.60
Business	3	10.71	0	0.00	3	9.09
Animal Husbandry	9	32.14	1	20.00	10	30.30
Total	**28**	**100.00**	**5**	**100.00**	**33**	**100.00**

Source: Present fieldwork.

Table 8.19: Secondary Occupation in the Lamahatta Bustee

Secondary Occupation	*Sex*				*Total*	
	Male	*%*	*Female*	*%*	*No.*	*%*
Agriculture	1	16.66	1	25.00	2	20.00
Pension-holder	0	0.00	1	25.00	1	10.00
Animal Husbandry	5	83.33	2	50.00	7	70.00
Total	**6**	**100.00**	**4**	**100.00**	**10**	**100.00**

Source: Present fieldwork.

Table 8.20: Secondary Occupation in the Lepchakha

Secondary Occupation	*Sex*				*Total*	
	Male	*%*	*Female*	*%*	*No.*	*%*
Agriculture	6	46.15	0	0.00	6	42.85
Animal Husbandry	7	53.84	1	100.00	8	57.14
Total	**13**	**100.00**	**1**	**100.00**	**14**	**100.00**

Source: Present fieldwork.

secondary sectors. But, there is a rise in the number of service holders. They live in the hills and practise indigenous method of cultivation. They do not use pesticide and fertiliser. Instead they prefer to use cow dung as manure and rotten leaves.

Income variation could be seen in two areas as the Dukpas of Lamahatta earn more in average than the Dukpas of Lepchakha. This is probably because of income opportunities in the remote Lepchakha. Whereas in the Lamahatta, both males and females are found to be engaged in different services. In general the majority of the earners are found to earn within Rs. 5000 to 10,000 per month in Lamahatta, but in Lepchakha the people mostly earn within Rs. 3000 (Tables 8.21 and 8.22).

Table 8.21: Family-wise Monthly Income and Expenditure in Lamahatta Bustee

Monthly Income Group	*Household*		*Monthly Expenditure Group*	*Household*	
	No.	*%*		*No.*	*%*
Below 1000	5	16.67	Below 1000	4	13.33
1000–3000	4	13.33	1000–3000	7	23.33
3001–5000	4	13.33	3001–5000	3	10.00
5001–10000	11	36.67	5001–10000	11	36.67
Above 10000	6	20.00	Above 10000	5	16.67
Total	**30**	**100.00**	**Total**	**30**	**100.00**

Source: Present fieldwork.

Table 8.22: Family-wise Monthly Income and Expenditure in Lepchakha

Monthly Income Group	*Household*		*Monthly Expenditure Group*	*Household*	
	No.	*%*		*No.*	*%*
Below–1000	0	0.00	Below–1000	0	0.00
1000–3000	13	54.17	1000–3000	16	66.67
3001–5000	8	33.33	3001–5000	6	25.00
5001–10000	3	12.50	5001–10000	2	8.33
Above–10000	0	0.00	Above–10000	0	0.00
Total	**24**	**100.00**	**Total**	**24**	**100.00**

Source: Present fieldwork.

Maximum number of families in both the places has savings bank account due to the fact that the government has now started to send money for different schemes directly into bank accounts. The nearest branch of bank from Lepchakha is more than 15 kms.

away. It is very unusual for them to visit the bank for depositing money.

It is interesting to find that a symbiotic relationship has developed among the inhabitants of Lamahatta. The agricultural yields are often exchanged with other tribes. Sometimes, they also exchange dairy products with the vegetables.

The Dukpas, like the others, take part in festivals, rituals and marriage ceremonies etc. identified with other communities. The landlord-tenant relationship defining a sharecropper is based on annual leasing (*kut*) and half a share (*adhiya*). The *adhiya* system depends on the type of the crops that are produced, like cardamom, ginger etc.

The practice of cultivator-labour as such is not in practice. Family members in most cases would cultivate their own land, as workers or labourers are usually engaged in roadworks, construction etc. When they face a labour crisis from time to time, they have to stop their children from going to school, which ultimately leads to a sizeable number of dropouts from the schools.

Language

In Lamahatta the language spoken at home among the kin group is Nepali, while with others Nepali and Hindi are in use with only a few speaking English. No one in the whole population has a little bit knowledge about Dzhongkha. When asked about the reason, the old-aged people said that they have been living with the mixed population of several tribes and hence had to maintain a common language to communicate. The young children are completely unaware of Dzhongkha and are being taught in Nepali language in schools.

The script they use is mainly Devnagari. The older generation can speak their own language which has different dialects, but the dialect they mainly speak is Garchog. The scripts they use are the U-Chhen and U-Med of Tibetan Languages. In Lepchakha traditional language Dzhongkha is spoken by many people.

Social Organisation

The Dukpa society is divided into some exogamous clans (*Thar*). It is interesting to find that the clans present among the Dukpas of Lamahatta is different from the Dukpas of Lepchakha. The clans found in Lamahata are Fensap, Bindup, Ishap, Bechamphu, Onda,

Aamchocey, Lama, Paljar, Pathip, Sakchopo, Siyap, Yatop, Feusa, Lasa and Gain. The clans found in Lepchakha are Dogop, Lhasa, Nalong, Nalop and Yalop (Tables 8.23 and 8.24).

Table 8.23: Clan-wise Family Distribution of the Dukpas in Lamahatta Bustee

No. of Clans	*Households*	
	No.	*%*
Aamchocey	2	7.41
Bechamphu	1	3.70
Bindup	2	7.41
Fensep	3	11.11
Feusa	1	3.70
Gain	1	3.70
Ishap	4	11.11
Lama	1	3.70
Lhasa	3	11.11
Orda	1	3.70
Paljar	1	3.70
Pathip	2	7.41
Sakchopo	1	3.70
Siyap	2	7.41
Yatop	2	7.41
Total no. of households having clans	**27**	**100.00**
Total no. of households	**30**	

Source: Present fieldwork.

Table 8.24: Clan-wise Family Distribution of the Dukpas in Lepchakha

No. of Clans	*Households*	
	No	*%*
Dogop	1	4.17
Lhasa	1	4.17
Nalong	14	58.33
Nalop	7	29.17
Yalop	1	4.17
Total	**24**	**100.00**

Source: Present fieldwork.

Life Cycle Rituals

Since the Dukpas follow Buddhism, the Lama performs all the rituals starting from birth to death.

Birth: There is no name-giving ceremony as such after birth of child. On the third day of the delivery a religious purification ceremony, called the Lhabsang ceremony, is observed. The outsiders can visit the house only after this ceremony. On any day after Lhabsang, parents can ask the Lama (priest-monk) to name the child, alter studying the horoscope. There are no ceremonies or rituals to observe childhood, adolescence etc. This is followed in both the studied areas.

Marriage rituals: A marriage is usually conducted through negotiations and the parents usually take part in it. The go-betweens are usually the maternal uncles. There are examples of marriages with other communities, but they prefer to arrange marriages within the community. The parents of the groom usually start the negotiations for marriage. In the marriage arrangement, the uncles have a great role. In Lamahatta, marriage is arranged by the matchmaker called *Bhatkhawre*.

After having conveyed the mutual consent of parents on both the sides, the go-between uncles of the groom along with the father go to the house of the bride, on an appointed day known as *khachang* to finalize the engagement, the date and terms and conditions. The visiting party has to offer gifts like *Chhang* (country liquor), pork, clothes, money etc. to the parents, brothers and sisters of the would-be bride. In absence of *Chhang Ram* is offered in Lamahatta. Here ritual of *Mangni* or engagement is practised. Exchange of ring and *Khada* is important *Rit* (name of this ritual).

Unlike the practice in District Darjeeling, the Dukpas, who mostly are from *Sarchhog* do not follow the *Bhorim* (milk-price) practice. The *Khachang* is followed by the *Shangchhang* (marriage day), which takes place within a short time (from a week to four weeks). Before marriage the Lama worship god by offering dry fruits and *Khada*. Marriage takes place in the paternal house of the bride. On the marriage day, a sumptuous feast is arranged by the bride's party, its sumptuousness determined by the economic capacity of the family. The invitees are kins, friends, and relatives, who offer to the newly wed the white scarves (*Khadog* or *Khada*) used on every occasion and festival, along with gifts in cash. The consummation of the marriage is made with the blessings of the parents of the bride.

The newly-wed couple stays in the bride's house or the paternal house of the bride for three days, after which they leave for the paternal house of the groom, where a similar party is arranged.

On the fourth day, when the bride leaves her paternal home, she carries along with her the gifts she has received. The ceremony is called *Tonglen*. The sign of a married woman is the coloured apron known as *Pangden*, which is tied at the waistline on top of the *pokho* and hangs down to the knee. Usually, the newly married couple resides at the paternal house of the groom, but there is a growing preference for neo-local arrangements due to many reasons, including economic and social. The final return of bride to the groom's house is called *Durhan* in Lamahatta.

Death: The death rituals are followed very strictly. A white cloth is thrown over the face of the corpse, and no person is allowed to touch the corpse, till the time comes to remove the body for cremation. A priest is appointed to perform the rituals for the dead; he is known as *Pho-Bo* (extractor of the consciousness principle). Meanwhile, a *Tsi-Pa* or astrologer-Lama is engaged to cast a death horoscope, the proper method of disposing of the corpse, the time and manner of the funeral and the sort of rites to be performed for the benefit of the departed spirit. Then the dead body is tied up to a sitting posture (the embryonic pasture), symbolical of being born out of this life into the life beyond death.

So long as the mourning continues, the dead body, thus, tied is placed in the corner of the room, where the spirit of the deceased is offered a part of all food, both solid and liquid, from each meal. After the dead body has been removed from the house for the final departure, an effigy of the deceased is put in the corner of the room occupied by the corpse and before this effigy, food continues thus to be offered, for forty-nine days (*Shib Chu Se Gu*).

After the funeral, the Lama returns to the house of the deceased, once a week, until the forty-ninth day. It is, however, a common practice, under economic and other kinds of constraints, that they intermit one day of the first week of each of the succeeding periods, in order to shorten the service, so that they return after six, five, four, three, two and one day, respectively, thus concluding the reading in about three weeks. On the completion of the first year after death, a yearly ceremony, the *Ski-Du*, is held. They also erect prayer-flags (*lungdar*), attached to a bamboo pole, in the manner of the Tibetans and Sikkimese in Sikkim, on occasions of death, *Losar* etc.

Inheritance: Sons inherit the property in equal shares. The house usually goes to the youngest son. The elder sons who are married and have jobs or other sources of income are considered mature. The married daughters do not usually inherit anything from the parents, but can receive gifts. The unmarried daughters are allowed to have a share of the property and are allowed to live in the paternal house.

Religious Practices

Both the populations of Dukpas follow Buddhism. They erect a sacred flag (*lung-dar*) on a bamboo pole which also serves as an identification mark for a Dukpa settlement. The Dukpas keep faith on the ghost and evil spirit.

Yankhu Puja as observed in Lamahatta: Every year in the month of January they worship goddess Yankhu for getting rid of the evil spirits and for benefit of the house. The preparation and the actual *puja* continue for five days. Five Lamas come to the house of the Dukpa for worshipping. The date for worshipping is fixed by the Head Lama. The day before actual worship, an idol is prepared by one Lama with flour, wax, Dalda (a kind of butter) and colour. The idol looks like a king, red in colour. It is known as *Jhapsi* which is required for *Graha-jop* (appeasing the planets). Another idol depicting a pole with flower is prepared symbolising goddess Yankhu (similar with Lakshmi among the Hindus).

We saw the *puja* at Tashi Dukpa's (one of the respondent in Lamahatta) house. The idol is worshipped inside the room. They worship goddess Kali before this *puja*. From morning they start this *puja*. Outside the house a table and chair is put for worshipping the god. The Lama utters *mantra* by beating the bells and *Damaru*. They read *Damang* (sacred text). They create fumes by burning Dhupi tree leaves. They believe that this fume helps in take away the evil spirit of the house. The Lamas enlighten the *deep* and worship the nature. Inside the house the Dukpas keep different idols in a special room (those who have space). Every year after this *puja*, they keep the idol inside the safe and worship everyday. They change the idol every year replacing the old one. This helps in protecting the family wealth.

On this occasion they worship nature and erect sacred flag of five colours depicting natural objects like Yellow for soil, Red for fire, Blue for water, Green for tree and White for peace. The head of the family and his wife remain present on this occasion.

This might be a local tradition and it is not found in Lepchakha.

Festivals

The people observe several ceremonies, e.g., the Sonam Lossar, the Losoong, the Sagadawa etc. The Sonam Lossar is associated with the harvest and is known as the peasants' New Year, and is observed within families. Gewa Lossar or the Tibetan New Year is also observed between February-March every year. The Sagadawa is observed for one month in the fourth month of the Tibetan calendar, which is believed to be a particularly auspicious month. The full moon day (the fifteenth day of the Tibetan fourth month) is the most important celebration of the community. On this day, the Sakyamuni Buddha was born, attained Buddhahood and achieved *Kaha pari Nirvana* as well. The major sacred centres for pilgrimage are Tashiding, Pemayangtse, Rumtek. Dharmo Chokro Centre, in Sikkim; and Paro Tag Tahang in Faro-Bhutan; they also visit Sarnath, Bodhgaya, Lumbini etc.

Folk Tales, Song and Dance: From ancient times the Dukpas are known for their skill in wood-carving, carpentry, weaving etc. But these arts are declining fast with a dwindling market for their produce. The community has a rich tradition of numerous folk tales, like the Phum-Kha-Sem, Gyab-Khesa etc. But the community has forgotten most of its folklore and folk songs. The musical instruments played by the Dukpas include the Dram-Mye, Inga etc. The Dukpa *vis-à-vis* other communities can enter and visit the holy places of other communities.

Socio-political Administration: The Dukpas have the Kyi-dug, like the Tibetans in Sikkim, to look after the welfare of the community. This is an independent regional body. The members of the Kyi-dug have some moral responsibilities as well as duties. The Kyi-dug is an organisation which always stands beside the people of the community in their hour of need. Every family has to pay a certain amount of money, fixed by the working members of the Kyi-dug, as subscription at proper intervals.

Like the Tibetans, Dukpas too have to spend a big amount of their income when a death strikes a family. When it becomes difficult, with the economic pressure it brings upon the family, the Kyi-dug steps in with all kinds of help. Every member of a family is expected to be present and help the family in need. When a family fails to send a member of its family, a sum of money is demanded as punishment.

Every 2-3 years, election takes place, and a new set of people are assigned to run the Kyi-dug. However, there are Panchayats, which look after the village locality, to which members are elected and are officially entrusted by the Government to look after the people. The Panchayat is responsible for looking after the day-to-day affairs of the locality, roadways, irrigation, land, law and order, land conservation, better seed distribution etc. People avail of different rural development schemes offered by the Government.

Traditional Dress and Ornaments: The dress worn by both male and female are mainly hand-woven. The dress of the male and female are known as *pho-kho* and *hho-kho*, respectively. The *pho-kho* is worn to a little below the knees, with long sleeves; the *hho-kho* is worn down to ankle length and has no sleeves. The *hho-kho* is a long shawl-type dress and is worn with the help of a brooch (*khow*).

To fasten the dress, they use a *sash* (hero), a little above the waistline; the upper part of the dress forms into a kind of pocket, where they usually keep some beetles, a purse etc. Males wear the *kabhi*, a white, handloomed shawl and the female wear the *khatri*, a coloured handloomed one. Their dress has changed more recently, as they now wear more European dresses.

The man usually does not wear any ornaments, except a gold ring studded with stones like turquoise (*gyu*) and coral (*byuru*). Ornaments worn by women include the Kho, the Kye-Kho, the Na-Gyan, the Grob-Dub and the A-Long which are usually made of gold and studded with *gyu-hyuru*, Baidurya etc.

Food and Drinks: The Dukpas are non-vegetarian, taking pork, beef, chicken, and mutton. In Lamahatta Bustee, there were some families who strictly opposed the intake of mutton. Only a few poor families take buffalo meat. Rice is the staple food but some have taken to *chapatis*. Usually, their food is prepared very hot with lots of green and red chillies. They take pulses like *urad*, *moong*, *masur* and *mashem* (a type of bean). Mustard and rapeseed oil are the more common mediums of cooking. They also use pork fat. The roots and tubers consumed by them are simal torul, ghar torul, ban torul, squash root etc., and they are all raised in their fields. The Dukpas of Lamahatta Bustee primarily consume what they grow in their fields.

The habit of consuming alcohol is common, as with most other hill communities. Women take alcohol only on special occasions, and even then it is confined mostly to the married and the old.

Fig. 8.1: A Dukpa House at Lepchakha

Fig. 8.2: A Kitchen of the Dukpas at Lamahatta

Men drink regularly, taking almost all the types of alcohol that are available in the market or are brewed at home.

Development Initiatives: Education for girls is still not popular in the community, specially in Lepchakha due to unavailability of

Fig. 8.3: A Dukpa Lady

Fig. 8.4: A Dukpa Man

higher education facilities. Though hospitals and other medical facilities are commonly available, they are often inaccessible to the Dukpas inhabiting the high and remote areas like Lepchakha. The diseases most common in Lepchakha are stomach ailments as they drink tap water directly without filtering or boiling.

The Dukpas of Lamahatta Bustee were provided with seeds and seedlings of different vegetable plants to support their food supply as well as to maintain their economy from the NABARD. No such efforts were seen to be provided from the government for the Dukpas of Lepchakha.

The Dukpas of both the areas draw weekly rations from local N.R. shops, where they get sugar, rice etc. There are complaints, however, of the irregularity in the supply of necessary items.

General Observation and Conclusion

The Dukpas are migrant community in West Bengal. Now, the Dukpa families are dispersedly scattered in different areas of North Bengal. Even some of them also live in Kolkata. But in Lepchakha, old Dukpa settlement could be found. A considerable number of Dukpa families are also settled in Lamahatta. The Dukpas of Lamahatta depict a mixed cultural pattern.

Being Buddhist, the Dukpas of both Lamatta Bustee and Lepchakha shows a resemblance in their religious activities, but the isolation of the Dukpas of Lamhatta made them preserver of traditional religious traits. The two populations belong to different sects of Buddhism.

The contradictory nature of isolation and communication is clearly noticed when the differences between these two populations are observed. On one hand, we see the Dukpas of Lamahatta gradually becoming as modernised and empowered like any other communities in and around the area. On the other hand, we see the Dukpas of Lamahatta still holding on to their tradition and are separated from all other communities around the area. Access to basic amenities reaches faster in Lamahatta than in Lepchakha. Lepchakha has been a popular tourist spot for years now, but not everyone can reach there, the place being so hard to trek to. Lamahatta has been recognised as a tourist spot, too, recently but it is gaining popularity at a faster rate. People coming from different places are definitely going to spend time with the Dukpas in Lamahatta Bustee, sharing their respective cultures and views. In a decade, we may notice the differences between the two studied populations gotten farther than it is presently.

Not messing with isolation of the Dukpas in Lepchakha, the provisions of the basic facilities to them should be more transparent. Lepchakha is on the Indo-Bhutan Border and hence have SSB (Sashatra Seema Bal) camp inside the village. One of the SSB officers told us that Lepchakha is still in Bhutan and Indian Government is paying taxes to Royal Bhutan Government for using it as Indian land.

References

Bisht, Narendra S. and Bankoti, T.S., 2004. *Encyclopaedic Ethnography of the Himalayan Tribes*, Delhi: Global Vision Publishing House.

Bisht, Ramesh C., 2008. *International Encyclopaedia of Himalayas*. New Delhi: Mittal Publications.

Choudhury, Maitreyee, 2008. *Himalayan Studies in India*. New Delhi: Mittal Publications.

Singh, Kumar S., 1994. *The Schedules Tribes*. New Delhi: Oxford University Press.

9

Media and Nation Building

An Empirical Study with Special Reference to Tribals Living in Birbhum District, West Bengal

Debasis Mondal

Introduction

Ideally, media is a functional tool in dissemination of news, information, ideas and innovative thoughts and so on. Media itself has different forms to share valuable information from person to person and develop social and political consciousness among the people of rural society in particular. In rural society, media works as the disseminator of information, facilitator of development and the agents of social change. Indeed, media provokes thought process of the individuals and its function for the progress of advanced civilization. Besides that, electronic media such as radio and television usually provides encouragement to tribal youth through their several programmes. Additionally, media is also mobilizing the most oppressed sections of the society, especially the tribal women and ensures their participation in nation building process. Sometimes, media organizes debates about various facets of our daily lives that would generate a healthy public discussion for betterment of the tribal society and its culture. Since last seven decades, the role of media in nation building has been well recognized and firmly regarded as a forum of public discussion. It helps to maintain a friendly and harmonious relationship between varied groups in order to unify society in particular and national solidarity of a country in general. Moreover, due to immense impact of media, people are aware about variety of issues such as education, health, electoral participation etc. In new India, media really holds a significant position in rural society and its impact deeply affects mindsets of the rural people. In this sense, media is the most effective and popular method of reaching the public with its informative content that are the present requirement for bringing out the changes and development in contemporaneous tribal society. In this endeavour, media is utilized in variety of ways in order to promote socio-economic reforms of a country that would extend towards the growth of a transforming nation.

Review of Literatures

Dash (2009) pointed out that despite these aberrations, the media does play a role in nation building. The owners and managers of the media must realize their responsibility towards society and aim to provide information that is clean, transparent and reliable. There are many things that are wrong with the society, and the media should engage itself in the betterment of society and the nation as a whole. By addressing itself to the needs of the people, it can strengthen the very root of democracy.

Dutta (2011) stated that media which was thought to be an agent of ushering in social change through development programmes directed at the non-privileged and marginalised sections of the society. He further told that though media at times successfully played the role of a watchdog of the government functionaries and has also aided in participatory communication, a lot still needs to be done.

Sen Choudhury (2011) opined that right from its inception, development communication has been pursued by all kinds of media, both traditional and new. However, sadly enough, it had been put into more theoretical use. Its possibilities, people's change of demand and opportunities, have not been to its limit to get an overall success. Both the strength and weakness of the media and the message and access of people to these medium should be considered to achieve success in real sense and not only in pen and paper.

Schramm (1964) asserted that it is extremely difficult to imagine that the national and economic development can be achieved without the input of external information irrespective of this complexity and indirectness. Thus, the fact remains that development related information must reach the population if any positive change is to bring about, but when the bulk of population live in less accessible and isolated villages both in plains and hills, such an effective communication is very difficult to take place. In this situation mass media are extremely important in stimulating a sense of involvement which is essential for development. Mass media create empathetic spirit, widens people horizon and conducive climate for social change.

Singh (2006) viewed that media as communicational instrument that society needed to expand its frontiers, both intellectual and technical. It could humanise society. To extend its capacity; to cope up with new problems, to provide a common context for democratic decision-making and to break the aristocratic monopoly of knowledge. Mass media made mass society a viable institution.

Objectives of the Study

The objectives of the study is to explore the role played by media in the process of nation building with special reference to tribals of Birbhum District, West Bengal. Specific objectives are—

(1) To find out different types of media used by tribals in the studied villages.
(2) To assess the educational status of tribals in the surveyed villages.
(3) To study the electoral participation of the tribal people in the studied villages.
(4) To determine the awareness level of tribals regarding different Government developmental schemes.
(5) To analyse the role media in nation building.

Methodology

Research Approaches

Qualitative and Quantitative research, both the approaches were employed for picking up the empirical data from the field.

Methods and Techniques

The survey and interview methods were applied by following in-depth interview techniques for gleaned up the primary data from the field. Structure interview schedule and some open ended questions were utilized as the tool of primary data collection. Moreover, the secondary data were picked up from various sources like books, journals, articles, conferences, published and unpublished research work etc.

Area and People

The present study has been conducted in eight villages, such as Kurumba Ghosh, Donaipur, Bondanga, Jaljalia, Padmabatipur, Durgapur, Fuldanga and Dhultikuri of Birbhum District, West Bengal. Four tribal groups of Birbhum are the main units of this research problem such as Kol, Kora, Oraon and Santal.

Sample Size

Total sample size is 341 out of which 8 Kol, 33 Kora, 45 Oraon and 255 Santal families were the main respondents of this empirical study.

Results and Discussion

In rural India, media motivates the tribal people to take part in the process of nation building. Media plays very crucial role to make individuals informative and knowledgeable. It also increases public involvement in national development programmes such as ensuring education for all, electoral participation and awareness about different Government developmental schemes etc. In this connection, media exposes public feelings about Government developmental policies and programmes and bring out the needs and demands of the poor and socially disadvantaged people to the forefront of the society. The Government is trying to uplift the conditions of the tribal people in regard to educational and political spheres of lives. It plays a key role by propagating useful information regarding education and political participation with a view to bring social changes in the society. Indeed, media is firmly recognized as an agent of social change because it provides strength to the democratic institutions, ensuring public participation in national building process.

Table 9.1: Distribution of Households of the Tribal in Eight Villages of Birbhum District, West Bengal

Villages	*Total*	*%*
Kurumbo Ghosh	8	2.34
Donaipur	12	3.52
Jaljalia	17	4.98
Padmabatipur	42	12.32
Bondanga	52	15.25
Durgapur	53	15.54
Phuldanga	60	17.59
Dhultikuri	97	28.44
Total	**341**	**100**

Source: Present fieldwork.

In Table 9.1, village-wise total households have been distributed by the studied villages of Birbhum District, West Bengal. In village Kurumbo Ghosh, there are total 8 households and their percentage is 2.34. In Donaipur village, the total number of households is 12 and their percentage is 3.52. In village Jaljalia, there are total 17 households and their percentage being 4.98. In village Padmabatipur, there are total 42 households and their percentage is 12.32. In Bondanga village, the total number of households is 52 and their percentage is 15.25. In village Durgapur there are total 53 households and their percentage is 15.54. In Phuldanga village, the total 60 households are there and their percentage is 17.59. In Dhultikuri village, the number of households is 97 and their percentage is 28.44.

Table 9.2 is the distribution of population of the eight tribal villages of Birbhum District, West Bengal. The village Kurumbo Ghosh is consisting of 24 individuals, out of which 13 are male and 11 are female. In Donaipur village, the number of total individuals is 56, out of which 28 are male and 28 are female. The village Jaljalia is consisting of 78 individuals, out of which 42 are male and 36 are female. In village Padmabatipur the number of total individuals is 177, out of which 86 are male and 91 are female. The Bondanga village, there are 229 individuals, out of which 115 are male and 114 are female. In village Durgapur, there

Table 9.2: Distribution of Population of the Tribals in Eight Villages of Birbhum District, West Bengal.

Villages	*Male*	*%*	*Female*	*%*	*Total*	*%*
Kurumbo Ghosh	13	0.86	11	0.73	24	1.60
Donaipur	28	1.86	28	1.87	56	3.73
Jaljalia	42	2.79	36	2.41	78	5.20
Padmabatipur	86	5.71	91	6.09	177	11.80
Bondanga	115	7.63	114	7.63	229	15.26
Durgapur	115	7.63	113	7.56	228	15.20
Phuldanga	150	9.96	160	10.71	310	20.66
Dhultikuri	204	13.55	194	12.99	398	26.53
Total	**753**	**49.99**	**747**	**49.99**	**1500**	**100.00**

Source: Present fieldwork.

are 228 individuals, out of which 115 are male and 113 are female. In village Phuldanga the number of total individuals is 310, where 150 are male and 160 are female. Lastly, the Dhultikuri village is consisting of 398 individuals, out of which 204 are male and 194 are female.

Table 9.3: Different Types of Media Used by the Tribal Households of Eight Villages of Birbhum District, West Bengal

Media Used by the Villagers	*Total*	*%*
Print Media (Newspapers)	13	3.81
Electronic Media (Radio, Television, Mobile telephony)	263	77.13
Media Non-Used by the Villagers	65	19.06
Total	**341**	**100.00**

Source: Present fieldwork.

Table 9.3 shows that different types of media using habit of tribal people in the studied villages. The study showed that only 3.81 per cent tribal households are using print media like newspapers in the villages. Besides, 77.13 per cent are habituated to use electronic media like radio; television and mobile telephony; while at the same time 19.06 per cent do not use any kind of media in their homes. Almost all of the villages have access to electronic media like radio, television and mobile telephony but they are not connected by roads and railways in all the cases.

Table 9.4: Educational Status of the Tribals in Eight Villages of Birbhum District, West Bengal

Class Standards	*Male*	*%*	*Female*	*%*	*Total*	*%*
Non-literate	149	19.79	266	35.61	415	27.67
Can Sign Only	180	23.90	173	23.15	353	23.53
Primary (I-IV)	118	15.67	87	11.64	205	13.67
Intermediate (V-VIII)	145	19.26	105	14.06	250	16.66
Secondary (IX-X)	126	16.73	87	11.65	213	14.20
Higher Secondary (XI-XII)	23	3.05	17	2.28	40	2.67
U.G.	9	1.2	12	1.61	21	1.4
P.G.	3	0.4	–	–	3	0.2
Total	**753**	**100.00**	**747**	**100.00**	**1500**	**100.00**
Literacy Rate	**80.21%**		**64.39%**		**72.33%**	

Source: Present fieldwork.

Table 9.4 signifies the literacy rate and level of education of the tribal in eight villages. The data showed that 19.79 per cent male and 35.61 per cent female are illiterate. Only 23.90 per cent male and 23.15 per cent female can sign; 15.67 per cent male and 11.64 per cent female have primary education (standard I-standard IV) and even 19.26 per cent male and 14.06 female are having intermediate education (V-VIII). Hence, a total of 16.73 per cent male and 11.65 per cent female have obtained secondary education (IX-X). There were only 3.05 per cent male and 2.28 per cent female who have either achieved or enrolled in the Higher Secondary (XI-XII) level. Eventually, only 1.2 per cent male and 1.61 per cent female obtain the degree of under-graduate (UG). There were 0.4 per cent male found who has achieved post-graduate degree. Moreover, the total male literacy rate is 80.21 per cent and female literacy rate is 64.39 per cent among the varied tribal groups. The data means that educational status has increased up to secondary level.

Table 9.5: Participation in Electoral Process of the Tribal in Eight Villages of Birbhum District, West Bengal

Participation in Electoral Process	*Male*	*%*	*Female*	*%*	*Total*	*%*
Number of Villagers Participating	458	89.11	477	88.33	935	88.74
Number of Villagers Not Participating	56	10.89	63	11.67	119	11.29
Total	**514**	**100.00**	**540**	**100.00**	**1054**	**100.00**

Source: Present fieldwork.

Table 9.5 shows that the villagers are participating and not participating in the electoral process. 458 (89.11%) male and 477 (88.53%) female are taking part in the voting process. Out of the total population, 56 (10.89%) male and 63 (11.67%) female are not taking part in voting process. The data means that the villagers are actively taking part in electoral process of the country.

Table 9.6: Awareness Level of Tribals about Different Government Development Schemes through Media

Different Government Development Schemes	*Aware*	*%*	*Note Aware*	*%*
Pradhan Mantri Gram Sadak Yojana (PMGSY)	300	87.97	41	12.02
Mahatma Gandhi Rural Employment Guarantee Act (MNREGA)	309	90.61	32	9.38
Right to Information (RTI)	14	4.11	327	95.88
Indira Awas Yojana (IAY)	288	84.45	53	15.54
Right to Education (RTE)	72	21.11	269	78.88
Self-Help Groups (SHGs)	318	93.25	23	6.74
Janani Suraksha Yojana (JSY)	319	93.54	22	6.45

Source: Present fieldwork.

Table 9.6 describes awareness of the villagers about different Government Developmental Schemes that have dissipated through media. The data showed that total 87.97 per cent households are aware about Pradhan Mantri Gram Sadak Yojana (PMGSY). A total of 90.61 per cent households are aware of Mahatma Gandhi Rural Employment Guarantee Act (MNREGA). Only 4.11 per cent households are aware about Right to Information Act (RTI). Next, 84.45 per cent households are aware regarding Indira Awas Yojana (IAY). Out of total 341 households, only 21.11 per cent households are aware about the scheme of Right to Education (RTE). Here, 93.25 per cent households are aware regarding Self-Help Groups (SHGs). Eventually, 93.54 per cent are aware of Janani Suraksha Yojana (JSY). It means that media is successful to generate social awareness among the villagers regarding various rural development schemes that I studied in the selected villages except Right to Information Act (RTI) and Right to Education.

Media has succeeded to promote educational and political awareness among varied tribal groups in the studied villages. Media, either print or electronic, tries to bring out social changes in various aspects of their lives. It does a tremendous work to build awareness of ensuring villagers participation for social and political process of national development. I observed in the villages that media has a great impact on the studied four tribal groups. As a result, changes in terms of education are taking place in the studied tribal areas. I also found from the field that the elders of every tribal group now understand the importance of education and send their children to school. The data showed that most of the villagers can sign only, followed by primary level (I-IV), intermediate (V-VIII) education and secondary level (IX-X) education (Table 9.4). But in some cases, it showed that positive attitudes of the villagers towards education have occurred due to immense effect of media.

Media basically propagates electoral information to the people and ensures people's participation in the political process of the country. For a long time, tribals are keeping themselves away from the political process of participation. Presently, they are educated through media and very much conscious about the political situation of the country. The information about voting rights is provided by the Election Commission through various types of media. Media plays positive role in this concern and insists the tribal communities to apply their voting rights during election in order to choose a Secular and Democratic Government. In this sense, media also ensures the participation of women and push them to take part in electoral process. The data showed that the villagers are actively participating in the voting process during election time, guaranteed by Indian polity (Table 9.5). Media creates peaceful environment and encourages them to apply their voting rights during election. The discussion emphasises that only proper awareness can change the life of the Scheduled Tribes in the villages. Due to media boom the villagers under my research area are participating actively in electoral process. This helps to join hands with mass leaders and administrators of the country who frame nation building process. The tribal people mostly watch television and listen to radio in order to keep themselves informed and entertained in the spare time. I observed in the field that the villagers are mostly using electronic media in their homes

(Table 9.3). They are watching several programmes in the time between 6 p.m. to 9 p.m. in the evening after getting free from all sorts of household work. Media ushers several schemes of the Government which are contributing in the process of national development.

Moreover, the villagers are aware about different Government developmental schemes that have disseminated through media. Media informed about all these programmes with a view to bring these welfare activities into the public notice (Table 9.6). Electronic media is too useful for the propagation of valuable information and promotion of knowledge regarding several rural development programmes. Further, the proliferation of several local media is helping to spread information to the tribal communities and trying hard to fulfil the planned goals of the Government.

Media is working as the peace builder in tribal society and plays a significant role to prevent political conflicts between intra- and inter-villages that probably takes place during election time. It also reduces the communication gaps between various groups and tries to promote peace in society. In the grassroots level, political conflict often takes place due to inadequate information and misunderstanding. Insufficient information creates suspicion among the tribal groups and results in conflict across tribal areas. It leads the tribal people towards peace by providing necessary information for ending political conflict in villages that taken place during election time. Sometimes, local media brings out issues of political conflicts and report the reasons. As a result, the Government circulates relevant information through media to solve the political conflict that arises at the local level. Reasons of conflict cannot be traced at a primary stage without intervention of media. The tribal people of such villages are considered politically violent. Conflict is often aroused among intra- and inter-groups. In these circumstances, media seeks the reasons behind the conflicts and reports the situation. The tribal people are nature lover and peace minded. From the beginning of their life, they are being traditionally educated to maintain peace in society. They like to live in peaceful environment, but get violent with the slightest notion of security threat. The study found that media plays a positive role to manage the tribal groups under such situations. It bridges the Government and sufferers. It exchanges the information between the duos and does best to control situation. So, media acts as a mediator and peace building agent of the society.

It has prevented political conflicts occurred in the studied tribal village.

The study also observed that political violence is often taking place during recent times in the villages. Thereby, the tribal chief of all the studied groups are influenced through media by watching different programmes of national integration and trying to maintain peace in the tribal society. Moreover, media has positive effect on tribals regarding peace building and national integration. It informs voters about the nominated persons, highlighting their profiles, so that they can vote for the right candidates. Recently, voters are introduced about, ballots papers, electoral machines and symbols of the candidates etc. Additionally, it sets out a conducive environment at the grassroots level for making the elections free and fair as well.

Conclusion

The study came to a conclusion that media broadly performs its functions across two areas such as social and political spheres of tribal livelihood in the studied villages. Media insists the tribal groups to become self-reliant and self-dependent. Ultimately, it promotes the idea of self reliance among socially varied groups. Media transforms social status of the tribal groups in many ways. Its active motivation helps illiterates to become literates, acquiring knowledge and adopting changes that occur through the ages. It tries to establish equality among all the classes and castes and promotes respect for mankind. Media gives emphasis on right to information campaigns. These campaigns strengthen the tribal groups and increase self-confidence among them. This self-confidence assists the tribal people to take part in nation building process. The enhancement of political awareness has enabled tribal groups to participate in the electoral process of a nation. It is media which showed the importance of the tribal communities for nation building and encourages them to co-operate actively towards national development.

References

Dash, S., 2009. Role of Media in Nation Building. *Odisha Review*, January: 50-51.

Dutta, S., 2011. Social Responsibility of Media and Indian Democracy. *Global Media Journal*, June: 1-8.

Schramm, W., 1964. *Mass Media and National Development*. California: Stanford University Press.

Sen, Choudhury, P., 2011. Media in Development Communication, *Global Media Journal* – Indian Edition 2(2):1-13.

Singh, N., 2006. Role of Mass Media. In *Development of Political Consciousness*, Delhi: AAYUSH Publishing House.

Sopory, A.K., 2008. *Modern Media and Social Change*, New Delhi: Cyber Tech Publications.

10

Social Media and Tribal Development

A Case Study of Bolpur, Birbhum District, West Bengal

Munshi Ismotara

Introduction

The term "Social Media" refers to the use of web-based and mobile technologies to turn communication into an interactive dialogue. Social media takes on many different forms including magazines, internet forums, weblogs, social blogs, microblogging, wikis, podcasts, photographs or pictures, video, rating and social bookmarking. With the world in the midst of a social media revolution, it is more than obvious that social media like facebook, twitter, whatsapp, myspace, skype etc., are used extensively for the purpose of communication. This form of communication can be with an individual or a group of persons. Today most of the people specially the youngsters are hooked on to the different social media platforms for keeping in contact with their peers. Social media is media for social interaction as a superset beyond social communication. There are pros and cons to the use of social media. One most important advantage is the online sharing of knowledge and information among the different groups of people. This online sharing of information also promotes the increase in the communication skills among the people especially among the specific community like same profession, organisation, student of same class etc.

Definition of is 'development'—"a process which enables human beings to realize their potential, build self-confidence, and lead lives of dignity and fulfilment" (*Oxford English Dictionary*). It is a process which frees people from fear of want and exploitation. It is a movement away from political, economic, or social oppression. Through development, political independence acquires true significance. And it is a process of growth, a movement essentially springing from within the society that is developing. The basic objective of human development is to enlarge the range of people's choices to make development more democratic and participatory. And Choices include: decent wages and employment opportunities, education, healthcare, clean and safe environment, ability to participate in community decision-making, and enjoyment of basic human, economic and political freedoms. Development is the process of expanding the freedoms that people enjoy and requires removing barriers to freedom. And barriers include: poverty, tyranny and unaccountable government, lack of opportunity, systematic social deprivation, lack of functioning infrastructure, and repression. Development depends on people's ability to make good choices in their economic, political, and social lives.

The term "tribe" originated around the time of the Greek city-states and the early formation of the Roman Empire. The Latin term, "tribus" has since been transformed to mean, a group of persons forming a community and claiming descent from a common ancestor. Tribals are those who live in relatively isolation, marked with distinctive culture, language and religion. In the contemporary world they are considered as a weaker section of the society. India being the second largest tribal dominated area after Africa is one of the most fascinating Nations of World from anthropological point of view. The total tribal population of India is 8.08 per cent. As many as 427 tribal communities are residing in India, of whom 75 are declared as primitive tribal groups who are spread across the country. Bhill, Gond and Santal are the major tribes of India, while Onje, Andamanese, Chenchu, and Mankirdia are the minor tribes of India. The tribal communities in India are largely concentrated in Central India region and North-East India region, which are specially treated under 5th Schedule and 6th Schedule to the Constitution of India respectively.

Birbhum is a tribal dominated District with the largest number of tribal communities, representing major linguistic groups like Dravidian, Austro-Asiatic and Indo-Aryan. They have been found at varied levels of acculturation, integration and assimilation with the caste Hindu societies of the District. Almost 44.21 per cent of the total land area in Birbhum has been declared as Scheduled area. The total tribal population of the State is 8.15 million, who constitute 22.13 per cent. Of 19 administrative districts, 3 districts like Birbhum, Bankura and Purullia are declared as fully Scheduled districts. Whereas there are 7 other districts declared as partially Scheduled districts.

Birbhum District Overview: The district of Birbhum lies between the latitudes of 23°23′30"N and 24°35′00"N and occupies the western parts of the state of West Bengal. The district has an area of 4545 sq. kms. The eastern most extremity of the district is marked by 88°01′40"E longitude and its western most extremity by 87°05′25"E longitude. The District is sharing 5.12 per cent of the land area of the State, but 3.76 per cent of its total population, indicating a relatively lower density of population per square kilometre in the district (663) *vis-à-vis* the state (903). The district is characterized by an undulating topography caused by the Chhotanagpur Plateau that passes through the Western borders of the district. The land terrain slopes down towards the east and merges with the alluvial plains of the Ganga. The district borders the states of Jharkhand and Bihar on the west, and lies at the eastern end of the Chhotanagpur Plateau. The district is triangular in shape with the rivers Ajoy forming the base of the triangle. The river forms the boundary between Birbhum and Burdwan (now Barddhaman) districts. Another important river is Mayurakshi, on which a river valley project that includes the Tilpara Barrage. The comparatively fertile eastern portion, constituting the north-eastern Rarh region, merges with the Gangetic plain. Important geographical features in Birbhum are the Khoai, the red soil, with palm trees visible from a long distance and protected forest areas on the western side.

Tribal Profile of the District Birbhum is one of the tribal dominated districts of West Bengal, which has been declared as the tribal district of the State. With three Sub-divisions Rampurhat and Bolpur are the part of the plain areas and Suri-I, is the tribal dominated region of the district. There are 15 types of tribes residing in the district. Out of 19 Blocks the tribal's are more concentrated in Khoyrasole, Dubrajpur, Rajnagar and Suri Blocks where the population varies from 70 per cent to 80 per cent of the total population of respective Blocks. The tribes constitute 56.6

per cent of total population of the district, though the population of Birbhum is only 6 per cent of the State's total population. Birbhum district is known for their rich tribal cultural heritage, mining and mineral resources. Due to development interventions in the form of mining activities, it is observed that certain changes in the life and livelihood of the Santals and the Mundas in few pockets. These changes are observed in the literacy status, educational achievements and their employment status. But, by and large the benefits of development programmes are yet to reach the tribal population in general. The State needs to understand the linkages between the development activities, livelihood requirements and natural resource base of the tribal communities and the development of these regions. Perhaps these processes have started and need to be strengthened in coming days if adequate resources are converged into the development processes of the district.

The Santal represents more than half of the total tribal population of the State (51.8%). Oraon (14%), Munda (7.8%), Bhumij (7.6%) and Kora (3.2%) are the other major tribals having sizeable population. Along with Santal, they constitute nearly 85 per cent of the State's total Tribal population. The Lodha and Mahali are the remaining tribals, and having population of one per cent or more. The rest of the tribals are very small in population size. According to 2001 Census, Birbhum houses 13 tribes. The major tribes inhabiting in Birbhum are Santal, Oraon, Kora, Lodha, Bhumij, Munda, Mahali etc. Linguistically, Austric and the Indo-Aryan language groups are dominated in tribal population of Birbhum. Tribal communities like Santal, Munda, Ho, Oraon, Mahali, Kol, and Bhumij speak their own languages. Rest of the tribal communities of the district are speaking Bengali and mixture of languages. In Bengal, four tribal communities developed their own script out of which two tribal communities inhabit in Birbhum, namely Santal and Munda. Santal is the largest tribe of the district scattered concentrated all over Birbhum. Their main occupation is agriculture and agricultural labourer. They are very conscious about their identity and culture. Santal is one of the largest and advanced tribes of India too. They developed their own script Olchiki and have been continuing language movement in Eastern India. Mahali is the only tribe well known in Bengal for his bamboo craft making skill. In order to have an educationally stable social order, it is necessary to minimize regional variation in literacy rates at micro-level with an uniform spread in education amongst the population. For this purpose, an attempt has been made to see the literacy variation in Birbhum District at village level.

Methodology

This is a descriptive type research. The study has been conducted at Bolpur, Birbhum district in West Bengal. This research paper is a combination of primary and secondary data. The Secondary data has been taken from different research reports, books, journals, articles, websites, research papers, conferences, published and unpublished research work etc.

Research Approaches—Both Qualitative and Quantitative research approaches were employed for picking up the empirical data from the field. Hereafter, the secondary data were picked up from various sources like books, journals, articles, conferences, published and unpublished research work etc.

Methods and Techniques—The structure schedule and some open ended questions have been utilized as the tools of primary data collection. After that a critical analysis was carried out of the collected facts and figures.

Universe and Population—The research universe of this present study is only the tribal people (Santal, Oraon and Kora) of Kolapukur, Bagantola, Pathorghata nearby villages from Bolpur, a semi-town in Birbhum district of West Bengal to the fulfilment of the purpose of this research study.

Sampling—Sample of the study was composed of 150 respondents and the sample was chosen using Purposive Sampling Technique in which the researcher selects a particular group or category from the population to constitute the sample because this category is considered to mirror the whole with reference to the characteristic in the schedule.

Results and Discussion

To explore the relationship between social networks and their impact on tribal people, a sample of 150 respondents (Santal, Oraon and Kora) of Kolapukur, Bagantola, Pathorghata nearby villages from Bolpur, a semi-town in Birbhum district of West Bengal were chosen who were in the age bracket of 15 to 35 years. Amongst the respondents the gender distribution shows that there is 60 per cent of women and 40 per cent men (Table 10.2). The research universe of this present study is only the tribal people (Santal, Oraon and Kora) of Kolapukur, Bagantola, Pathorghata nearby villages from Bolpur, a semi-town in Birbhum district of West Bengal shows that they are quite exposed to the city culture and the literacy rate is almost 45.33 per cent (Table 10.3).

Table 10.1: Distribution of Tribal Population in Birbhum and West Bengal

West Bengal Total Population	*Birbhum Total Population*	*Tribal Population of Birbhum*	*% Tribal*	*% WB*
80176197	3015422	203127	6.74	4.8861

Source: According to the 2001 Census data.

Table 10.2: Gender Distribution of Respondents

Gender	*Percentage*
Male	40
Female	60

Source: Present fieldwork.

Table 10.3: Age-wise Literacy rate of the Respondents

Age	*Non-Literate*	*Literate*
15 to 25	55	40
25 to 35	27	28
Total		**68 (45.33%)**

Source: Present fieldwork.

Uses of Social Media

From a sample of 150 tribal people we found that 58 per cent (Fig. 10.1) of them use one or the other social media. The social networking sites that they use include YouTube, Whatsapp and Facebook. Whatsapp was used as much as Facebook. Twitter was the least used of all the websites. Any other social media included WeChat, Google+, hike etc. The respondents found Facebook and Whatsapp easier to use.

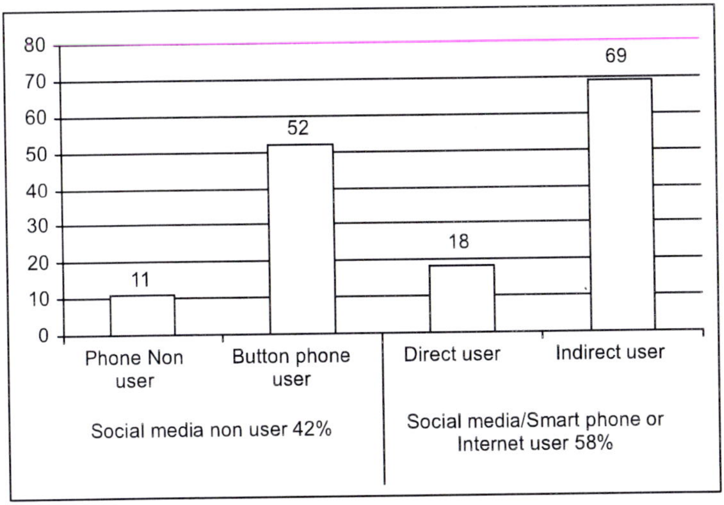

Fig. 10.1: Social Media Exposure of Respondents
Source: Present fieldwork.

The respondents reported the number of hours they spent on social networks per day 16 per cent spent one hour per day 44 per cent spent two hours per day and 21 per cent spent more than two hours. They were only few respondents (9%) who spent zero hours on the social networks. The consumption levels for more than two hours are the highest (Fig. 10.2).

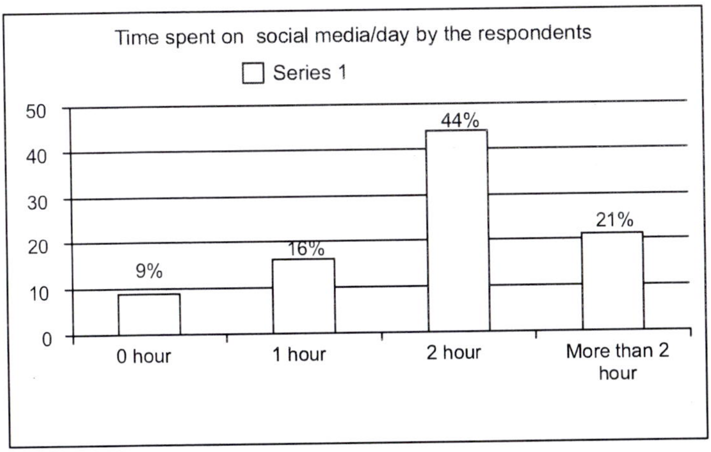

Fig. 10.2: Time Spend on Social Media/Day by the Respondents
Source: Present fieldwork.

Purposes of Using Social Media

The next variable in this assessment was the purposes for which the tribals use social media. The tribal people were able to point out the different purposes for which they used the social media. It is observed that the highest score of 60 per cent is for downloading music and videos. 6 per cent used for posting photos, 12 per cent used it for chatting. Downloading music and videos were not only educational but consisted of several genres. The highest score revealed that the tribals used it for downloading music/videos. Posting photos and chatting can be categorized as entertainment use. Educational activities like publishing articles, participating in quizzes/poll, communicating with teachers comprised of a lesser score. Only 10 per cent used social media for uploading videos. Two per cent for creating quizzes/poll 4 per cent for blogging, 3 per cent for submitting articles, 2 per cent communication with teachers. This reflects that social media were used by tribal people used for entertainment mostly and less for education purpose (Table 10.4).

Table 10.4: Percentage of Usage of Social Media by the Respondents

Purposes	*% of Respondents*
Downloading music/video	60
Uploading music/video	6
Posting photos	12
Chatting	10
Blogging	2
Creating polls/quizzes or surveys	4
Submitting articles to website	3
Communication with teachers/class fellows	2
Any other	1

Source: Present fieldwork.

Role of Social Media

Any development programme implemented by Government to reach people needs a better communication. Social media has an essential role as a catalyst, to facilitate a link between information and communication. The information is available but it does not get circulate. Then Social media or Social networking such as Facebook, Whatsapp, Blogs and Twitter, which are predominantly used by young tribal people. These findings claim that social networking is further isolating people from necessary face-to-face communication, which is a characteristic of tribal behaviour, but the continuous flow of information claim that it is a force that will create a new and powerful paradigm of tribalism. Human beings are social animals and need some form of community. Since the time our ancestors gathered together in caves for protection and food we have formed tribes and exhibit tribal behaviour. As civilization advanced the tribes got more numerous and specific, developed into institutions, communities and countries. The predominant characteristic of tribes throughout time is the need to communicate. So, when in one hand Social media is making the rise of modern civilization with its secularism and isolationism, on the other hand it has done much to break down the tribal culture. Social media has given them the platform to attach with the outer world as a social responsibility. Modern human tribes are based on the need to use language to communicate. With the growth of the social media with its capacity to communicate 24/7 everything and anything to anyone on the planet, Social media have created the ultimate platform for tribals to not to be isolated. The power of Social networking, combined with the Internet, can literally change cultural or social landscape rapidly.

Conclusion

These observations drawn from empirical data shows tribal people have started using social media for various purposes which is making them empowered unknowingly. While some perceived social media as a distraction and were hesitant to share their feelings, a high percentage of respondents found it an avenue to search for information, join educational networks and look for career opportunities. The use of social media gave them a sense of belonging to a community and not dependent on others. The flow of information's favoured academic through Social media. The use of these media has to be disciplined as it can lead to isolation which is the key feature of tribalism by the misuse of social media. The research also concludes that social media if designed and tailoured to the specific needs of tribal people then it can be a useful instrument for development of Tribal people of Bolpur, Birbhum, and West Bengal.

References

Arya, S.R.S. and Shah, 1987, New Technology Rain-fed Agriculture and Identification of Constraints on its Adoption in Midhills of Uttar Pradesh, *Agricultural Situation in India*, 34:139-184.

B.B. Pawde, V.B. Bhise, S.R. Takle, 2008, *Adoption and impact of new agriculture technology on tribal agriculture*, Serial Publications, New Delhi.

Bhagat, L.N., 1983, Factors Determining adoption of new agriculture practices in tribal areas—A Quantitative analysis, *Agricultural Situations in India*, 33: 77-80.

Dua and Gupta, 2002, *Television and its impact on rural areas: A Doordarshan Study Media and Development*, Har-Anand Publications, New Delhi.

Ghurye, G.S., 1943, *The Tribals so called and their Future*, Gokhale Institute of Politics and Economics, Poona.

Gupta, V.S., 1996, *Media strategist for Rural Development*, Publication Division, Ministry of I&B, New Delhi.

Oxford English Dictionary, IX, 1933, p. 339, as cited in Fried, 1975, p. 7.

Verma, P., 1960, *Socio-Cultural Organisations of Tribals*, Metro Publishers, Jaipur.

Verrier, Elwin, 1943, *The Aborginals*, Oxford University Press, New Delhi.

Vidyarthi, L.P., 1976, Development Plans of the Tribes of Andaman & Nicobar Islands, *Journal of Social Research*, 19: 74-85.

Index

Advancement of education, 21
Agricultural land, 8, 10–11, 84, 88, 91, 139, 153–54
Alcohol, 163
Alien language, 102
Alienation, 142
Amarkantak, 27–29, 31, 34, 36, 40–42, 44, 46, 48, 51, 55
Ancestral fields, 19
Animal husbandry, 8, 118, 149, 154
Ayodhya Hills, 80, 123

Backward classes, 99
Backward regions, 133
Barriers, 1–3, 10, 15, 79, 180
Basic amenities, 146, 149, 166
Basque country, 37
Bastar region of Chhattisgarh, 135
Benefits, 101–2, 136, 139, 160–61, 182
Bengali, 79
Betel nuts, 11–12
Biodiversity, 2, 11
Birbhum houses, 182
Birth Rituals, 92
Blacksmiths, 78, 89
Blesso Montessori School, 21
Bondanga village, 171
Brick manufacturing factory, 88–90
Bride, 94–95, 151, 159–60
Bridegroom, 94
Buddhism, 158, 161, 166
Buxa hills, 146–47, 149
Buxa reserve forests, 10

Cardamom, 154, 157
Case study method, 69
Caste-panchayat, 95
Chalauni tea garden, 80
Chhotanagpur Plateau, 181
Child labourers, 155
Children education, 21, 68
Christian education, 22
Christian missionaries, 18, 20, 22
Christian rituals, 97
Christianity, 3, 6, 16–23, 97
Clan-based village council, 17
Cleanliness, 19–20
Code number, 30
Colonial government, 18
Common land, 142
Communication, 16, 18, 33, 122, 148–49, 166, 179, 186
- effective, 169
- face-to-face, 187
- gaps, 176
- participatory, 168
- problem, 121
- skills, 179
- social, 179

Communicational instruments, 169
Communities
- hill, 163
- migrant, 146, 165

non-tribal, 146
owning, 154
vulnerable, 132
Community cultivation, 11
Comparative Literacy Rate, 82
Cone Chart of Occupational Distribution, 74
Configuration of livelihood economy, 46, 55
Constitution of India, 180
Contemporary situation, 35
Cow dung, 93, 95
Crater rims, 28, 35, 43
Cultivable land, 10, 12
Cultivation, 8, 10–12, 38, 85, 140–41, 155
performed, 8
rubber, 11
seasonal, 11, 56
shifting, 140
wild edible, 56
Cultivator-labour, 157
Cultural community life, 20
Cultural development, 64
Cultural landscape, 33
Cultural life, 141
Culture, tribal, 187

Death rituals, 96, 160
Decimal land, 84
Deforestation, 2, 133
Delineation, 2
Demography, 27, 37, 41, 48, 51
Development
activities, 10
of communication, 16
initiatives, 163
interventions, 38, 182
programmes, 35, 100, 168, 182, 186
projects, 3, 8, 35, 38, 50–51, 131–32, 135, 142–43
scheme, 55, 101
of thrifting habit, 99
of tribes, 51
Dharmo Chokro Centre, 162
Dhultikuri village, 171–72
Directive principle of state policy, 16
Discrete groups of people, 37
Displacement, 55, 131–32, 134–36, 139, 141–42
development-caused, 132
discourse, 136
extent of, 134
families, 141
forced, 135
frequent, 99
induced, 135
involuntary, 143
Division of Labour, 87
Divorce, 151
DMS
benefit of, 121
initiation of, 103–4
savings account, 116
Dravidian group, 35–36
Dudhi River, 27, 32–33
Dukpa
communities, 146
House, 164
settlement, 161
Dzhongkha, 148, 157

Ecological wisdom, 27, 37, 39, 46, 49, 55
Economic
conditions, 88, 139, 141
development, 2, 15, 18, 168
growth, 63–64, 83, 133, 136
life, 98
problems, 87
Education/Educational
backwardness, 18
compulsory, 16
development, 65
expansion of, 16
free, 26

growing, 23
networks, 187
primary, 69, 173
rudimentary, 20
secondary, 173
Electoral participation, 168–70
Electoral process, 173–75, 177
Electronic media, 167, 172, 175–76
Empirical study, 167, 170
Ethnicity of tribal identity, 41
Evil spirit, 161
Exchange of bride, 151

Female empowerment, 42
Female literacy rate, 81, 173
Fertile soils, 33
Festivals, 20, 56, 96–98, 156, 159, 161
Field survey, 5
Financial
exclusion, 102–3
problems, 97
Fishery purposes, 118
Focused Group Discussion (FGD), 5, 137
Forest
adjacent, 11
based biodiversity management, 131
cleared, 65
committee, 142
coverage, 28, 34
deciduous, 28
dense, 35–36
dwellers, 25
eco-system, 39
fringe areas, 3, 13
habitat, 39
land, loss of, 142
legislation, 132
livelihood intervention, 12
management, 39
natural, 2
policy, 2
protection, 12
reserve, 140
resources, 1–2, 10, 140
strong, 39
thin, 147
upland, 27
Forest Conservation Act, 140
Forest Rights Act, 10, 13
Forest Rights Rules, 2
Forestry, 56

Geographical areas, 56, 64
Girls dormitory, 20
Government
functionaries, 168
initiative, 50
policy, 16
schemes, 44
Gradual development, 121
Grass land, 33
Grazing land, 142

Health Centre, 139
Herbal medicine, 39
Herbal parts, 45, 47, 49, 54
Holy Spirit School, 21
Home garden, 12
Homelessness, 135
Homestead land, 8, 83, 138
Human
capital, 63–64
development, 180
groups, 132
Habitation, 32
Hurlung village, 80

Impoverishments, 135, 142–43
Improvement, 100–101, 132
Inclusive education, 142
Income generation, 56
Indigenous
communities, 3, 131
knowledge, 11
method of cultivation, 155

Indira Awas Yojana (IAY), 174
Individual Level Variables, 6
Individualistic life, 141
Indo-Aryan language groups, 182
Indo-Mongoloid group, 3
Industrial Estate, 135
Industrial projects, 133, 135, 139
Inevitable circumstances, 56
Information
  campaigns, 177
  electoral, 175
  external, 168
  gathering, 100
  strengthen, 56
  validated, 50
Information Act, 174
Interests of cultivation, 141
Intergenerational wisdom, 39
Internal problems, 90
Intervention of media, 176
Intra-and-inter groups, 176
Intractable realities, 27
Invaluable knowledge, 56
Iron smelting, 80, 85–86, 88, 96–97
Irrigation, 11, 55, 163
Isolation, 39, 165–66, 180, 187

Jalpaiguri, 79, 81, 87, 89, 95–96
Jhuranti Tea Garden, 80, 90, 97

Kali Puja, 86
Kin groups, 157

Labour, 16, 56, 69, 87, 91, 97
  agricultural, 36, 73, 76, 87, 97
  bonded, 133
  contractual, 90, 97
  crisis, 157
  daily, 74, 76
  garden, 92
  hard, 88
  manual, 87–88, 97
  market, 69
  migrant, 87
  migratory, 6, 10
  permanent, 91
  temporary, 86, 91
Land
  alienation, 133
  conservation, 163
  distribution, 34
  owners, 84, 87
  survey, 138
  terrain slopes, 181
Landlessness, 135
Language movement, 182
Life cycle rituals, 92, 98, 158
Life style, 21–22, 37, 40–41, 145
Linguistic groups, 180
Literacy rate, 16, 81, 152, 173, 183–84
Literate, 19, 70, 72, 81, 113, 177
Livelihood
  basket, 135
  earning, 42
  economic, 33, 37
  economy, 46, 55
  loss of, 133, 135, 142
  patterns, 41, 132
  promotion, 13
  requirements, 182
  resources, 140
  rural, 44
  sustainable, 131
  tribal, 133, 177
Living
  condition, 3, 6, 15
  index, 5, 8

Maikal hills, 34
Mainstream society, 16, 64, 122
Marginal workers, 42
Market economy, 44, 46, 49
Marriage
  ceremonies, 157
  rituals, 94, 159
  early, 82
  inter-tribal, 21
  tea gardens inter-caste, 93
Mass media, 169

Matriarchal society, 3
Media boom, 175
Media works, 167
Medical treatment, 19, 120, 122
Medicinal plants, 33, 40, 45, 47, 56, 131
Micro-Credit Loan (MCL), 118-19, 122
Migration, 45, 50–52, 86, 146–47
Mini Bank, 103
Ministry of Environment and Forest, 2
Ministry of Tribal Affairs, 38, 50
Missionaries, 18–19
Mobile telephony, 172
Modern education, 21
Modernisation, 20–21, 23, 26, 55–56
Modernity, 26, 51
Money-lenders, 101
Motorway, 26
Mudumalai Wildlife Sanctuary, 3
Multi-purpose dam projects, 133

Nagaisuri Tea Garden, 81, 87, 90, 97
Nandigram, 135–36
Nation building, 167–70, 177
National Aluminium Company (NALCO), 133
National development, 175, 177
National Forest Policy, 2
National integration, 177
National Sample Survey Office (NASSO), 38, 52
Network chain, 12
Non-forest areas, 141
Non-profitable conditions, 86
Non-Timber Forest Products (NTFPs), 8-9, 12, 33, 35, 44-45
Non-tribal areas, 16
North-eastern India, 18
Nuclear families, 150

Occupational change, 78, 98
Occupations, 4, 10, 74, 78, 83, 85–86, 92, 97, 154
main, 182
primary, 6, 88–90, 154–55
secondary, 84, 90, 155
subsidiary, 139
Odisha Forest Act, 140
Odisha Survey and Settlement Act, 141
Ownership of Agricultural Land, 84

Paddy, 5, 8–12
Panchayats, 46, 92, 162–63
Panchmarhi Biospere Reserve (PBR), 28, 33
Parental generations, 6
Patalkot Valley (PKV), 26, 28, 30, 32-3, 35-6, 39-40, 43-5, 50, 55
Paternal house, 159–60
Peaceful environment, 175–76
Periphery development, 143
Pilgrims, 28, 34, 37, 55
Policies, 2, 38, 51, 57, 141, 143
government developmental, 170
national development, 1
Political conflicts, 176
Political fields, 21
Pradhan Mantri Gram Sadak Yojana (PMGSY), 174
Predominant characteristic, 187
Professional knowledge, 27
Progressive generations, 123
Protected forest, 140–41
Pteridophytes, 47
Pucca houses, 149
Purposive Sampling Technique, 183

Quality of life, 68, 123, 132

Rain-fed land, 88
Real estate, 55
Record of Rights (ROR), 141

Regions
  geographical, 51
  hilly, 36
  humid, 28
  natural resource, 133
  rural, 38
  tribal, 133
Rehabilitation and Resettlement Act, 142
Rehabilitation and Resettlement Policy, 132
Rehabilitation Colonies, 137
Religious Occasion, 96
Reproductive diseases, 47, 49
Reproductive health problems, 48
Research problem, 170
Reservation, 141
Resettlement Act, 142
Rice, 95, 154, 163, 165
Right to Education (RTE), 174
Rights, 3, 51, 55, 136, 140–41
  human, 136
  legal, 10
  voting, 175
Ritual
  bath, 93
  practices, 92
  traditional, 97
Rural development schemes, 163

Sacred centres, 162
Santal community, 65
Savings habit, 100
Scheduled Districts Act, 1
Self-Help Groups (SHGs), 100–1, 103–4, 106, 109–164, 118, 120, 122-3, 174
Sex-ratio, 80, 147
Social change, 16–17, 22, 38, 167–71, 174
Social development, 63
Social landscape, 25, 187
Social life, 20, 23
Social media, 179, 184, 186–87
  misuse of, 187
  purposes of, 186
  revolution, 179
  role of, 186
Social networking, 65, 186–87
Social networks, 183, 185
Society
  civil, 143
  complex, 51
  co-operative, 99
  human, 35
  mass, 169
  patriarchal, 68
  rural, 167–68
  tribal, 18, 65, 167–68, 176–77
  urban, 50
Special Economic Zones (SEZs), 136, 139
Spiritual well-being, 20
Standard of Living Index (SLI), 5, 8
Sustainable development, 143

Tea Estate, 84
Tea garden, 80, 83, 86–87, 89–93, 97
Temporality of development, 35
Terrace hill cultivation, 153
Thrifting habit, 99, 101, 113, 121, 123
Traditional
  centre, 20
  knowledge, 11–12, 40, 55
  occupation, 85–86, 92, 97, 149
  Panchayat, 97
Tribal
  belief, 26
  communities, 2, 15, 38, 57, 65, 80, 86, 92, 99, 133, 140–41, 175–77, 180, 182
  districts, 181
  dominated districts, 180–81
  families, 16, 91
  feuds, 23
  identity, 41

individuals, 51
knowledge, 35, 56
skill, 23
welfare, 44
wisdoms, 46, 55
Tribalism, 49, 187
Upheaval land, 45

Visva-Bharati, 67, 69, 74–76
Voting process, 174–75

West Bengal Cooperative Societies Act, 100
West Bengal Tribal Development Cooperative Corporation Ltd. (WBTDCCL), 99–100
Wildlife Protection Act, 2
Women empowerment, 100
World Health Organization, 39

Xaxa Committee, 50
Yankhu puja, 161

YouTube, 184

Zamindar, 91